SERIES ON
ECONOMIC DEVELOPMENT
AND GROWTH VOL. 2

ELDERLY ENTREPRENEURSHIP IN AN AGING US ECONOMY

IT'S NEVER TOO LATE

Series on Economic Development and Growth   (ISSN: 1793-3668)

Series Editor: Linda Yueh (*University of Oxford & London School of Economics and Political Science, UK*)

Advisory Board Members: John Knight (*University of Oxford, UK*)
Li Shi (*Beijing Normal University, China*)

SERIES ON
ECONOMIC DEVELOPMENT
            AND GROWTH VOL. 2

ELDERLY ENTREPRENEURSHIP IN AN AGING US ECONOMY

IT'S NEVER TOO LATE

Ting Zhang, Ph.D.

George Mason University, USA

World Scientific

NEW JERSEY · LONDON · SINGAPORE · BEIJING · SHANGHAI · HONG KONG · TAIPEI · CHENNAI

Published by

World Scientific Publishing Co. Pte. Ltd.
5 Toh Tuck Link, Singapore 596224
USA office: 27 Warren Street, Suite 401-402, Hackensack, NJ 07601
UK office: 57 Shelton Street, Covent Garden, London WC2H 9HE

Library of Congress Cataloging-in-Publication Data
Zhang, Ting, 1978–
    Elderly entrepreneurship in an aging US economy : it's never too late / Ting Zhang.
        p. cm. -- (Series on economic development and growth, 1793-3668 ; v. 2)
    Includes bibliographical references and index.
    ISBN 978-981-281-449-4 (wood-free papers)
    1. Older people--Employment--United States. 2. Self-employed--United States.
3. Entrepreneurship--United States. I. Title.
    HD6280.Z53 2008
    658.1'108460973--dc22

                                                    2008030257

British Library Cataloguing-in-Publication Data
A catalogue record for this book is available from the British Library.

Typeset by Stallion Press
Email: enquiries@stallionpress.com

Printed in Singapore.

DEDICATION

This book is dedicated to my mother, who was fighting against extreme cancer pain until the last moment of her life and whose wisdom, courage, and persistence encouraged me throughout this entire adventure.

Aiyu Yu
1948–2008

ACKNOWLEDGMENTS

I am deeply indebted to my advisor and mentor Prof. Laurie Schintler, who has been extremely resourceful, patient and approachable throughout the course of my book writing. I am also indebted to Prof. Roger Stough, Prof. David Wong, and Prof. Zoltan Acs from George Mason University whose help, provoking suggestions and encouragement helped me throughout my study and my research of this book. I would also like to thank my external reader Prof. Maryann Feldman from University of Georgia whose encouragement and inspiration made this book more possible.

I want to thank the School of Public Policy at George Mason University for providing me important knowledge and skills to start and finish this book project. I particularly thank faculty members of the School of Public Policy for offering me sustainable financial, knowledge, and network support to finish this book. Among them, I am particularly obliged to Prof. Naoru Koizumi, Prof. Jeremy Mayer, Prof. Kingsley Haynes, Prof. Jean Paelinck, Prof. Stephen Fuller, Prof. Stephen Ruth, Prof. David Hart, and Prof. Ann Baker. Prof. Richard Florida has helped me understand his concept of "creative class" and with data on Social Tolerance Index. My further thanks would be extended to Dr. Jules Lichtenstein from the AARP whose interests in my research encouraged me and to the Ewing Marion Kauffman Foundation whose fellowship program financially supports my research.

My colleagues from the School of Public Policy of George Mason University supported me in my research work. I want to thank them for all their help, support, interest and valuable suggestions. Especially, I am obliged to Lisa Fowler, Chunpu Song, Adriana Kocornik-Mina, Shaoming

Cheng, Lei Ding, Qingshu Xie, Henry Vega, and Huaqun Li. I also want to thank Mr. Raj Kulkarni for all his assistance on the GIS. My sister, Qun Zhang looked closely at the final version of the book for English style and grammar, correcting both and offering suggestions for improvement.

Finally, I would like to give my special thanks to my husband Gary Armstrong whose patient love enabled me to complete this work.

The author can be contacted at tingzhangphd@gmail.com

FOREWORD

Laurie A. Schintler
Associate Professor, School of Public Policy
George Mason University

The world around us continues to get grayer. According to the United Nations, the number of people aged 60 and over could reach 2 billion by the year 2050, which would be an increase of 217% above the current level. Many parts of the developed world experienced baby booms following WWII and are now seeing accelerated aging rates as a result. Improvements in health care, and consequently higher fertility rates and longer life expectancies are also helping to augment the trend. In the United States, individuals of age 65 or above are currently the fastest growing age group and their share out of the total population is ballooning and is expected to expand even further in the coming years. The United States Census estimates that by 2030, 1 out of 5 will fall into the older age cohort.

For some, the trend has presented itself as an opportunity. Seniors have become big business. In recent years a whole new market of products and services has surfaced targeted to the specific needs and interests of older individuals, many of them are aging boomers who are now reaching their retirement years. One area where this is highly visible is in the real estate industry, which has productized the concept of "senior living" and created a new breed of housing developments designed specifically with the lifestyle of the active adult in mind. The business of selling to seniors has also taken off on the Internet, which is becoming an increasingly popular venue for seniors to seek out information, obtain custom services or products or even to do social networking.

The graying population has also come at some cost to society. For one, older individuals are generally more prone to chronic diseases and disabilities, and such conditions can result in a cessation of driving and constrained mobility, a strain on friends and family who must take on the role of caretakers and in the end, costly institutionalized care. Medicaid disbursements and the share of the national budget dedicated to providing the entitlement program are both continuing to grow. There are also the more difficult quantity reductions in productivity that can result from diminished work performance or absenteeism on the part of ailing seniors or their caretakers.

Another concern is the possible labor force shortage and fiscal crisis that could in the near term result from the exodus of seniors from the workforce. Statistics show that individuals are retiring earlier, as Dr. Zhang's book delineated. One reason for this trend stems from the variety of impediments that older individuals face in wage and salary employment. Perceived or actual age discrimination, health- or mobility-related issues and pension plans that penalize late retirement are some of the factors that discourage later retirement. If, as the population gets older, an increasing share of the workforce retires, then a labor shortage could be imminent. This also raises concerns about the future of the Social Security Fund, which some speculate could run out as a growing number of individuals retire from the labor force.

Numerous solutions to the problem have been proposed. One is to capitalize on the growing immigrant population and to provide incentives that encourage their further participation in the labor force. Such a policy however, is controversial and politically difficult to implement. Other policy measures are targeted specifically at alleviating some of the obstacles that seniors face in wage and salary positions. Programs aimed at promoting elder mobility through transportation coordination, currently being implemented in some states, are an example of this strategy. Telework and flexible work hour programs in the workplace have also been discussed as a way to maintain seniors' participation in the workforce. It is unclear, though, whether these and other similar measures can be effective on a large enough scale to mitigate a labor force shortage and fiscal crisis; nor, are any a holistic fix to the problem.

An emergent trend that could, interestingly, offer an effective solution to the imminent labor force shortage and fiscal crisis is senior entrepreneurship, as this book indicates. Within recent years, the face of the entrepreneur has begun to change. The young, hip business person of the dot com era is now being replaced by individuals who are much older. Statistics show that, in fact, seniors are more likely than their younger counterparts to be self-employed and the number of senior entrepreneurs continues to rise.

Self-employment offers a number of benefits to the senior and those could help explain why we are seeing a recent surge in start-up activity by that population cohort. As owners or managers of their own business, older individuals are afforded more scheduling flexibility. This, in turn, allows them to more easily manage any health conditions they may have, carry out their roles as caretakers of others, spend more time with grandchildren or other family members and engage in leisure activities. Seniors may also experience secondary health benefits as a result of the feelings of empowerment and self-worth that self-employment engenders.

In the knowledge economy, seniors are well-positioned to continue working as entrepreneurs well beyond their retirement years; this is part of the message this book delivers. The more-physically demanding occupations of the Fordist economy have now been replaced by those centered more on the processing of information, creative tasks and communication. Advanced technologies as well as the Internet are making it easier to work remotely. It is also being increasingly recognized that seniors bring years of experience, knowledge, business contacts and maturity, in many ways, beyond that their younger cohorts have to offer. It is not difficult to imagine a scenario in the future where outsourcing to senior-owned companies to take advantage of these assets is commonplace.

While there is a relatively substantial and growing body of research that looks at entrepreneurship in general, the senior entrepreneur and his/her role in the context of the new economy has been relatively unexplored. This book begins to fill that gap and provides new insight and knowledge in the area. It gives us with a better understanding of who the older entrepreneur is, the factors that motivate them to become self-employed, the regional economic and fiscal benefits of senior entrepreneurship and the policy tools that can be effective in fostering further start-up activity by older individuals.

It is interesting to find from the book that seniors themselves could be a solution to the economic and fiscal crisis that their aging is predicted to result. In the context of a "senior entrepreneurial milieu" that fosters diversity, creativity and social openness and incentivizes self-employment across different socio-demographics through appropriate tax policies and other measures, the self-employment of seniors in the aggregate can be expected to help supplant the labor force, stimulate regional economic growth and reduce the burden on the Social Security Fund. In certain respects, the benefits of senior entrepreneurship could be even more powerful than those associated with younger individuals or the population as a whole. These findings and other knowledge contained in the book truly broaden our understanding of the senior entrepreneur and the positive role the elderly can play in society as pioneers of their own fate.

FOREWORD

Roger R. Stough
Vice President for Research and Economic Development
NOVA Endowed Chair and Professor of Public Policy
George Mason University

Dr. Ting Zhang has identified a totally missed aspect of the renewed interest in entrepreneurship as a public policy vehicle in her investigation of entrepreneurship among the elderly. It offers new insight and thus input to several of the great debates of our times. First, it shows that the elderly have surprisingly high rates of entrepreneurship compared to younger groups in the labor pool. Thus, the elderly contribute disproportionately to job creation and support and probably could do more if the incentives were higher. Further it suggests that the elderly might be able to contribute more to staving off shortfalls in Social Security funds that are forecast in the face of a population pyramid that is flipping or reversing. Finally, in a knowledge economy the physical skills required to remain in the labor force are less important than in the industrial age. Thus, health policy and services are important not only for extended life quality but also to enable seniors to remain productive longer than in the past. In short, Zhang's work provides fresh and new insights into public policy issues regarding the aging of society, maintenance of economic productivity, job creation, maintenance of the social security system and the role of the elderly in society, i.e., whether they will in large measure remain a large dependency group or far more economically productive one. Dr. Zhang's research suggests significant new approaches may be available to transform a part of the elderly dependent group into a highly productive one that not only creates jobs for its own but also for other younger persons in the labor pool.

CONTENTS

ABSTRACT[1]

This study addresses elderly entrepreneurship in the setting of an aging population, the prognostic labor fiscal crises, and the "knowledge economy". After interpreting the special role that elderly entrepreneurship could play for the aging population and the opportunities that elderly entrepreneurship faces in the "knowledge economy", this study focuses on exploring old-age effect on entrepreneurship propensity, sources of seniors' entrepreneurship, regional dynamics of elderly entrepreneurship, and the economic, fiscal, and labor impacts from elderly entrepreneurship. After reviewing the current theories and literature, four hypotheses are tested through two binomial logit models, an extended log-linear growth model with spatial and sensitivity analysis, and a path analysis model. This book builds on the utility maximization theory, economic growth theories, and social theories of aging. The empirical tests find out that seniors are more likely to be entrepreneurs, tax policies and social tolerance level matter to elderly entrepreneurship, and elderly entrepreneurship has positive impacts on regional economic growth, labor force size, and the amount of Social Security fund contribution. This book concludes with policy implications.

End note

[1]   This research was funded in part by the Ewing Marion Kauffman Foundation. The contents of this publication are solely the responsibility of the author.

LIST OF ABBREVIATIONS

ACS:	American Community Survey
AARP:	American Association of Retired Persons
BEA:	Bureau of Economic Analysis
BLSs:	Bureau of Labor Statistics
CBR:	Crude Birth Rate
CED:	Committee for Economic Development
CMSAs:	Combined Metropolitan Statistical Areas
CPS:	Current Population Surveys
DR:	Dependency Ratio
EDR:	Elderly Dependency Ratio
ERIPs:	Early Retirement Incentive Programs
FIRE:	Finance, Insurance, and Real State
GDP:	Gross Domestic Product
GEM:	Global Entrepreneurship Monitor
GIS:	Geographic Information System
GMP:	Gross Metropolitan Product
GRP:	Gross Regional Product
HRS:	Health and Retirement Study
LM:	Lagrange Multiplier
LQ:	Location Quotients
OASDI:	Old age, Survivors, and Disability Insurance
OECD:	Organization for Economic Co-operation and Development
OLS:	Ordinary Least Square
MSAs:	Metropolitan Statistical Areas
MLE:	Maximum Likelihood Estimation
NAICS:	North America Industry Classification System
NOWCC:	National Older Workers Career Center
NSF:	National Science Foundation

PMSAs:	Primary Metropolitan Statistical Areas
PUMAs:	Public Use Microdata Sample Areas
PUMS:	Public Use Microdata Samples
RHSs:	Retirement History Surveys
R&D:	Research and Development
SHRM:	Society for Human Resource Management
SIC:	Standard Industrial Classification
SOCs:	Standard Occupation Classification system codes
SSA:	Social Security Administration
SSB:	Social Security Bureau
TEA:	Total Entrepreneurial Activity
U.S.:	United States
YDR:	Younger Dependency Ratio

PART 1
INTRODUCTION

CHAPTER 1

INTRODUCTION

An aging population is predicted to cause two economic problems — a labor force shortage and the Social Security fund exhaustion. In academia, although aging, as a demographic phenomenon and trend in many countries, has been heatedly discussed in health research, welfare benefit discussions, labor force shortage concerns, and fiscal policies, most of these researches have treated older people as a burden of the economy.

While numerous policy approaches have been discussed in the literature to deal with the above two problems, a labor force shortage and the Social Security fund exhaustion, limited attention has addressed entrepreneurship among the elderly (called "elderly entrepreneurship" throughout this book[2]) as a viable solution to the aging-related social and economic problems. Involving more seniors in the labor force, particularly as entrepreneurs, can possibly not only enlarge the labor force size, but also increase the Social Security Trust Fund. This would in turn have a positive impact on regional economic growth. Although some literature suggests involving seniors in the labor force, the focus of most of this line of literature does not fall on seniors who are older than average retirement ages. Instead, younger seniors who are about to retire or even younger are typically the subjects in this line of literature.

There also exists an issue on how to motivate skilled seniors to remain in or return to the labor force. Forcing them to continue working after the age they wanted to retire is not necessarily a good strategy because it could result in seniors' reduced life satisfaction. Compared with wage-and-salary jobs, elderly entrepreneurship has its special advantages. In wage-and-salary workplaces, there exists social discrimination against seniors; wage-and-salary jobs typically do not offer enough flexibility to meet seniors' needs and time arrangements. On the other hand, entrepreneurship can offer more flexibility, and more importantly, more control that could enhance seniors' life satisfaction. In this background, elderly entrepreneurship can potentially become a viable solution to involving seniors in the labor force. Hence, it is an interesting research question whether developing elderly entrepreneurship could be an effective way to retain seniors in the labor force.

However, entrepreneurship is typically perceived and described as a privilege and opportunity for younger people and whether the elderly population can be as entrepreneurial is in question. There is also a question as to whether elderly entrepreneurship, if it is existent and possibly even prevalent, can have a significant positive impact on regional economic growth and can help mitigate the related prognostic labor and fiscal crises, and if so, how large these impacts could be.

At the same time while demographic challenges approach us, the economic transition to the "knowledge economy" (or the "knowledge-based economy" or the "new economy") might provide some special opportunities which might help to mitigate the potential problems that are related to the aging population. The discussion on this economic transition centers on the shift from the old so-called "Fordist economy" to a "knowledge economy" and on the role of entrepreneurship in the "knowledge economy". Although entrepreneurship, particularly new-technology related entrepreneurship or innovation entrepreneurship according to Baumol (1993), is not typically associated with older people, the "knowledge economy" may offer special opportunities to the elderly[3]. The "knowledge economy" emphasizes the role of knowledge and brainpower. This new economy (i.e., "knowledge economy") is less physically demanding and it offers more locational flexibility that is facilitated by the information technology. Many seniors have rich accumulated knowledge and work-related skills that are particularly valuable assets in the "knowledge economy". The lower physical requirement in the "knowledge economy" makes it more possible for seniors to participate in economic activities.

At this historical juncture where an aging population and "knowledge economy" coexist, it could be extremely relevant and meaningful to explore entrepreneurship among the elderly, to explore the economic role of elderly entrepreneurship, if existent, in boosting the productivity in an aging society, and to explore the possibility and magnitude for elderly entrepreneurship to mitigate the potential aging-resulted crises. If it were found that elderly entrepreneurship has a positive role in regional economic growth, employment contribution, and the Social Security fund, encouraging elderly entrepreneurship would be extremely beneficial and critical to our aging society. This above statement is made under the assumption that developing elderly entrepreneurship will not reduce seniors' life satisfaction. In fact, developing elderly entrepreneurship is a process of recognizing seniors' human capital and brain power, which would elevate social respect toward seniors, reduce social discrimination against them, even increase seniors' wealth, and eventually enhance seniors' life satisfaction.

In this context, it would also be important to explore the factors that drive elderly entrepreneurship and therefore to derive policy implications from these findings. Thus, while the body of research and literature on this topic is very thin, elderly entrepreneurship is worth investigating. This book addresses the dynamics and the role of elderly entrepreneurship in the U.S. economy.

1. Definitions

This book defines three terms: elderly, entrepreneurship, and "knowledge economy". The *elderly* are defined as those aged 62 or above. The rationale of using this definition is based on two facts: First, the average retirement age in the United States is 62 (Gendell, 2001); second, age 62 is the initial eligibility age to receive Social Security benefits in the United States.

The measure that this book uses for *entrepreneurship* is the knowledge-based unincorporated and incorporated self-employment[4]. According to other studies, particularly in the elderly entrepreneurship literature, self-employment is a best-available measure for entrepreneurship (Evans and Leighton, 1989; Blanchflower *et al.*, 2001). However, there are three drawbacks of using self-employment as a measure for entrepreneurship: first, it does not emphasize knowledge intensity and it does not address the notion of innovation; second, it tends to refer to sole proprietors and partnership owners in most datasets and thus excludes incorporated business owners or those business owners who count themselves as employees in survey data; third, using seniors' self-employment rate as a measure does not necessarily characterize establishment of the new startups by the elderly of a region. In another word, this concept reflects entrepreneurship stock, not flow.

To avoid the first drawback, only knowledge-based self-employment is used in the definition of entrepreneurship in this book. Although knowledge intensity and innovation is not always argued to be a necessary key element of entrepreneurship, it is through new technology and innovation that the value of entrepreneurship was identified in economic growth (see Schumpeter, 1950). In this case, the knowledge base of business ownership would help to delineate entrepreneurship.

To avoid the second drawback, this book includes incorporated business owners in self-employment data. Incorporated business ownership is an important part of entrepreneurship.

For the third drawback, current data does not offer information on newly established business owners who are aged 62 or above. Using the marginal increase in elderly knowledge-based self-employment over years was once considered to measure the establishment of new businesses by the elderly. However, regional change in elderly self-employment does not necessarily reflect the level of elderly startups. Firm survival and migration (and immigration) could contribute to the change as well.

The measure of entrepreneurship that is employed in this book, i.e. the knowledge-based incorporated and unincorporated self-employment, is, therefore, the best available proxy measure to entrepreneurship.

Additionally, using knowledge-based unincorporated and incorporated self-employment to measure entrepreneurship avoids some of the problems associated with other measures that are typically used in the literature. One measure, regional R&D expenditures tend to underestimate small-business entrepreneurship (Acs and Audretsch, 1990). Another measure, startups (Audretsch and Keilbach, 2004), only emphasize the first stages of a venture's development and ignore whether or not a firm survives. Although it is possible to use the available data to create a time series measure of new companies in a region by year (Acs *et al.*, 2007), which seems to in part address this issue, this measure has a high requirement on data and it requires data to have consistent measurements across all years. Most importantly, those alternative measures typically do not offer information on business owners' age, which makes it inconvenient to conduct research on elderly entrepreneurship.

In this book, the measure of entrepreneurship, instead of measuring its flow, measures its stock at a location at a certain time. Elderly entrepreneurs thus include two groups of seniors: (1) those seniors who establish new businesses after the age of 62, and (2) entrepreneurs who continue to be entrepreneurs after the age of 62.

This book also defines the *"knowledge economy"*. It is in the knowledge-based economic context that elderly entrepreneurship becomes more possible and especially valuable. The knowledge base relies on human capital and the "knowledge economy" is less physically demanding. The reliance on human capital instead of physical labor in the "knowledge economy" makes it more possible for seniors to stay in the labor force and makes seniors' cumulated insights, skills, and business ties particularly valuable.

The scale or size of the "knowledge economy" (or knowledge-base sectors) is defined by the "creative class" employment that is addressed in Florida (2004)[5]. The term "creative class" has a clear occupational classification[6] and delineates creativity, knowledge base, and innovation. Reich (1992), a previous attempt to describe the "knowledge economy", defined those in the knowledge-based occupations as "symbolic analysts". According to Reich (1992), symbolic analysts solved, identified, or brokered problems by manipulating symbols or abstract images using analytical tools (such as mathematics, financial gimmicks, and legal arguments). Eventually, the work of the symbolic analysts transforms the symbols into products and services or, thus, reality. Reich's concept was interesting, but he did not offer a clear operational definition that could provide a classification of occupations. Florida (2004) addressed this concern and provided a definition for the "creative class" under the U.S. Standard Occupation Classification System Codes (SOC). The creative class jobs include knowledge-intensive jobs, such as scientist, engineers, and other professional occupations. Although Florida's creative class was intended to address human creativity[7], his classification was conceptually quite similar to Reich's characterization of knowledge-based occupations. Florida observe that creativity was becoming more valuable in today's global economy and found that the creative class comprised about 30% to 40% of the current U.S. labor force. Within the last decade, this segment of the labor force had increased a great deal.

2. Research Hypotheses and Data

This book specifically examines seniors' propensity to become entrepreneurs, the factors that contribute to this propensity, and at a macro level, the regional economic, labor, and fiscal impacts of elderly entrepreneurship. The existent literature has not address the importance of elderly entrepreneurship in the knowledge-based economic setting and in the aging demographic setting; it sheds only a partial light on the relationship between old age and entrepreneurship; it does not examine the effects of social policies and related factors on elderly occupational choice studies; it has not focused on the regional distribution of elderly entrepreneurship; it has not addressed the impact of elderly entrepreneurship on the regional economy; it has not considered elderly entrepreneurship as a possible solution to the aging-related labor and fiscal crises. This book attempts to bridge these gaps in the literature and address and even empirically test the propensity, factors, regional distribution, and economic, labor, and fiscal roles of elderly entrepreneurship. The initial research questions to be explored in this book are:

> Is entrepreneurship an effective way to retain or attract seniors back in the labor force? What are the reasons that offer the possibility and necessity for elderly entrepreneurship? What are the sectoral preferences of senior entrepreneurs and is the "knowledge economy" a fertile economic environment for the elderly to become entrepreneurs?

Then, further testable research questions that will be addressed with empirical evidences include:

(1) Are seniors more likely to be entrepreneurs than those in younger working cohorts?
(2) What are the social or policy-related factors that contribute to elderly entrepreneurship? How do seniors' individual characteristics affect their propensity to become entrepreneurs?
(3) Does elderly entrepreneurship tend to cluster with certain proximity? Are there regional disparities in elderly entrepreneurship distribution in the United States? Do regional entrepreneurship environments and knowledge base affect the regional level of elderly entrepreneurship?
(4) Does elderly entrepreneurship have a positive impact on regional economic growth, and if so, how significant is the impact?
(5) Does elderly entrepreneurship help to increase the labor force size and existent Social Security fund contribution?

The above research questions motivate the following hypotheses that will be addressed in the book:

(1) Entrepreneurship is an effective way to retain or attract seniors in the labor force due to many personal reasons and social readiness that provide seniors the possibility and necessity to become entrepreneurs. The "knowledge economy" offers a fertile economic environment for seniors to become entrepreneurs.
(2) Older age is a significant factor that positively affects a person's probability of being an entrepreneur. There is a higher self-employment

rate in senior labor force than that among the younger labor force, particularly in the knowledge-based sectors. Seniors are more likely to be entrepreneurs than the younger persons in general.

(3) Policy indicators, such as R&D environment, tax policies, and social tolerance level, are among the factors that affect elderly self-employment rate, as well as some personal factors.

(4) There exist regional disparities for elderly entrepreneurship distribution in the United States. Regional entrepreneurship environment and knowledge base tend to be associated with regional elderly entrepreneurship levels.

(5) Elderly entrepreneurship is positively related to regional economic growth. The more elderly entrepreneurs a region has in its labor force, there is an evidently higher regional economic growth rate, *ceteris paribus*.

(6) Elderly entrepreneurship has a statistically significant and positive impact on increasing labor force size and Social Security fund contribution and hence helps alleviate prognostic aging-related labor shortage and Social Security fund exhaustion.

3. Methodology

The analysis builds on utility theories, economic growth theories, and social gerontology theories and previous literature. This book uses empirical data, descriptive statistics, and tests through two binomial logit models, an extended log-linear growth model with sensitivity and spatial analysis, and a path analysis model to test the hypotheses and evidences of the theories interpreted in the book.

Data sources for the analysis in this book include the Census Public Use Microdata Samples (PUMS), Bureau of Economic Analysis (BEA), American Community Survey (ACS), and Social Security Bureau (SSB). It heavily relies on PUMS 2000 one-percent data because these data sets offer detailed individual level employment, demographic and other socioeconomic information of seniors aged over 62. BEA data is used to measure the physical capital of the metropolitan areas. ACS data is used to measure the regional economic growth after year 2000 that is the year of most independent variable values. Using this method captures the lagged effect of the independent variables. SSB data measures the Social Security fund contribution.

The descriptive statistics calculate and compare ratios and proportions, graph and tabulate those basic statistics, and visualize relationships between key variables through scatter plots. This method is typically used in an exploratory research. In this book, descriptive statistics are heavily used when exploring elderly self-employment rates, the sectoral distribution of elderly self-employment, the relationship between age and entrepreneurship (see Chapter 6), the regional disparities of elderly entrepreneurship, and the association between regional entrepreneurship environment or regional knowledge base and elderly entrepreneurship (see Chapter 8).

The logit models are used because the dependent variable is a binary variable that measures the propensity of being entrepreneurs; logit models are used in previous empirical studies on seniors' self-employment (such as Quinn 1980; Bruce *et al.*, 2000). The modified log-linear Solow growth model extends Audretsch and Keilbach (2004) who tested the regional economic impact of entrepreneurship. This book indicates the limitations of the Audretsch and Keilbach model and extends their model with spatial and sensitivity analysis. The path analysis is an exploratory study: a logical association path is observed, but no previous empirical studies or models are found to test the labor and then fiscal impacts of elderly entrepreneurship. Spatial autocorrelation is also considered in this path analysis model.

4. Roadmap of this Book

This book includes eight parts and six major topics. The first part (Chapter 1) overviews this book. Then each major topic composes a part and contains at least one chapter. The first topic is on population aging. On this topic, Chapter 2 explains the crises that come with an aging population and the proposed solutions to those crises. The second topic explains why elderly entrepreneurship is the key concept in this book. Chapter 3 theoretically interprets the possibilities and necessities for elderly entrepreneurship to retain or attract seniors in the labor force. This chapter highlights the importance of researching elderly entrepreneurship instead of just elderly labor force as a solution to the aging population. The third topic introduces current literature and theories that is related to or can be used to associate with elderly entrepreneurship, under which Chapter 4 provides a review of the empirical literature relevant to elderly entrepreneurship and Chapter 5 introduces economic and gerontology theories that underlie this book. Some gaps in the literature and previous theories are identified in those two chapters.

The following three topics address the aforementioned hypotheses and interpret the results of data analysis and empirical tests. The fourth topic addresses the possibility and situation of entrepreneurship of seniors. Under this topic, Chapter 6 explores the relationship between age and entrepreneurship and Chapter 7 examines the social and individual factors that are related to the development of elderly entrepreneurship. The next topic focuses on regional dynamics of elderly entrepreneurship. Under this topic, regional distribution of elderly entrepreneurship and the association of elderly entrepreneurship with regional entrepreneurship environment or regional knowledge base is analyzed in Chapter 8. In Chapter 9, the role of elderly entrepreneurship in regional economic growth is tested. The last topic addresses the fiscal and labor role of elderly entrepreneurship. In Chapter 10, the labor and fiscal impact of elderly entrepreneurship is tested to examine whether elderly entrepreneurship can help mitigate the potential labor shortage and Social Security fund exhaustion that are resulted from the aging population.

Finally the last part after the six topics, i.e., Chapter 11, provides a summary of the research and its conclusions. It also provides a discussion of the public policy implications and recommendations based on the empirical based findings and presents directions and topics for future research.

End notes

[2] Elderly persons in this book are classified as people who aged 62 or over. There are two reasons of this definition: (1) 62 is the current US average retirement age; (2) 62 is the initial eligibility age of Social Security claim.

[3] This book tries to define entrepreneurship as inclusive as possible. Baumol (1993) has categorized entrepreneurship into innovation entrepreneurship and business organization. Reynolds *et al.* (2005) defined necessity entrepreneurship as a start-up that occurs because of missing alternatives (e.g., out of unemployment) and define opportunity entrepreneurship as a new business that is set up to pursue an opportunity. With strong focus on the knowledge base, entrepreneurship defined in this book emphasizes the innovation aspect of it; with seniors' management skills, business organizational perspectives would be a necessary component of elderly entrepreneurship addressed in this book; for seniors who like to continue staying active in economic activities, opportunity entrepreneurship would be relevant; for seniors who need extra income but are not welcome in wage-and-salary employment, necessity entrepreneurship would be an important component.

[4] As indicated earlier, this book tries to incorporate several important components of entrepreneurship that are applicable to the elderly. Those components include: innovation entrepreneurship and business organization (Baumol, 1993) and opportunity entrepreneurship and necessity entrepreneurship (Reynolds *et al.*, 2005). Innovation entrepreneurship emphasizes the innovation and high technology focus of entrepreneurship. Business organization recognizes the organizational skills as a necessary part of entrepreneurship. Opportunity entrepreneurship is defined as a new business that is set up to pursue an opportunity. Necessity entrepreneurship is defined as a start-up that occurs because of missing alternatives (e.g., out of unemployment).

[5] It is necessary to note that this book only uses Florida (2004)'s occupation classification for Creative Class, which differs from his Creativity Index or Global Creativity Index. His Creativity Index (see Florida, 2004) is a composite measure that is based on four indices: the Innovation Index, High-Tech Index, Gay Index, and the Creative Class. His Global Creativity Index (see Florida, 2005) is composed of an equally weighted combination of the Talent Index, Technology Index, and the Tolerance Index.

6   Those occupations include management, business and financial operation, computer and mathematical, architecture and engineering, science, legal, education, arts and media, health care practitioners, and high level sales management occupations.

7   Among his creative classes, Florida (2004) further distinguished Super-Creative Core from other Creative Professionals. Arts, design, entertainment, sports, and media occupations were included in the Super-Creative Core; the Super-Creative Core was argued to be more creative and contributive to the economy than Creative Professionals. This book does not focus on this interpretation of creativity by Florida (2004), but his occupational classification for the Creative Class in general fits the purpose of defining knowledge-based occupations in this book.

PART 2

AGING …

CHAPTER 2

SOCIOECONOMIC BACKGROUND: AGING
POPULATION, RESULTED LABOR AND FISCAL
CRISES, AND THE POSSIBLE SOLUTIONS

1. Aging Population

The U.S. population is aging. Seniors continue to comprise a larger proportion of the population. As a result of a declining mortality rate and
staying low fertility rate, the U.S. population is aging. On the one hand,
continuously enhancing health care and living conditions reduce the mortality rate of Americans. Enhancements in medical and health conditions
have been reducing the mortality rate of Americans and lengthening the
life expectancy. As illustrated in Figure 2.1, the U.S. average life
expectancy at birth in 1900 was only 47 years; a baby born in 2000 can
expect to live till 76.9 years; in 2050, this figure is projected to reach 82.6
(U.S. Census Bureau, 2001).

On the other hand, fertility rates of the U.S. population stay no higher
than the replacement rate that is 2.11 births per woman. In 2000, the
U.S. total fertility rate is 2.056; in 2001, this figure shrinks to 2.034
(Haub, 2003; Population Research Bureau, n.d.); in 2005, this figure is
estimated as 2.08 (CIA World Factbook, 2005). Consequently, older
people who aged 65 or over take a growing proportion among total U.S.
population. As shown in Figure 2.2, people aged over 65 in 1900 only
accounted for approximately 4% of the U.S. population. Now, the size
of the cohort aged over 65 has grown to 35 million and accounts for
12.4% of the U.S. population (U.S. Administration on Aging, 2002; CIA
World Factbook, 2005).

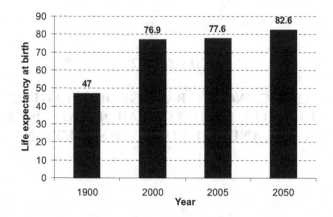

Figure 2.1 Life Expectancy at Birth in the U.S., 1900–2050

Data Source: U.S. Census Bureau (2001); CIA World Factbook (2005).

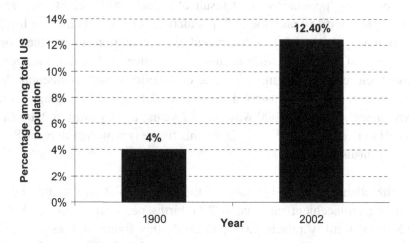

Figure 2.2 Proportions of U.S. Older People, 1900 versus 2002

Data Source: U.S. Administration on Aging (2002).

The baby boomer generation (i.e., those who were born from year 1946 to year 1964) expedites the aging process in the next decades. This baby boomer generation has created population driven dynamics in U.S. society at each of its development stage: from the moment when baby boomers were teens to their adulthood and to their current senior ages.

This generation has affected U.S. society from every aspect, such as education, employment, and consumption. When this generation was around teen, education resource was a major issue; when this generation reached employment ages, policies were created to settle their jobs; now when this generation approaches retirement ages, Social Security, Medicare, and many other aging-related issues become more prominent.

Age pyramid of the U.S. population also illustrates the aging process and trend through an increasingly large proportion of older persons in the total population. Appendix 2.1 contrasts the age pyramids of the United States in the years 1975 and 2000 and projected population pyramid of 2025 and 2050. In these pyramids, each horizontal bar represents a 5-year birth cohort. The younger birth cohorts are located at the bottom of the pyramids and the top ones represent the older birth cohorts. The population pyramids, from the census population estimation in 1975 to its population projection in 2050, show a ballooning top: during the period of 1975–2050, the shape of the population pyramid changes from approximately triangle-like pyramid in 1975 to a rectangular cylindrical form in 2050, with even a ballooning top for ages over 85. In the year-1975 age pyramid, the bottom bulge for ages 10–29 represents the baby boomer generation. In the year-2000 age pyramid, the middle bulge represents the baby boomer generation and the bottom bulge represents the echo boomer generation. The Echo boomer generation is composed of the offspring of baby boomers and therefore is called "echo" of the baby boomer generation. In the year-2025 age pyramid, the top bulge is for baby boomers and the middle bulge is for echo boomers. However, the bulges in the year-2025 age pyramid are not as evident as the year-1975 and year-2000 age pyramids. In 2050, there seem no bulges any more; instead, the age pyramid is transformed into a rectangular shape. The shift from a triangle shape to a rectangular shape pyramid indicates that the U.S. population is aging and older people take a bigger and bigger proportion among total population. This ballooning top in the 2050 population pyramid is especially prominent for women aged 85 and above.

Although baby boomers that are entering retirement age are normally considered a reason for the population to age, they are not the only source for the aging population. Instead, this trend of aging is projected to be inevitable as the fourth stage of demographic transition process, according to Warren Thompson's "Demographic Transition Model".

The "Demographic Transition Model" is an idealized model that describes population changes over time, based on the experience of Western European developed countries. In this model, the population change is presented through the relationships between the birth rate (e.g. Crude Birth Rate or CBR), the death rate (e.g. Crude Death Rate or CDR), and the population growth (Weeks, 2005). The whole population growth experience is divided into 4 stages:

I.   Pre-industrial,
II. Transitional,
III. Industrial, and
IV. Postindustrial stage.

As shown in Figure 2.3, Stage I shows a primitive low-growth balance, called the "primitive stability", between a high birth rate and a high death rate. Then, the improved food, nutrition, health and medical conditions brought about a "mortality transition". With this "mortality transition", Stage II is comprised of a high birth rate, a low death rate, and thus a high population growth rate. Followed by the high population growth are migration and urbanization. In Stage III, due to feminism movement and cultural changes, the birth rate starts to decline as well as the death rate. The declining birth rate is called "fertility transition".

Starting from the "mortality transition" in Stage II, people begin to live a longer life, and the total population becomes older. The "fertility transition" occurred since Stage III accelerates the population to become even older; in Stage IV, with a low fertility rate and a low mortality rate, the population is stably aging. This stability is sometimes called "modern stability" to contrast to the "primitive stability" in Stage I.

The experiences of the current developed countries are similar to the above model and most of them are now in Stage IV, including the United States.

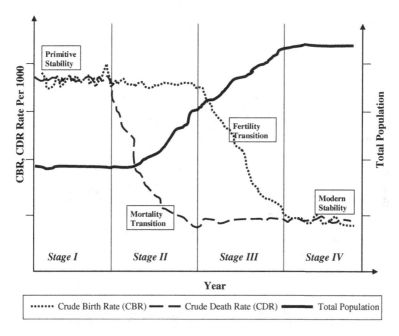

Figure 2.3 The Demographic Transition Model

Note: This figure is drawn based on Warren Thompson's Concept of Demographic Transition Model in Weeks (2005).

Shown in Figure 2.4, the U.S. population entered Stage IV in the 1990s and this status of the "modern stability" with aging seems to persist for another many more years. Since Americans are living longer and the fertility rate still stays below the replacement rate, the U.S. population will continue the trend of aging. This aging trend is not necessarily resulted from baby boomers.

The second wave of the CBR curve in Figure 2.4 indicates the baby boomers. Although this wave is evident, it is not the only force that determines the general aging trend. As shown in Figure 2.4, in the U.S. population history, baby boomers only compose a small part of the U.S. demographic transition chart. Although the aging of baby boomers expedites the U.S. population aging process, the general trend of population aging seems inevitable, even without baby boomers. This aging trend will

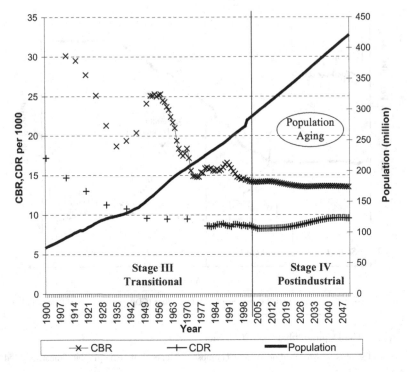

Figure 2.4 Demographic Transition Model in the U.S.
Data Source: U.S. Census Bureau.

not disappear with the disappearance of baby boomers. Although the demographic transition model did not consider cross-country migration and although immigrants in the United States contribute to the U.S. population and economic growth, international immigrants still stay a relatively low proportion among the total U.S. population. The limited quantity of immigrants has a limited impact on the general trend of the overall U.S. population.

Since the aging trend will possibly not disappear with the exit of baby boomers from the population, mitigating the aging related crises will not be meaningful just for the next decade or two. Concentrating on the issues resulted from an aging population will relate to the long-run future of the U.S. economy.

2. Aging Labor Force and Labor Force Shortage

As a result of an aging population, the U.S. labor force is also aging. Younger cohorts are shrinking and younger workers comprise a declining proportion of total employment. Based on data from the U.S. Bureau of Labor Statistics (BLS), Figure 2.5 exhibits the dramatic change in the age structure of the labor force. From 1994 to 2002, employment growth rate for younger people (aged 25–54 in this figure) shows a slowdown and eventual declines following 2000. As a contrast, employment growth rate for people aged 55 and over (this includes the leading edge of baby boomers) is rising at an increasingly fast rate. With more and more baby boomers reaching retirement ages, the U.S. labor force is expected to age even more in the next two decades.

While the U.S. labor force has continued to age, *the average retirement age* has actually *declined* since 1950 (Social Security Administration, 1999). Between 1970 and 2000, the average retirement age decreased

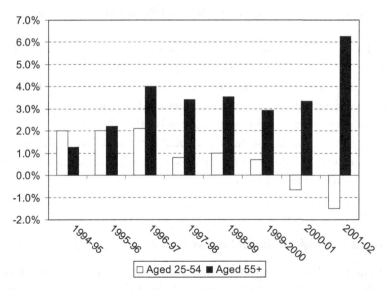

Figure 2.5 Percent Change in the Number of Employed Persons Aged 25–54 and 55+, 1994–2002

Source: U.S. Department of Labor, Bureau of Labor Statistics January 1995–January 2003.

from 66.2 (Ippolito, 1990) to 62 (Gendell, 2001). Ippolito (1990) indicated that the average retirement age from full-time and part-time work declined from 66.2 in 1970 to 64.1 in 1985. In 1995, the average retirement age for American men was 63.6 and for women was 61.6 (Blöndal and Scarpetta, 1999). Although Johnson (2001) critiqued on Blöndal and Scarpetta's (1999) measurement of average retirement age, the average retirement age estimated by the BLS and Social Security Administration was basically consistent with Blöndal and Scarpetta (1999): the average retirement age for the period of 1995–2000 was about 62.0 for men and 61.4 for women, though the estimation from Social Security series was normally slightly higher than the labor force series (Gendell 2001).

With current policies and various historical incentives for early retirement, most workers aged 55 or over will possibly withdraw from the labor force soon. Additionally, with the withdrawal of baby boomers from the labor force but insufficient supplements to the labor force from the younger cohorts, the U.S. labor force will continue to shrink. If there are no dramatic technological innovations, a short-run labor force shortage could consequently result, as Peterson (1999) and Schetagne (2001) realized.

Several policy options have been proposed to mitigate the labor force shortage, but they all have limitations. For example, although this labor force shortage has been in part and will likely in part be offset by immigrants, politically the United States cannot admit too many immigrants and cannot totally rely on immigrants to solve the labor shortage problem. The later section (Section 4) in this chapter summarizes the policy options that are proposed to mitigate the labor shortage. This section also evaluates their limitations in details.

3. Financial Crisis of Social Services

In addition to the looming labor shortage crisis, a financial crisis would result from the aging population as well. With the increasingly large retirement cohort and under current policy conditions, a financial crisis of social services is imminent. Moreover, the earlier retirement age, as indicated in the previous section, and thus longer life after retirement would further deepen this labor shortage.

As shown in Figure 2.6, the elderly dependency ratio (defined by age in this figure) is increasing. The dependency ratio, expressed through age, is the ratio of the economically dependent part of the population to the productive part. The dependent part includes both seniors who are aged over 64 (the elderly dependent part) and children who are aged below the age of 15 (the younger dependen part). Therefore, the dependency ratio is equal to the number of individuals aged below 15 or above 64 divided by the number of individuals aged 15 to 64, expressed as a percentage. By 2050, the total dependency ratio is projected to surpass 65%, and this increasingly high dependency ratio is largely the result of the enlarging retirement population. In another word, it is the Elderly Dependency Ratio (EDR), instead of Younger Dependency Ratio (YDR), that leads to the increase in the overall dependency ratio. It should be noted though that the dependency ratio does not accurately reflect the ratio of non-working people to working people. This is because age is not necessarily the determinant of a person's participation in the labor force. In this case, the age-defined dependency ratio is used only as a proxy to the ratio of non-working people to working people.

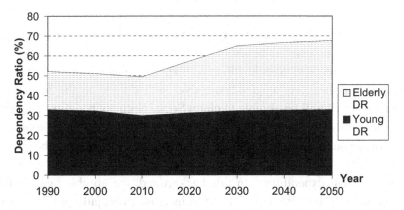

Figure 2.6 Dependency Ratio (DR) in the United States, 1990–2050

Data Source: U.S. Census Bureau.

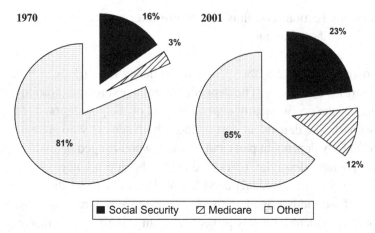

Figure 2.7 Federal Budget Allocation I 1970 versus 2001
Note: This figure is drawn based on Hooymann and Kiyak (2005).

What is behind the increasing dependency ratio is not just the looming labor shortage, but also the fiscal crises. Social Security, Medicare, and national health expenditures on the senior population comprise an increasingly large percentage of the federal budget. In 1970, Social Security represented 15.5% of federal budget and Medicare about 3.2%; in 2001, these percentages had increased to 23% and 12%, respectively (Hooymann and Kiyak, 2005). This is illustrated in Figure 2.7.

Callaban (2000) also indicated that Americans aged 65 or over consumed 36% of national health expenditures, which is 4 times higher than that for younger cohorts (with ages less than 65). The U.S. Census projects that the number of Americans aged 62 and over will double in the next three decades and all will be eligible to claim Social Security benefits. This will mean seniors will consume at least 8 times higher national health expenditures than younger cohorts in the next three decades, assuming the size of younger cohorts stays the same. This will surely add much more pressure to government expenditure. In this background, the eligible age for full Social Security benefits is legislated to increase eventually to 67 so as to reduce the fiscal pressure (Social Security Advisory Board, 1999; Bruce *et al.*, 2000). Duval (2003) noted that early labor market withdrawal came at the expense of living standards of the later generations because retirement benefits were financed through payroll taxes. Greenspan (2004) thus emphasized the need for the government to recalibrate public programs, or the economy would not be able to deliver sufficient benefits to retirees.

Social Security income is an important source of income for seniors. The initial Social Security Act (Act of August 14, 1935) paid retirement benefits only to the primary workers and Social Security benefits was not meant to support all needs of individuals in the old age but rather as a supplemental resource; however, the Social Security benefits have been expanded over the past decades and nowadays comprise an important part of income to many seniors. According to Social Security Administration (2004), Social Security benefits comprised 39 percent of the aggregate income of the aged population (of age 65 and over) in 2003; Social Security was the only source of income for 21 percent of American seniors in 2003, and it comprised over 90 percent of the total income for 34 percent of American seniors in 2003.

Without altered policies, the financial crisis in the coming decades will be worse. Bruce *et al.* (2000) indicated that under the current policies and the Social Security Trustees' intermediate assumptions, annual expenditures on the Old Age, Survivors and Disability programs (OASDI) would be expected by the year 2016 to exceed the OASDI tax income that would come from the payroll. This will also exceed all sources of income. These sources of income include the taxes and interest earned on Trust Fund Reserves that are expected to come in by 2025. The Board of Trustees (2000) indicated that by 2037, the accumulated OASDI trust funds could be exhausted, and anticipated receipts would be able to cover only about 70% of anticipated expenditures.

4. Policy Options for the Labor Force Shortage and Expenditure Pressure

To avoid the potential labor and financial crises, some are considering various policy options (see Peterson, 1999; Herman *et al.*, 2003). These include cutting back benefits, raising taxes, and taking measures to enlarge the labor force.

4.1. *Cutting benefits and raising taxes*

As mentioned earlier, if the dependency ratio keeps increasing and there are more and more people who demand but not produce social products, the macroeconomic pressure will keep increasing. To solve this problem, several approaches are suggested to cut benefits. Pension privatization is a heatedly discussed strategy that proposes to reduce government cost for retirement benefits. However, the transition cost for privatization is huge, and privatization could generate higher taxes (Peterson, 1999). Another way to cut welfare benefit for older people is to reduce health care cost. Let alone the rising living standard and growing individual demands for health care, the new medicine and treatment are increasingly expensive. All this made it less possible to largely reduce health care cost. During these recent years, the required benefit cuts under Bush's proposal have caused a huge debate on Social Security. Directly cutting benefits seems against the social progress expectation and seems difficult to the policy implementation.

Instead of cutting benefits, increasing taxes to pay for the welfare for seniors is another approach intended to directly mitigate government expenditure pressure, but this approach transfers the government expenditure pressure to workers. The high tax in European has ended up with more working-age people dropping out (Peterson, 1999). There is no guarantee that the similar situation would not occur in the United States if higher taxes were levied. Additionally, tax in the United States has already been as high as 32% of GDP (Peterson, 1999).

To indirectly reduce government pressure for health cost, filial obligation and family care giving have been emphasized. Researches have argued that filial obligation and family care could not only reduce health cost, but also generate bigger life satisfaction for older people (Hooyman and Kiyak, 2005). However, with limited number of young people and with such huge social responsibility to create enough output, future family care from the younger generation can only be limited.

4.2. *Enlarge the labor force*

To alleviate the government expenditure pressure, enlarging labor force is an alternative strategy other than cutting benefits or raising taxes. Since the strategies to cut benefits might not work well, it is necessary to evaluate approaches to enlarge the labor force. The strategies to increase the labor force include attracting more immigrants to the U.S. labor force, encouraging greater labor force participation by women, shortening current education length requirements, and increasing productivity through, for example, developing new technologies and innovations to further supplement human labor (Crown and Longino, 2000; Herman *et al.*, 2003). All of these strategies have certain limitations.

Enlarging the labor force include enhancing per worker productivity and increasing quantity of workers. Due to the excitement created by the technological progress, machine operating (Herman *et al.*, 2003) and technological and organizational innovation (Crown and Longino, 2000) have been heatedly discussed as approaches to enhance per worker productivity and to reduce the need of human labor. However, machines cannot totally replace human labor. Without human capital such as creativity and innovation, machines would not perfectly replace human labor. Developing and using technological and organizational innovation need people and funding as well. Also, it is not possible for machines and innovation to replace human labor in a huge magnetite within a short period of time.

In addition to enhancing per worker productivity, involving more workers into the labor force is critical to enlarge the labor force. Absorbing immigrants to make up for the American labor force shortage has been considered as a possible approach (Herman *et al.*, 2003). However, politically a country cannot admit huge quantities of immigrants over a short period of time. The U.S. national security issue is the first reason many Americans will oppose increasing the size of immigrants. Also, with the economic development in developing countries, fewer and fewer people of those countries would want to leave home for career opportunities in the United States. Moreover, it is necessary to offer working immigrants similar social benefits as to American citizens, as many recent immigration policy debates argue. Unfortunately, improving welfare benefits to immigrants will add financial pressure to government. The recent immigrant workers' riot in France is a lesson of the situation that immigrant workers are used as only labor, but not necessarily provided with social welfare.

Attracting more women to work is another approach to add more workers to the labor force (Herman *et al.*, 2003). Liberating women from housework has been a milestone of cultural progress and that largely resulted in the "fertility transition" in Stage III of the "Demographic Transition Model" (Figure 2.3). During the past decades, women's participation in the labor force has been increasing, which has partially resulted in the decrease of fertility rate. Although promoting female labor force could help to bridge the labor force shortage, this approach has two limitations. First, many American women have already been in the labor force and the effect from putting more women to work could be limited, relative to attracting seniors to the labor force. Second, putting more women into work could possibly further endanger the fertility rate or influence education for children. More flexible work schedule may help women to balance work and family. In general, unless there is a whole series of policies and technology possibilities to ensure the fertility rate and children's education performance, adding women to the labor force would not be a long-term thorough approach to mitigate the looming labor shortage.

Herman *et al.* (2003) also included promoting practical education as a way to fill in the labor force shortage. This approach emphasizes that current education is obsolete for job skill needs and it is necessary to adapt young students with the technology change. Thus, shortening current education length and putting young graduates to work sooner can enlarge the current size of labor force. This may be a fairly effective approach, except that change in education policy is never a short-term practice. Another advantage of shortening schooling time span and involving more young graduates into labor force is the possibility of increasing fertility rate and thus downsize the population age. However, if no better policies could solve the conflicts between raising children and pursuing individual career goals, the win from increasing children will be partially traded off by fewer women would participate into labor force.

4.3. *Involving seniors in the labor force as an option*

All the above approaches could help to reduce the labor force shortage; however, in addition to enhancing productivity per worker by developing technology and increasing the size of working age labor force by involving more women and early graduates into current labor force, working longer and retiring later might solve the labor force shortage in a big magnitude. Encouraging older people to remain in the labor force could be a feasible and effective strategy to mitigate the labor force shortage crisis. First, as mentioned earlier, the aged cohort is growing. Second, this strategy could help to reduce the number of senior dependents, improve the elderly dependency ratios and consequently, contribute to the Social Security fund contribution. Lastly, this strategy could even improve seniors' satisfaction of life (Hooymann and Kiyak, 2005).

According to the age pyramids in Appendix 2.1, there will be an increasingly large senior population in the future decades and seniors will take a bigger and bigger proportion among total population. Plus, encouraging a longer working life will not exclude other approaches mentioned above. These older people include women and immigrants. If everyone could work a bit longer with their accumulated working experience and skills, the elderly "dependents" could turn into elderly "supporters". Since people are living longer, healthier, and better educated than before, why cannot people work longer? Early retirement incentive was applied in a certain historical period, but this approach may not be necessary any more. In addition, continuing working is consistent with the concept of "successful aging" that implies that keeping active and productive in late life can increase older people's life satisfaction (Hooymann and Kiyak, 2005).

In response to the fiscal and labor crises, Bruce *et al.* (2000) predicted that future generations of workers could decide to remain in the labor force longer than current workers, and that these workers would rely more on earnings rather than Social Security funds for their economic well-being in the later stages of life. Duval (2003) also offered a similar insight and suggests, based on theoretical and empirical analysis, that seniors' participation in the labor force could ease the adjustment to aging population by curbing the rise in age-related spending. Actually, the enlarged labor force participation through increased seniors' involvement can result in higher tax revenue and thus generate a better financial basis for an enhanced welfare system to seniors as a whole.

However, there are also many disincentives as well as incentives for older people to join the labor force. The next two sections thus focus on exploring the disincentives and incentives for delaying retirement age.

5. Disincentives for Elderly Employment

Although seniors' participation may help reduce the labor force shortage, the issue of retiring later in life is a controversial concern for both employers and seniors themselves. First, in the private sector, many employer pension plans penalize older workers through benefit calculation rules that reduce the value of expected pension benefits for additional years of work on that job (Bruce *et al.*, 2000). Second, employers are concerned about the higher cost[8] and lower productivity generated by older people[9] (Crown and Longino, 2000). Another similar major concern is that older people are perceived as being technically obsolete. Last, there are many other personal and social factors that discourage an older person to continue working beyond retirement. Some of these factors include increased income[10] (Clark *et al.*, 1999), their own failing health or their family members' failing health, financial incentives for early retirement (Ippolito, 1990; CED, 1999; Crown and Longino, 2000; Remery *et al.*, 2003), job loss, difficult bosses or coworkers, and age discrimination (Rix, 2004).

As indicated earlier, historically, there is a trend of early retirement since the 1950s. This trend of early retirement is resulted from various factors. Personal decision of retirement is from the labor supply side, which differs from the reasons of the labor demand side. The incentives for early retirement from the labor demand side include policy incentives for early retirement in some companies, new technology requirement, and stereotypes against seniors. Crown and Longino (2000) also indicated that some policies encouraged early retirement, such as financial incentives for Social Security and private pension plans. The following subsections explain those incentives in details.

5.1. *Factors affecting individuals' retirement decisions*

Although retirement is basically a voluntary decision in the United States, there are many personal factors influencing older people to decide the timing of retirement, in addition to policy incentives for early retirement and age discrimination. Clark *et al.* (1999) compared data across states in the United States and found that increases in income per capita over long periods played a significant role in the decline in older men's labor force participation rate. With the income increase, many young older people (aged 65–74) choose to retire for leisure travel that is prevented by their working schedules. However, leisure travel is not the only attraction for Americans to retire. Many of them retire because they need to offer care to their beloved ones, or because of their own failing health, or because they do not obtain enough happiness from work, which could result from indirect age discrimination. Research from American Association of Retired Persons (AARP) Public Policy Institute has found that job losses, health problems, and care giving responsibilities as well as difficult bosses or coworker and age discrimination (Rix, 2004) are among the incentives to appeal for retirement.

5.2. *Public policy and financial incentive for early retirement*

Public policy usually plays an important role in intervening market behavior, particularly when the policy can be used for profitability. The Early Retirement Incentive Programs (ERIPs) in the late 1970s and early 1980s have been very effective and its influence can still be seen now. ERIPs was developed to vacate more working opportunities to the large young baby boomer cohort and thus gave older people more time to enjoy the rest of their life. However, it has been used as an excuse for employers to reduce their older personnel for cost consideration without exposing themselves to charges of age discrimination (Crown and Longino, 2000). Now facing the workforce shortage, public policy tend to orient later retirement, but those polices do not seem as effective as the ERIPs. Although 1978 Amendments to the Age Discrimination in Employment Act, 1983 Social Security amendments, and Social Security Retirement Trust Fund contained several provisions designed to encourage later retirement, those policies are only partially effective and receive smaller than anticipated effects (Crown and Longino, 2000).

Among public policies, financial policies normally strongly influence people's decisions to retire. CED (1999) suggested that private pension plans and Social Security discourage older people to continue working because they penalized work after some age, often as low as age 55. Working after this age will reduce the value of lifetime pension benefits and thus creates an implicit "tax". Remery *et al.* (2003) concluded Dutch employment for older people and directly pointed out that older workers tended to be a particularly vulnerable position during economic recession because early retirement was often seen as a less painful approach to reduce the labor supply than large-scale layoffs. The U.S. economic sluggish in the late 1980s and early 1990s compounded with early retirement wave has downsized the age of the U.S. labor force and many older workers have exited from the labor force. In 1950, the labor force participation rate of older people aged 65 or over was 42%; in 1970 this figure declined to 27%; by 1985, this labor force participation rate for older people dropped to only 16% (Ippolito, 1990). Although recent labor force participation rate of older people began to slightly rebound due to various reasons (see Appendix 2.2), according to data from BLS early retirement trend still has its momentum so that the actual retirement age in 2000 has not yet increased much from the age of 62.

5.3. *Structural disincentive for late retirement and cost of employing older people*

In addition to older people's voluntary decisions of withdrawing the labor force, there are also structural and cultural disincentives for them to continue working. Crown and Longino (2000) indicated that older people tended to be at odds with technology innovation associated with the increased training needs. Older people are more vulnerable to skill obsolescence, which shrinks their value to employers. For those older people who retired for a while and who had been working for an employer for a long time and did not change jobs as often as the younger ones, lacking job hunting techniques is another structural disincentive for older people to continue working (Hooyman and Kiyak, 2005).

Many employers concern about the higher costs and lower productivity generated by the older employees, relative to younger ones (Crown and Longino, 2000). Productivity, to a large extent, depends on workers' skill levels. Older people's obsolete skills devalue their productivity or profitability toward employers, which thus composes a big reservation of hiring older people. Employing older people is normally associated with higher labor cost because of higher income matching with their longer working experiences, higher level of absenteeism, higher health insurance cost, some government regulation of employee benefits, and pensions.

Although pensions are fading from the equation of labor cost for employers, realities between older workers' earnings and health insurance cost still worry employers. Thurow (1975) introduced a "Seniority Principle". This principle suggests that income and productivity are not always related across a worker's career. During the first phase of workers' career while they are younger, their earnings are lower than their productivity; during the second phase with older ages, their earnings are higher than their productivity (Lazear, 1998). During the older ages, when productivity begins to decline, their earnings do not necessarily decline; but the "overpaid" earnings are normally a signal of the end of their employment due to profitability for employers. Hence, realities between older workers' earning partially contribute to the high cost of hiring older people. CED (1999) pointed out that employers' willingness to hire or retain older employees depends on availability of their labor, level of their productivity, and associated costs. This is consistent with social exchange gerontology theory that emphasizes the reciprocal benefit between older people and others (Hooyman and Kiyak, 2005). Hence, unless older workers continually upgrading their skills, desirable well-paid jobs needing new technology and skills will not open to them.

5.4. *Stereotype and myth of the old*

Although public policy currently prefers older people to continuing to work, at corporate level, employers tend to be culturally biased against older workers and tend not to design programs to retain them (AARP, n.d.; Barth *et al.*, 1993; Guillemar *et al.*, 1996; Taylor and Walker, 1998; Wagner, 1998;

Henkens, 2000). In addition to possible higher labor cost of hiring older people due to seniority principle and obsolete skills of many older employees, older people are typically perceived in public culture as ailing, less efficient, with slow reaction, limited learning capacity, etc. (Sokolovsky, 2000). All those contribute to barriers preventing hiring older people and preventing older people from seeking for training and job opportunities.

Actually, various studies show that age is a poor indicator of work performance and the variations in performance within the same cohorts far exceed the average differences between cohorts (Human Resources Development Canada, 1999; Sterns and McDaniel, 1994). Using data on U.S. General Motor employees, Florida State University Psychology Department and Pepper Institute on Aging and Public Policy have found that older workers are not less productive or valuable in the workplace, despite their longer learning processes (Charness, 2004).

Even for the new skills related to high technology, research also shows that seniors' deficiencies in computer skills, for example, are really a function of socially driven motivation (Friedberg, 2003; Resnick *et al.*, 2004). Lawton and Nahemow's (1973) Competence Model can be used to explain this phenomenon. This model is composed of environmental press and individual competence. Environmental press refers to social and physical environments; individual competence refers to the theoretical upper limit of an individual's adaptability to environmental change.[11] Older adults still have the ability to learn new technologies and gain further skills. The key to this is how much the social environment facilitates and encourages them to learn these skills. Once older people learn new skills, their individual competence improves and they can handle a higher level of environmental press.

6. Incentives for Elderly Employment

There are also positive incentives for elders to stay in the labor force and these factors have contributed to the recent increase in older people's labor force participation rate (see Appendix 2.2). First, improved health conditions, more often physically, enable seniors to continue working after retirement. Second, the emergence of the "footloose" "knowledge economy" and an increasing public attention paid to the workforce barriers of the physically challenged, are making it easier for seniors to participate in the workforce. Third, financial reasons, such as the inability to afford retirement and fear of losing access to health insurance, encourage seniors to continue working (Brown, 2003; Rix, 2004). Fourth, the improvements in quality of life that result from continuing to work provide another motivation for seniors to remain in the workforce (Research from CED, 1999; Hooyman and Kiyak, 2005). Fifth, innovative arrangements, such as more attractive part-time jobs, more flexible schedules, phased retirement opportunities, and teleworking possibilities also encourage older people to postpone their retirement. The flexibility offered by the teleworking options allows seniors to tend to personal or family health-related needs and enables workers to combine employment and leisure (RoperASW, 2002; Herman *et al.*, 2003; Rix, 2004). Sixth, the work disincentives associated with Social Security are going away. Those who have reached the normal retirement age are no longer subject to an earning test. This situation allows seniors to earn any amount of income without the fear of losing Social Security benefits (Burtless and Quinn, 2000; Bruce *et al.*, 2000). Also, as mentioned earlier, the normal retirement age for Social Security eligibility in the United States has been raised from 65 to 67. This trend may continue to push up the average retirement age and legislative efforts to raise the initial eligible age for Social Security to beyond 62. Last, seniors' human capital is being recognized and paid increasing attention to. The following subsections give more details of the above points.

6.1. *Improved health conditions*

As indicated in the last section, individual decisions of later retirement are normally determined by the factors of their health, financial affordability, life satisfaction through work, etc. Although poor health of some older people and their family members prevent them from continuing to work, health condition for older Americans generally keeps enhancing, due to improving medical care, medicine and immunization technology, living conditions, and social attention to nutrition. Americans now live longer and healthier. Hayflick's (1980) rectangularization of the survival curve theory captures this change. Because people are living a longer and longer life, percentage of people surviving till age 100 is approaching 100% and thus approaching the rectangular shape with which 100% of people can survive till age 100. Hayflick (1980) delineated the trend of surviving curve rectangularization according to American demographic history.

In addition, factors, such as the development of "footloose" economy and more and more public attention paid to handicapped people's accessibility and mobility, reduce physical constraints for older people to work. In fact, by 1970s when physically demanding manufacturing industries dominated job markets, seniors used to work till their 70s. Now with a less physically demanding industry mix, why can't the elderly work longer? According to the labor force data from BLS, over the period of 1950–1980, labor force participation rate of older people was higher and people retired later than the period of 1980–2000. Although early retirement programs and other factors have withdrawn many older people from workforce, as introduced in the previous section, health condition is generally not a key factor preventing older people from working longer, comparing the historical period before 1980.

6.2. *Other personal incentives for late retirement*

Financial reasons are normally a key reason for older people's decision of retirement. The 2003 random telephone survey from AARP indicated that financial concerns represented the primary reason for older people to continue working (Brown, 2003). Rix (2004) also indicated that, if seniors were physically capable of working, lacking affordability to retire and fear of losing access to health insurance would for older people to work. However, if older people continue to work for merely lack of financial support, this situation will imply that older people are forced to continue working and it will reduce older people's life satisfaction, which is inconsistent with social progress expected by Americans. The policy proposal that purports a legal retirement age as late as 67 or even 70 is not included in policy considerations of this study.

Rather than out of financial necessity, many older people believe that work is also a source of life satisfaction, which is consistent with the promotion of "successful aging" or "productive aging". Working can not only make older people feel more productive and valuable, but also keep them active in many social relationships, particularly when older people have had established comfortable networks. Hooyman and Kiyak (2005) stated that, in addition to financial need, desires to feel productive, job restructuring and contingent and temporary service jobs were other reasons making older people seek employment. A 2002 AARP survey which examined older people's working attitudes disclosed that 76% of those surveyed considered work satisfaction as the major reason to continue working; 68% chose to work because they liked being productive; 68% worked because they felt themselves useful (AARP, n.d.). Research from CED (1999) also pointed out that psychological life satisfaction was an important reason for older people to work, in addition to their own economic status and other social factors.

6.3. *Older workers' human capital*

Many people are recognizing the value of older people's human capital. The 2003 SHRM/NOWCC/CED[12] Older Workers Survey identified the following reasons to hire or retain older workers: invaluable experience, established business ties, strong work ethic, loyalty to company, adding diversity of thoughts and approaches, and mentoring to younger workers (Collison, 2003). Jimmy Carter also concluded wisdom of older people as experience, guidance, leadership, and comfort (Peterson, 1999). Technology and skill obsolescence is a concern preventing employing older people; however, older people do have valuable human capital that younger people may not possess.

Although older people are typically associated with obsolete technology and skills, research shows that older people are not naturally disconnected from new technology; instead, it is the environment that makes older people give up accepting training for new technology and skills. Friedberg

(2003) found that not only investment in computer use made older people retire later, but also people who had planned to retire later were more likely to accept training and invest in computer use. Although marketing and training for new information and communication technologies (ICT) has focused mainly on younger people due to stereotype about older people's learning capacity, recent studies from Resnick *et al.* (2004) demonstrated that older adults could learn to use the Internet and that web use can improve elders' quality of life.

Lawton's (1973) Competence Model can also explain these phenomena. Older adults still have ability to learn new technology and skills. The key is how much the social environment facilitates and encourages them to do so. In terms of new skills and technology, if the society generally doubts elders' learning capacity and discourages them to learn, or if the new technology and skills are totally disconnected with older people's original skill base, older people sense a strong environmental press, which may prevent older people from updating their skills; however, if elders are encouraged to learn new skills and technology related to their original skills, older people sense a limited environmental press and their individual competence can lead them to learn. If older people are totally disengaged from working responsibilities and there is no need to learn new skills while they are still in good shape, they will face too low environmental press and feel bored or become dependent on others. Hence, creating a comfortable learning environment that encourages elders to learn is helpful; disengaging older people while they are still competent for many jobs will possibly either reduce their life satisfaction due to boredom or make them dependent on others due to learned helplessness resulting from too low environmental press.

Another major concern from employers or general public is that older people are perceived to be less productive than younger people, but this perception could be wrong. People's intelligence is composed of Crystallized Intelligence and Fluid Intelligence (Hooyman and Kiyak, 2005). Crystallized Intelligence is a form of acquired knowledge and is usually stable until very late life; Fluid Intelligence refers to ability to quickly solve novel problems and shows declines from the 20s or 30s

(Schulz and Salthouse, 1999). Although older people may have disadvantage for fluid intelligence, they may not have disadvantage for crystallized intelligence. Thus, older people may have more difficulty than younger ones for learning brand new knowledge, but it does not necessarily mean they are less productive. Human Resources Development Canada (1999) evaluated older people aged over 45 in Canada and found that there was no significant overall difference between the job performance of older and younger workers and variations within an age group far exceeded the average differences between age groups in almost every study. Although this study used a difference age definition for older people and the research samples are of Canadians instead of Americans, the result still shows a possible wrong stereotype of older people in terms of their productivity. Research done by Florida State University Psychology Department and Pepper Institute on Aging and Public Policy used data from U.S. corporations such as from General Motor and found that age is not a good predictor of worker productivity: although age may make older people's learning slower and take longer, age does not make significant difference in work performance and productivity (Charness, 2004). This result is consistent with research done 10 years ago by Sterns and McDaniel (1994) who indicated that age was a poor predicator of job performance.

6.4. *Flexible work schedule adjustment*

Economic background is an "invisible hand" influencing the timing of retirement. Current U.S. economy has transferred from a manufacturing dominant economy to a service dominant economy. The development of information technology also makes "footloose" economy possible. In this background, flexible work schedule becomes more and more possible, which offers an environmental incentive for older people to retain working. Hence, more attractive part-time jobs, more flexible schedules, phased retirement opportunities, and teleworking possibilities would encourage older people to postpone retirement because the flexibility allows for older workers' personal health related needs and also enable workers to combine employment and leisure (Herman *et al.*, 2003; Rix, 2004). A national survey conducted for AARP introduces phased retirement as an approach that enables older workers to reduce their work schedules and thus prolongs their work life, particularly for the retention of skilled workers (RoperASW, 2002).

7. Increasing Labor Force Participation Rate Among Seniors

These years, older people's labor force participation rate has begun to increase. In Europe, the "Dutch miracle" in the 1990s that reflects public attitude change from negative to positive on older people's involvement into the workforce has led to a high rate of employment growth and further stimulated early retirement reforms (van Dalen and Henkens, 2002). In the United States, data from BLS shows the upward trend over the past decade for older people's labor force participation rate and their employment-population ratio, shown in Appendix 2.2. Using random digit dialing, in 2003 AARP conducted a nationwide telephone survey of 2001 workers between the ages of 50 and 70 to explore their vision of retirement and found that majority of pre-retirees defined retirement to include some form of work (Brown, 2003).

Summary

- The aging U.S. population results in potential labor force shortage and Social Security trust fund exhaustion.
- Involving seniors in the labor force is an option to enlarge the labor force.
- Disincentives for seniors to be involved in the labor force include policy and financial incentives for early retirement, individuals' decision, structural disincentive for late retirement, and stereotype and myth of the old.
- Individuals' decision to stay outside the labor force is affected by needs for leisure, job loss, lack of happiness from work, health problems, care giving responsibilities, and age discrimination.
- The structural disincentives for continued employment include perceived skill obsolescence, lack of job hunting techniques, and

higher labor cost (i.e., higher wages, higher level of absenteeism, and higher health insurance cost).

- Incentives for seniors to be involved in the labor force include improved health conditions, inability to afford retirement and fear of losing access to health insurance, the improvements in quality of life that result from continuing to work, existence of innovative working arrangements such as phased retirement and teleworking possibilities, disappearing early retirement incentives, and being recognized seniors' human capital.

End notes

[8] Higher labor cost is because of higher level of absenteeism, higher health insurance cost, pensions, higher income level matching with their longer working experiences (Thurow, 1975; Lazear, 1998), and some government regulation of employee benefits.

[9] Perceived lower productivity is associated with their obsolete skills (Crown and Longino, 2000) and stereotype against them, such as ailing, less efficient, with slow reaction, limited learning capacity, etc. (AARP, n.d.; Barth *et al.*, 1993; Guillemar *et al.*, 1996; Henkens, 2000; Sokolovsky, 2000; Taylor and Walker, 1998; Wagner, 1998).

[10] Increased income accumulated throughout their life ensures seniors a more affordable and comfortable late life. This situation discourages to some extent, working beyond retirement if the continued working is only motivated by and targeted to getting more necessary income to increase the affordability to retire.

[11] With a too high environmental press surpassing individual competence, individuals experience excessive stress or overload; with a too low environmental press, individuals experience sensory derivation, boredom, helplessness, and thus depend on others (Hooyman and Kiyak, 2005).

[12] This survey is a combination of a team effort among the Society for Human Resource Management (SHRM), National Older Worker Career Center (NOWCC) and Committee for Economic Development (CED). A sample of

HR professionals was randomly selected from SHRM's membership database, which consists of more than 170,000 members. In November 2002, 2,500 randomly selected SHRM members received an e-mail invitation containing a link that directed them to the online survey. Of these, 2,143 e-mails were successfully delivered to respondents, and 428 HR professionals responded, yielding a response rate of 20%.

PART 3
WHY ELDERLY ENTREPRENEURSHIP?

CHAPTER 3

ELDERLY ENTREPRENEURSHIP TO SUSTAIN THE LABOR FORCE: POSSIBILITIES AND NECESSITIES

As indicated in the previous chapter, there are both incentives and disincentives for seniors to be involved in the labor force, at personal levels as well as social levels. Although motivating more seniors to remain in or reenter the labor force would possibly help our economy to mitigate the aging-related labor and fiscal crises, there is a problem on how to motivate seniors, particularly those skilled seniors, to continue contributing to the economy after their planned retirement age. Although many seniors would still prefer staying active in the economic society to avoid boredom in retirement, not all seniors would be happy to continue working. Many factors could contribute to this unwillingness of returning to the work place, such as the responsibilities to take care of ailing family members, their own health limitations, personal needs to travel and leisure, difficult bosses, unpleasant working environment, and even age discrimination at work. In those cases, unless their continued employment in the workplace could bring them more necessary income, they would not be much motivated to work after retirement age.

Entrepreneurship, compared to the wage-and-salary employment, could possibly offer more motivation for seniors to stay in the labor force. Entrepreneurship offers more flexibility than wage-and-salary employment. This flexibility allows for more personal needs in retirement life. That is why entrepreneurship or self-employment has been treated as a "bridge job" by Quinn (1980). For Quinn, the "bridge jobs" means a working position between full engagement in the labor force and retirement. In this situation, seniors can both consider needs in the retirement life and enjoy fun and income from working. Entrepreneurship, different from the wage-and-salary jobs, could possibly be an effective way to motivate seniors to remain in or even reenter the labor force. If this were true, when a positive social policy investment favors elderly entrepreneurship, many seniors would possibly be motivated to choose elderly entrepreneurship and participate in the labor force; this would eventually help to mitigate the labor and fiscal crises resulted from an aging population.

Specifically, two levels of possibilities and of necessities make developing elderly entrepreneurship a viable solution to enlarging the labor force to include more seniors in the aging economy. The two levels refer to the personal/individual level and the social levels. The following sections explain in details those possible and necessary factors to develop elderly entrepreneurship for an aging society.

1. Social Possibilities

Among the social possibilities, the most important one is the economic shift to the "knowledge economy". The emergence of the "knowledge economy" elevates the importance of mental power, reduces requirement for physical labor, is less restrictive to physical locations and thus becomes more "footloose", and generates many new technological possibilities.

In the "knowledge economy", human capital, brainpower, and innovation become the key factor driving economic growth and physical labor becomes less important. This situation makes seniors' reduced physical labor power less disadvantageous and instead makes their cumulative working skills and knowledge more valuable in the new economy. The "knowledge economy" encourages innovation and entrepreneurship. The "footloose" property of the "knowledge economy" increases teleworking possibilities and encourages seniors to become or continue to be entrepreneurs. The "footloose" and less physically demanding feature of the "knowledge economy" reduces location and physical limitations for seniors to participate in the labor force; the innovative and entrepreneurial focus of the "knowledge economy" makes elderly entrepreneurship more possible.

Assisted technology also makes elderly entrepreneurship more possible. With more seniors in the population and with an increasing concern about handicapped people, assisted technology has been of public focuses. Information technology further expedited the development of assisted technology by reducing geographic limitations. The assisted technology makes it easier for seniors to work and therefore increases the opportunity for seniors to become or continue to be entrepreneurs.

Additionally, more and more people begin to recognize seniors' special human capital and the social respect toward seniors are increasing. Seniors' special mental value that has been aware of in literature include invaluable experience, established business ties, strong work ethic, loyalty to the company, adding diversity of thoughts and approaches, mentoring to younger workers (Collison, 2003), guidance, leadership, comfort, and wisdom (Peterson, 1999). The positive attitude toward seniors would further encourage seniors to become or continue to be entrepreneurs.

2. Personal Possibilities

At the individual level, improved health conditions and enjoyment from working, particularly as an entrepreneur, makes it more possible for seniors to become or continue to be entrepreneurs. Over the past decades, human's health conditions are much improved and life expectancy becomes longer. This enhanced health condition and longer life biologically makes it possible for seniors to be involved in entrepreneurial activities. The biological background also guarantees seniors to enjoy their work more than before. Retirement while being physically active increases boredom to many seniors. Instead, many seniors enjoy working rather than retiring. Researches have evidenced the improvements in life quality that resulted from continuing to work rather than retirement (AARP, n.d.)[13].

Compared to wage-and-salary employment, entrepreneurship offers more flexibility, control, and freedom, which would offer more life satisfaction.

Therefore, the improved health conditions and enhanced life quality through working, particularly through entrepreneurship, increases the possibility for seniors to participate in entrepreneurial activities.

3. Social Necessities

There are not only social and personal possibilities for seniors to become entrepreneurs, there are also social and personal necessities. Elderly entrepreneurship is a necessary approach to solve the aging-resulted labor and financial crises. As indicated earlier, the aging population results in a potential labor force shortage and the Social Security fund exhaustion. On the one hand, the aging labor force will generate an increasingly large retirement population, while the working age population is not enlarging; on the other hand, retirement age is actually declining from 1970 to 2000 (Ippolito, 1990; Gendell, 2001). Assuming similar technological and policy conditions at the current level, a labor force shortage would be the result. Longer life and thus longer periods in retirements would even deepen this labor force shortage.

Accordingly, Social Security expenditures on seniors comprise an increasingly large share in the federal budget. Under the current policies and the Social Security Trustees' intermediate assumptions, Social Security expenditure will exceed the total of Social Security tax income and interest earned by 2025 (Bruce *et al.*, 2000). By 2037, the Social Security fund is predicted to be exhausted and anticipated receipts could only cover 70% of anticipated expenditures (The Board of Trustees, 2000).

Developing elderly entrepreneurship becomes a necessary approach to mitigate the aforementioned labor and financial crises, not only because several alternative policy options have limitations[14], but also because wage-and-salary employment is not an easy option for seniors. Pension privatization will generate huge transition costs and may result in higher taxes (Peterson, 1999). An increase in income taxes may result in higher dropout rates from the labor force, as occurred in Europe (Peterson, 1999). Politically it is difficult to put in place policies to absorb too many immigrants to fill in the labor force. Attracting more females in the labor force needs to settle daycare and schooling arrangements in order not to affect fertility rate and education quality, which might not be achievable in a short time period. Wage-and-salary employment does not offer sufficient flexibility and freedom as entrepreneurship and thus limits seniors' chance to retain or reenter in the labor force. Moreover, wage-and-salary employment only makes senior employees contribute 50% of the Social Security fund, but elderly entrepreneurship will make seniors contribute 100%. Compared to elderly wage-and-salary employment, elderly entrepreneurship can largely help to mitigate the aging related fiscal crisis.

Additionally, it is necessary to improve the public image of seniors. Successful elderly entrepreneurship can largely enhance seniors' public image and defeat the stereotypes against seniors. With an aging population and an increasingly large elderly population, the stereotype against seniors needs to be changed. Older people are perceived in the United States typically as being technically obsolete, slow, ailing, and some other negative images. All those negative images generate discrimination against seniors and harm seniors' late-life satisfaction. With more seniors in our society, improving seniors' life satisfaction becomes a general public issue that would concern more and more social members. Successful entrepreneurship, including elderly entrepreneurship, on the other hand, is concentrated with various positive qualities: high motivation, timely innovation, skillful management, established social and business ties, and strategic organizational behavior. Entrepreneurship could occur to the elderly and elderly persons actually have many advantages to be entrepreneurs, such as their cumulative job skills, management skills, mature social and business ties, and business experience.

4. Personal Necessities

There are also personal or individual level reasons that offer necessities for seniors to become entrepreneurs. On the one hand, financial situations force many seniors to participate in the labor force; on the other hand, wage-and-salary employment limits seniors' working opportunities.

Those financial reasons include the need for more income, inability to afford retirement, and fear of losing access to health insurance (Brown, 2003; Rix, 2004).

In the wage-and-salary workplace, many employers are still concerned about the higher cost and lower productivity associated with seniors rather than with younger workers. Higher labor cost is believed because senior workers tend to have a higher level of absenteeism, higher health insurance cost, higher income level matching with their longer working experiences (Thurow, 1975; Lazear, 1998), payment for pensions, and some government regulation of employee benefits. Lower productivity is believed because seniors are perceived to be associated with obsolete skills (Crown and Longino, 2000) and because of the stereotype against them, such as ailing, less efficient, with slow reaction, limited learning capacity, etc (AARP, n.d.; Barth *et al.*, 1993; Guillemar *et al.*, 1996; Taylor and Walker, 1998; Wagner, 1998; Henkens, 2000; Sokolovsky, 2000). In addition, there still exist some employer pension plans that reduce the value of expected pension benefits for additional years of work on the job after certain age (Bruce *et al.*, 2000). All those factors reduce the attraction of wage-and-salary workplace among seniors.

In addition to financial needs, many seniors need more flexibility and freedom beyond what wage-and-salary employment can offer. For seniors who want to or need to work after retirement but their own or their family's failing health require them a flexible schedule while working, self-employment or entrepreneurship is an option.

Foreseeable cuts in public pensions and even Social Security systems push seniors to tap new sources of income. For those who have enough income to retire, they need flexibility and time for leisure, if they choose to continue working. In this case, self-employment or entrepreneurship would possibly fulfill the needs better than wage-and-salary employment. Self-employment and working as an entrepreneur not only offers more flexibility for working seniors, but also offer more freedom and work satisfaction. Rix (2004) has noted that many seniors choose self-employment rather than wage-and-salary employment because of age discrimination, difficult bosses or coworkers, and job loss in wage-and-salary workplaces.

5. Elderly Entrepreneurship as a Means to Retain Seniors in the Labor Force

The above four sections explained the possibilities and necessities for seniors to participate in entrepreneurial activities. Due to those possibilities and necessities, elderly entrepreneurship becomes an effective approach, compared to wage-and-salary employment particularly, to retain seniors in the labor force. To empirically test this argument, this chapter uses the latest U.S. Census Public Use Microdata Samples (PUMS) data, i.e., PUMS 2000 data, to graph self-employment data by age versus wage-and-salary employment data by age. In this case, self-employment includes both unincorporated and incorporated self-employment date, according to the U.S. Census survey definitions.

Based on this dataset, the dropout rate for seniors in wage-and-salary positions is higher than that for seniors who are self-employed. Figure 3.1 shows that the proportion of wage-and-salary employees in the population as a whole begins a precipitous decline around the age of 50. Wage-and-salary employment rates in the population nearly mirror those rates associated with labor force participation and this is consistent across most age groups. Wage and salary employment and labor force participation rates drop much faster than the rates for self-employment[15] in the population. These findings are consistent with Quinn (1980), who found that the elderly who are self-employed tend to be less likely to retire than those seniors who are employed in wage-and-salary positions[16].

This smaller retirement rate in self-employment than in wage-and-salary employment could result from the aforementioned social level and individual level possibilities. Those possibility factors facilitate the development of

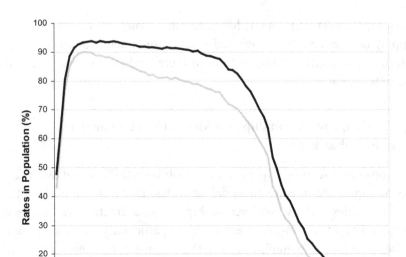

Figure 3.1 Self-employment Rates versus Wage-and-salary Employment Rates in Population by Age

elderly entrepreneurship and thus reduce the withdrawal rate from self-employment, considering the fact that entrepreneurship is a special type of self-employment.

Additionally, occupation transition from wage-and-salary employment to self-employment and from retirement to self-employment could also mitigate the reduction of self-employment in old ages. After many years of working experiences in the leadership role and with a highly familiar business ties in a certain field, many seniors have the capacity to step to personal businesses instead of working for their original companies. There are also some elderly entrepreneurs who startup new companies after retirement.

No matter what the reasons are, the smaller declining rate with old age in self-employment than in wage-and-salary employment results in a fact — self-employment retains the labor force in a much bigger magnitude than wage-and-salary employment. In this case, elderly self-employment, or elderly entrepreneurship, becomes an effective approach to retain senior labors. This would help to mitigate the labor shortage that is expected to result from the aging U.S. population.

6. Conclusion

The previous chapter introduced the labor and financial crises of the aging population and discussed the issues related to involving seniors in the labor force as a viable approach to the aging-resulted crises. This chapter further investigates the issue of involving seniors in the labor force and explains why developing elderly entrepreneurship, rather than developing wage-and-salary employment among seniors, is a necessary and possible approach to mitigate the labor and financial crises resulted from the aging population. The U.S. Census PUMS 2000 data further evidences the relevance of developing elderly self-employment to retain the labor force. According to this dataset, in comparison to seniors who are wage-and-salary employees, those who are self-employed have a higher likelihood to remain in the workforce. Age could be a significant factor for wage-and-salary employees to retire, but it does not lead to self-employment retirement with the same magnitude. This situation indicates that elderly entrepreneurship could be a viable approach to retain the labor force and thus mitigate the labor loss due to the aging population. Elderly entrepreneurship, compared to wage-and-salary employment, is a more effective and meaningful means to involve seniors in the labor force. In this case, the following chapters focus on elderly entrepreneurship and explores the possibility of entrepreneurship on seniors, factors driving seniors to become or continue to be entrepreneurs, regional distribution of elderly entrepreneurship, the role of elderly entrepreneurship in regional economic growth, and the impacts of elderly entrepreneurship on mitigating the labor force shortage and the Social Security fund exhaustion.

Summary

- Social possibility for seniors to become entrepreneurs:

  o The "footloose" less physically demanding "knowledge economy" encourages innovation and entrepreneurship and assisted technology reduces geographic and physical limitations.

  o Seniors' special mental values that include invaluable experience, established business ties, strong work ethic, guidance and leadership are being recognized and respected.

- Personal possibilities for seniors to become entrepreneurs:

  o Human's health conditions are much improved and life expectancy becomes longer.

  o Retirement while being physically active increases boredom to many seniors.

  o Entrepreneurship offers more flexibility, control, and freedom than working for others.

- Social necessities for seniors to become entrepreneurs:

  o Several alternative policy options to mitigate the potential labor shortage and Social Security crisis all have limitations.

- Personal necessities:

  o Financial reasons force many seniors to participate in the labor force.

  o There are limited opportunities in wage-and-salary employment.

  o Many seniors need more flexibility and freedom beyond what wage-and-salary employment can offer for various personal needs.

  o Foreseeable cuts in pensions and even Social Security systems push seniors to tap new sources of income.

- U.S. Census Public Use Microdata Samples data shows that wage-and-salary employment rate drop much faster than self-employment rate in the elderly population.

End notes

[13] For example, as indicated previously, a 2002 AARP survey on the attitudes of seniors found that 76% surveyed seniors considered work satisfaction as the major reason to continue working; 68% chose to work because they liked being productive; and 68% of the elders worked because they felt themselves useful.

[14] As is explained in the previous chapter.

[15] It should be noted though that difference in trends could be biased due to a relatively limited number of observations for very old ages.

[16] The data used in this figure is presented in Appendices 3.1 and 6.3.

PART 4

LITERATURE AND THEORIES ON ELDERLY ENTREPRENEURSHIP

CHAPTER 4

LITERATURE REVIEW: PREVIOUS STUDIES

The disadvantages of wage-and-salary jobs make entrepreneurship a special opportunity for the elderly. Chapter 2 concludes that there exist various barriers against seniors' employability, for a variety of reasons. This makes it difficult for seniors to obtain or maintain wage-and-salary employment during their retirement years, in comparison with their younger counterparts. On the other hand, providing seniors continued opportunities to stay active in the workforce could be beneficial to both seniors and the society. Seniors' continued economic activity could have positive effects on the economy through wage, labor, tax base expansion, and wealth creation; many seniors would possibly like to be actively involved in the labor force and feel valuable.

There is a paucity of literature on elderly entrepreneurship. This chapter details the specifics. In general, although personal factors associated with elderly occupational choice have been addressed in previous research, little attention has been paid to social and policy factors. The relationship between older age and entrepreneurship is unclear, based on previous empirical studies. Further, elderly entrepreneurship has not been addressed as a factor affecting regional economic growth. While aging population debates with respect to the labor shortages and the Social Security fund bankruptcy have been made, elderly entrepreneurship has not been suggested in previous studies as a possible solution to mitigate these problems.

This chapter reviews previous studies related to the topic of elderly entrepreneurship, outlines the theories this book relies on, and identifies some gaps in previous studies. The previous literature concerning elderly entrepreneurship addresses seniors' occupational choices, the relationship between age and entrepreneurship, and the personal factors that affect seniors' propensity to be entrepreneurs. This literature is summarized and assessed below.

There are factors, addressed in the previous chapter, that both encourage and discourage senior citizens to continue working after their retirement; this is introduced in Chapter 2. There are also many factors that offer necessities and possibilities for the elderly to be entrepreneurs; this is delineated in Chapter 3. Some of these discouraging factors for further employment are private-sector pension-plan penalties for seniors who work after a certain age, their own or family members' failing health, unpleasant working environment and, more specifically, difficult bosses. The encouraging factors for seniors to become entrepreneurs include the fact that seniors tend to have better interpersonal skills, managerial skills, and cumulated working experience. In addition to the pension-plan penalties from wage-and-salary jobs versus self-employment jobs[17] self-employment offers more time flexibility, provides a platform for seniors who have managerial skills to develop businesses by their own, eliminates the unhappiness generated by difficult bosses, and generates more self-control on their part. Various barriers to participating in or continuing to work in wage-and-salary jobs, as mentioned in Chapter 2, make self-employment an attractive alternative for seniors who would like to stay in the labor force. The fact that some seniors have built up assets and wealth over their lifetime means that seniors tend to have smaller liquidity constraints to start their own businesses. Lastly, foreseeable cuts in the generosity of public pensions and even Social Security systems may create the necessity for elders to tap new sources of income.

1. Occupational Choice, Retirement Decision Study, and Elderly Entrepreneurship

Previous aging studies have examined elderly retirement behavior and occupational choices that include withdrawing from the labor force, becoming wage-and-salary employees, or becoming an entrepreneur.

Although the topic of entrepreneurship in general has received extensive scholarly attention, aging and retirement issues are seldom addressed as relevant factors in the entrepreneurship literature. Quinn (1980) provided possibly the earliest research in this field. Using two waves of Retirement History Surveys (RHS) (Data from the 1969 and 1971 interviews of the RHS) and using data on 836 white married men aged 58–63 in 1969, Quinn found that lack of flexibility in hours worked, lack of compulsory retirement provisions, psychological and financial traumas of sudden retirement in wage-and-salary workplaces resulted in higher labor force withdrawal among senior wage-and-salary employees than among senior entrepreneurs. Quinn thus believed self-employment could be a "bridge job" between full engagement in the labor force and retirement. In addition, Quinn found that health status and Social Security benefits tended to be associated with higher withdrawal rates from the labor force.

Following Quinn (1980), several other researchers used the same survey, RHS, to investigate elderly occupational choices. Fuchs (1982) found that those with previous self-employment experience or white-collar workers with previous quasi-entrepreneurial occupations, such as managers and executives, tended to venture into entrepreneurship or venture creation before retiring. Berkovec and Stern (1991) had estimated a static and a dynamic programming model of job exit behavior and retirement. Both models displayed similar results — bad health, age, and lack of education increase the probability of retirement of older men. The method used was simulated moments[18]. The authors further noted that the job-specific differences were an important source of unobserved heterogeneity. Another study on older men, Blau (1994) used a hazard rate model with quarterly records from RHS and found that Social Security benefits had strong effects on the timing of labor force transition at older ages.

Bruce *et al.* (2000), using 1992 and 1996 Health and Retirement Study (HRS) data, examined the impact of health insurance coverage on labor market transitions of older workers and found that there was little impact of older workers' health insurance status and coverage on their choice between self-employment, wage and salary employment, and retirement. Based on the phenomenon of "insurance lock" that prevents movement toward self-employment because the entry rates to self-employment are higher but retirement rates are lower among those with no insurance than those with non-portable insurance, the authors divide elders' health insurance status into several categories: those who have no insurance, have "portable" insurance that is valid even if they change jobs, and have non-portable health insurance that will be lost if changing current employers.

With cross-country comparative time-series and micro-data evidence from the Organization for Economic Co-operation and Development (OECD) countries, Blanchflower (2000) found that self-employment rates rise with age, were higher among men, had nonlinear patterns with education, and vary across countries. Duval's (2003) OECD cross-country study suggested that the eligibility age of pension plans and unemployment rate had a significant influence on seniors' retirement decisions. Using a sample of 200 self-employed people from the British Retirement Survey (1988, 1989, and 1994), Parker and Rougaier (2004) found that greater actual and potential earnings were associated with a declined retirement probability among the self-employed; compared to wage-and-salary employees, gender, health or family circumstances did not appear to affect self-employment retirement decisions; a relatively limited number of employees and even fewer retirees switched into self-employment in later life; those who switched to self-employment in later life were less affluent and had weaker ties to the labor market. This British situation could differ much from that in the United States.

2. Previous Literature on Age and Entrepreneurship

The literature on the relationship between age and entrepreneurship is controversial. One stream holds the conventional view that seniors are less entrepreneurial than the young, i.e., less likely to start a new company. The Global Entrepreneurship Monitor (GEM) 2001 Executive Report conducted a global research and indicated that people aged 55–64 tended to be less entrepreneurial than the younger working-age groups in terms of Total Entrepreneurial Activity (TEA) opportunities, TEA necessity, and the quantity of nascent firms. GEM (2004) Executive Report also illustrated that, for countries with various income classifications — low-income, middle-income, and high-income, people of age 55–64 had a lower entrepreneurship prevalence rate than younger working-age groups. Although entrepreneurial activity does not necessarily mean self-employment, measuring and defining entrepreneurship is still a controversial issue in the academic field. Self-employment, which is used to measure entrepreneurship in many studies, is an important indicator of entrepreneurship. The findings by GEM (2001) mirrored the prediction by Johnson (1978) and Miller (1984) that younger workers, compared to older workers, would try riskier occupations first.

Another literature stream holds a neutral view on the relationship between age and entrepreneurship. Evans and Leighton (1989) found that the probability of switching to self-employment was roughly independent of age and total labor-market experience. Specifically, the fraction of the self-employed labor force increases with age until the early 40s and then remains constant until the retirement years.

The third stream of this exploration purports that seniors have a higher self-employment or entrepreneurial propensity. A cross-country study by Blanchflower *et al.* (2001) found that older workers were more likely to be self-employed. This study also explored latent entrepreneurship in those countries through surveying people's self-employment preferences. This study found that a higher proportion of younger people (than older ones) preferred to be self-employed, but a higher proportion of seniors than that of younger people were actually self-employed. This study further observed that a stronger preference for self-employment could be due to several reasons including psychological ones. Reardon (1997) also reached a similar conclusion for non-agricultural full-time self-employment based on empirical studies in the United States and Canada.

3. Previous Research on Factors Affecting Entrepreneurship Propensity

Numerous factors, such as wealth, employment status, and education, have been hypothesized and tested to influence a person's propensity to be an entrepreneur. One finding is that lack of capital is an impediment to becoming an entrepreneur. Using U.S. micro data from the National Longitudinal Survey of Young men for 1966–1981 and the Current Population Surveys for 1968–1987, Evans and Leighton (1989) and Evans and Jovanovic (1989) found that entrepreneurs face liquidity constraints that were expressed in the literature as family assets. Evans and Leighton (1989) also found that unemployed workers, low-wage workers, and workers who frequently changed jobs were more likely to be self-employed. Blanchflower and Oswald (1998) suggested that an inheritance or gift positively affected the probability of being self-employed. Blanchflower *et al.* (2001) conducted a survey of self-employment development in eighty countries and noted that old workers and men with more education were more likely to be self-employed in Europe. Using data for the U.S. and the Netherlands, van der Sluis and van Praag (2004) found that the returns to formal education for the self-employed were higher than for wage-and-salary employees. This finding was consistent with Lazear (2002) who indicated that people with many and broad skills were more likely to be self-employed than others.

Exploration of institutional factors that affect entrepreneurship is relatively limited. Those that have been identified include minimum wage legislation (Blau, 1987), immigration policy (Borjas and Bronars, 1989), retirement policies (Quinn, 1980), and tax policy (Long, 1982; Blau, 1987; and Schuetze, 2000). Schuetze (2000) compared self-employment patterns and trends in Canada with those in the United States and found that the self-employment rate increased with tax rates in primary jobs but not as much in secondary jobs. Schuetze noted that this tax-sheltering effect indicated a possibility that the self-employed were more likely to under–report.

There is also a body of literature that investigates the relationship between self-employment and the regional socioeconomic environment. Some literature finds that unemployment positively affects the probability of self-employment (Meager, 1992; Evans and Leighton, 1989; Bogenhold and Staber, 1991). Other investigators have found a negative relationship between regional unemployment and self-employment in cross-country studies (Blanchflower and Oswald, 1990; Acs and Evans, 1994; Taylor 1996; Blanchflower and Oswald, 1998). Schuetze and Bruce (2004) explored the complicated interplay between tax policy and entrepreneurial activity; Giannetti and Simonov (2004) found business environment, cultural values, and social norms were all related to entrepreneurship. Low *et al*. (2005) distinguished characteristics between urban and rural self-employed through a new measure of entrepreneurship — entrepreneurship breadth (quantity) and depth (value added). Blachflower (2000) did not find any evidence that the increase of the self-employment rate increases the real growth rate of the economy.

Other research investigates job creation, job satisfaction and gender issues as they relate to entrepreneurship. Using data from the BLS and CPS, Picot and Manser (1999) evidenced self-employment as a job creation engine in Canada and the United States. In Britain, Van Stel and Storey (2004) and Burke and Fitzroy (2006) also found evidence of a positive relationship between job creation and entrepreneurship, measured by firm birth and self-employment. Acs and Armington (2003) extended Davis and Haltiwanger (1992, 1996) methodology and concluded that the job creation function came from the business birth process, not business expansion. In terms of job satisfaction, Hamilton (2000) and Blanchflower (2000) both found that the self-employed were more satisfied with their jobs than wage-and-salary workers. This study indicated that the self-employed, despite pressure, stress, strain, worry, and exhaustion, were satisfied with their lives because they exercised control. Benz and Frey (2004) indicated that wage-and-salary employees were substantially less satisfied with their work than the self-employed, whose job satisfaction was not driven by higher pay, fewer working hours, or a person's personality, but rather by greater independence and autonomy. Taylor (1997) further indicated that the self-employed reported higher levels of job satisfaction with pay and work, but lower levels of satisfaction with job security, after tracing lifetime employment history in Britain since 1960 through data from the British Household Panel Survey. For gender issues, Carrasco and Ejrnas (2003) found that availability of part-time wage employment and childcare facilities mattered to female participation in self-employment through examining the experience in Denmark and Spain.

4. Limitations of Current Literature

Literature on the impact of age on self-employment shows inconsistent results. Some studies indicate that the elderly tend to be less entrepreneurial than the younger cohorts (Johnson, 1978; Miller, 1984; GEM, 2001, 2004); some show no correlation between age and self-employment propensity (Evans and Leighton, 1989); yet others find that elders are more likely to be self-employed (Blanchflower *et al.*, 2001).

The above-mentioned literature explores many factors that influence non-age specific entrepreneurship. Those factors include the availability of assets, tax policy, retirement policy, unemployment rate, education and skills, immigration policies, and business environment. The literature on seniors' occupational choice also identifies several other factors affecting elderly entrepreneurship, such as health, Social Security benefits, earnings, pension plan eligibility age, previous occupational experience, and demographic factors (including gender and marriage status).

However, previous literature has not emphasized the fiscal and economic impact of elderly entrepreneurship in an aging economy. In addition, the nature of a social environment that spurs elderly entrepreneurship has been minimally researched, compared to individual factors. Lastly, the literature on seniors typically addresses only young seniors (aged up to 59 in those studies) and ignores those who are even older. The labor force participation of those seniors aged over the average retirement age (62) is important to the calculation of aging-resulted fiscal and labor issues.

Part of the reason for the limited academic attention to the social environment of elderly entrepreneurship is related to the data set. The literature on elderly occupational choice around retirement age normally uses micro data sets. For the United States, HRS is typically used for the occupational choice model. Although HRS data provides extensive longitudinal detail on

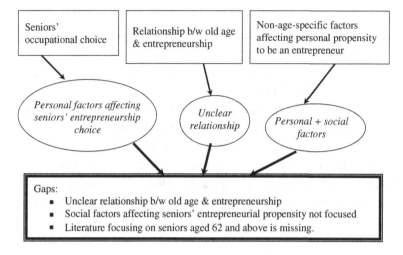

Figure 4.1 Previous Research Related to Elderly Entrepreneurship

health and labor force status of seniors aged 50 to 57 or even 59 (that is most updated age limit this dataset offers), geographically refined data at the metropolitan or county level data is not available. These limitations make it difficult to conduct regional analyses of elderly occupational choice and associated modeling, which limits the ability to examine the spatial aspects of the problem. This in turn could produce bias in the estimation of the model. Figure 4.1 summarises the previous literature and its limitations related to elderly entrepreneurship.

Summary

- Various factors were tested to relate to seniors' occupational choice, such as health, education, age, gender, and family circumstances.
- Numerous factors, such as wealth, employment status, education, tax policy, and business environment were tested to influence a person's propensity to be an entrepreneur.
- Despite pressure, stress, exhaustion, and even more working hours and not necessarily more pay, entrepreneurs were found to

be more satisfied with their life than wage-and-salary jobs, because of control, independence and autonomy.
- The previous literature on the relationship between age and entrepreneurship is controversial.
- Previous literature has not emphasized the fiscal and economic impact of elderly entrepreneurship in an aging economy.
- The nature of a social environment that spurs elderly entrepreneurship has been minimally researched, compared to individual factors.
- The literature on seniors typically addresses only young seniors and ignores those who are even older and who are important to the calculation of aging-resulted fiscal and labor issues.

End notes

[17]   Details of this is in Chapter 2.
[18]   This estimation method is used for a dynamic programming model of job exit behavior and retirement. The method allows for both unobserved individual effects and unobserved job-specific "match" effects. The model is estimated using two different assumptions about individual discount factors. First, a static model, with the discount factor equal to zero, is estimated. Then a dynamic model, with the discount factor equal to 0.95 is estimated.

CHAPTER 5

THEORETICAL FRAMEWORK

Deep population aging is occurring at a historically important economic moment — the shift to a so-called "knowledge economy"[19]. This shift presents special opportunities for seniors' economic activity, particularly elderly entrepreneurship. A major focus on this book is on the relationship between elderly entrepreneurship and regional and national economic growth. It is in the consideration of the looming labor shortage and Social Security fund exhaustion that elderly entrepreneurship is under discussion in this book; it is believed based on previous chapters that elderly entrepreneurship could help to mitigate the aging-resulted labor and fiscal crises. In this specific setting of economic discussion, elderly entrepreneurship becomes particularly important.

To interpret the specialties of the "knowledge economy" and the specific socioeconomic setting, this chapter introduces the major theories that this book underlies. Economic growth theories and regional theories are among the core of this book's theoretical framework. On the supply side, late life satisfaction offers additional perspectives of elderly entrepreneurship. Therefore, utility maximization theories and social gerontology are involved in the theoretical framework. This chapter reviews and interprets theories related to the topic of elderly entrepreneurship. It is based on these theories that further analyses are conducted in later chapter. This chapter starts with explaining the notion of the "knowledge economy" and reviews theories on regional economic growth, social gerontology, and seniors' utility maximization.

1. The Notion of the "Knowledge Economy" versus The "Fordist Economy"

The "knowledge economy" is different from the "Fordist economy" in that it is driven by knowledge and innovation rather than just capital and labor (see Table 5.1). Due to the diffusion of information technology, "footloose" information technology organizes business structures in a horizontal network that annihilates space differences, and thus many businesses have successfully outsourced engineering, accounting, etc. (Jarboe and Alliance, 2001). To increase the knowledge stock that is the driver of the "knowledge economy", education and training have become increasingly important. The U.S. Census shows that the population's educational attainment is continuing to increase[20]. Moreover, the traditional skills

Table 5.1 Some Attributes of "Old" and "New" Economy

Issue	Old Economy (Fordist)	"New Economy" (Neo-Fordist)
Economy-wide characteristics		
Organizational form	Vertically integrated	Horizontal networks
Production characteristics		
Growth driver	Material Resources: Capital and labor	Innovation, invention and knowledge
Role of research and Innovation in the Economy	Low moderate	High
Infrastructure characteristics		
Form	Hard (physical)	Soft (information and organizations)
Transport	Miles of highway	Travel time reduction via IT
Learning	Talking head, a skill degree	Distance learning, lifelong learning

Source: Adapted from Atkinson and Court (1998); Jin and Stough (1998).

required for the workplace are now being replaced by strong academic skills, thinking, reasoning, teamwork skills, and proficiency of using technology (21st Century Labor force Commission, 2000). Earning power is highly associated with education attainment, working experience, and interpersonal skills, as seen in job requirements. Because of the importance of knowledge and innovation in the "knowledge economy", service industries become increasingly critical in the U.S. economy; traditional sectors, such as manufacturing, mining, and agriculture, are shrinking. Knowledge workers[21] play a more and more important role in the U.S. economy (Reich, 1992). As an evidence of a transition to the "knowledge economy", the original Standard Industrial Classification (SIC) code was recently replaced with the new North American Industry Classification System (NAICS) code that includes categories for the sectors that define the "new economy". This transformation from the "Fordist economy" (or the "old economy") to the "knowledge economy" is also an element of the thinking that led to new developments in economic growth theory, as presented in the next section.

The characteristics of the "knowledge economy" offer more opportunities to the elderly than the "Fordist economy". On the one hand, since the "knowledge economy" is knowledge driven, human capital, which is characterized by such factors as experience, information, skills, education attainment, social network, and health (Becker, 1986, 1992, 1990, and 1993), has become a central element for economic growth in the "knowledge economy". Seniors possess many of these above factors through their cumulated working experience and many of them also possess management skills, mentoring skills, a mature social network, and job-specific skills.

The types of jobs that define the "knowledge economy" are not as physically demanding as in the more manufacturing based "Fordist economy", which makes it possible for seniors to be more involved in the labor force. The "footloose" characteristic facilitated by information technology reduces the limitation of older people's mobility, which may further enhance older people's human capital in the "knowledge economy". As indicated in the introduction section, this book therefore defines the "knowledge economy" through creative class occupations. *Creative class*, as introduced earlier, is a concept Florida (2004) uses to describe the characteristics of our current economy and is explained as a key indicator of growth. Florida classifies the following occupational sectors as creative class: management, business and financial operation, computer and mathematical, architecture and engineering, science, legal, education, arts and media, health care practitioners, and high level sales management.

2. Theories on Economic Growth

Economists have long attempted to understand the factors that drive growth. Traditional neoclassic growth models use physical capital investment and labor to explain the factors that through scale economies drive growth. These models are only partially able to explain growth in the "knowledge economy". Physical capital accumulation can only explain a small amount of the variation in economic growth across regions in the "new economy" (Cicone and Hall, 1996). Hence, economists have begun to explore alternative or enhanced models to understand the economic growth and that incorporates new elements as well as the traditional two factors.

2.1. *Neoclassical growth theory/Solow growth model*

The neoclassical growth theory, particularly the Solow (1957) models, is the most prevalent and widely accepted growth theory. Neoclassical growth theory is based on the basic production function[22], which assumes a diminishing marginal product of capital. Physical capital stock and labor are viewed as the two drivers of economic growth. Using the national income accounts identity for a closed economy, Solow (1957) argues that the economy ends up with a steady-state level of capital[23] because investment raises capital stock but depreciation reduces it.

The Solow model later generates a few extensions. The extended Solow models recognize the positive impact of population growth on the capital stock, but predict that higher population growth will generate lower levels of GDP per person. Support for this prediction was found by Barro and Sala-i-Martin (1995) and Barro and Lee (1994). Although technology was included as an economic growth driver in the analysis, neoclassical economists assumed technology to be an exogenous variable and the only factor that contributed to persistently rising living standards (Mankiw, 2005).

Neoclassic growth theory treats technology as an exogenous variable and does not integrate knowledge into the models. This theory emphasizes the role of two inputs — physical capital and labor — in production, but the economic growth predicted by the Solow models typically falls short of the actual growth observed. This is particularly so in the "knowledge-based economy". This difference between the predicted and observed growth is referred to as the "Solow residual". Although the extended Solow models incorporate the role of technology, they do not explain how the technology is generated and they only treat technology as an exogenous factor. Given the importance of technology and knowledge in the "new economy", neoclassical models do not well incorporate the new elements of the "knowledge economy".

2.2. *New growth theory/endogenous growth theory*

New (endogenous) growth theory does highlight the role of knowledge and considers technological change[24] to be an endogenous factor[25], similar to labor and capital, for the long-run steady state growth in a closed economy (Nijkamp and Poot, 1993). By incorporating knowledge and technology as endogenous factors, the new growth models account for a portion of the "Solow residual" and thus explain more of the variation in economic growth than the neoclassic growth models. The endogenous growth model also starts with a production function[26], but this function does not assume diminishing returns to capital and labor. While physical capital exhibits the property of diminishing returns, knowledge, treated as a type of capital, does not possess the property of diminishing returns. The new growth theory claims that knowledge is a non-rival, non-excludable, intangible, and reusable good with the marginal cost of production near zero (Romer, 1993, 1994; Mankiw, 2005). Further revisions add that knowledge is not always a non-rival and non-exclusive. The exceptions that generate this revision are patents, trademarks, and copyrights.

Endogenous growth theory helps explain long-run sustained regional economic growth in the high-value added "knowledge economy" and helps to reveal the positive (or partially positive[27]) externalities and spillover effects of knowledge capital. The new growth theory treats knowledge as basically (sometimes partially) non-rival and non-excludable[28]. This newer theory also posits that knowledge spillovers are an important mechanism underlying endogenous growth (Romer, 1986; Lucas, 1988; Grossman and Helpman, 1991).

However, this theory does not shed much light on how knowledge spills over and assumes that knowledge spillovers are automatic, costless, and unconstrained by spatial factors. This missing component of endogenous growth theory may be a crucial factor for a higher level of accuracy in predicting economic growth. According to Acs *et al.* (2004), evidence shows that it appears more correct to assume knowledge spillovers are costly, geographically constrained, and not automatic.

2.3. *Human capital theory*

New (endogenous) growth theory and human capital theory are related. New growth theory advocates that improvements in productivity are linked to the growth of the knowledge stock or innovation. With endogenous growth, knowledge stock is treated as a factor of production and a representation of human capital. Formal models of new growth theory elevate human capital, particularly knowledge, to an increasingly important role in the economics of growth (Romer, 1986; Lucas, 1988; Becker, Murphy and Tamura, 1990; Becker, 1992; Barro and Sala-i-Martin, 1992). The neoclassic growth model only considers the quantity of labor, but quality of labor is not formally modeled as an endogenous growth factor. The interpretation of human capital or knowledge as a factor that drives growth is a progress.

Human capital is typically associated with knowledge and education for most scholars. The seminal work of Schultz (1963) on human capital theory examined the impact of education investment on agricultural output. The work of Adam Smith, Alfred Marshall, and Milton Friedman, although more sophisticated, did not include education and training investment as factors that drove growth (Becker, 1992). Building on Schultz's theory, Becker (1992) defined human capital[29] to include knowledge, skills, health, and values, and measures human capital investment through expenditure on formal education, training[30], and medical care. Arrow (1962) interpreted human capital as learning-by-doing (Mankiw, 2005). Knowledge and learning include both formal codified knowledge and tacit knowledge (Lundvall and Johnson, 1994; Saxenian, 1994; Foray and Lundvall, 1996).

2.4. *Entrepreneurship capital*

Newer growth theories posit that the "Solow residual" is associated with entrepreneurship and innovation (Acs and Evans, 1994; Grossman and Helpman, 1994; Kirzner, 1997; Shane, 2000; Audretsch and Thurik, 2001; Audretsch and Keilbach, 2004). In fact, entrepreneurship is being increasingly recognized as a driver of economic growth. The economic connotation of entrepreneurship originated with Schumpeter (1950), who defined an entrepreneur as a person who was willing and able to convert a new idea or invention into a successful innovation — e.g., new products or new business models. Therefore, entrepreneurship forces "creative destruction" across markets and industries. It is through this "creative destruction" that industries acquire dynamism and contribute to economic growth over the long run. Baumol (2002) had argued that entrepreneurial activity might account for a significant amount of the growth left unexplained in the neoclassic growth models. Entrepreneurial activities contribute to part of the "Solow residual" and explain economic growth because entrepreneurship capital offers a mechanism that facilitates knowledge spillovers from the source creating that knowledge to its commercialization in a third-party (Acs *et al.*, 2004). Entrepreneurs' new ideas and innovation contribute to create new products, services or business models, reduce barriers to knowledge and information spillovers, and thus spur economic growth.

The link between entrepreneurship capital and economic performance still remains largely anecdotal or based on case studies (Evans and Leighten, 1989), though empirical testing on this topic has largely developed in the recent years. One problem is how to define and measure entrepreneurship capital. The concept of entrepreneurship varies from economic fields to management perspectives. There is no single, consistent definition for this capital. Audretsch and Keilbach (2004) developed a model of entrepreneurship that incorporated entrepreneurship capital into the neoclassical production function growth model. They defined entrepreneurship capital as the capacity of a society to generate new firms. However, there are two limitations of this model: 1. It does not control for regional economic scale effects and it ignores the problem of multicollinearity; 2. Spatial autocorrelation is not controlled.

2.5. *Limitations of current growth theories*

The above growth theories are not perfect yet and none of them includes age as a variable. Neoclassical economists treat labor, like physical capital, as a factor of production subject to diminishing returns (Mankiw, Romer and Weil, 1992). Although labor efficiency and productivity are considered, it is viewed as being driven by an externally given technology. New growth theory attempts to interpret the sources of technological change; however, endogenous growth models are not yet fully accepted and the theory requires empirical verification. Neither theory considers age as a factor that influences economic growth. Human capital theories have been mainly applied to the analysis of children and younger cohorts and focused on the role of education. Human capital theory has seldom been utilized to analyze older people's contribution to economic growth.

Figure 5.1 briefly summarises the theories on economic growth and indicates a new direction of those theories — extending to include the role of elderly entrepreneurship.

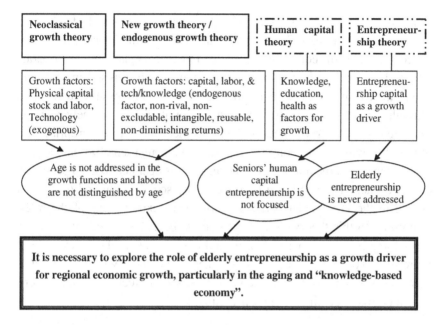

Figure 5.1 Theories on Economic Growth

3. Social Gerontology Theories Related to Elderly Labor Force Participation

Social gerontology theories are more concerned about seniors' well being, but these theories present conflicting views on whether to involve the elderly in the labor force. Role theories (Cottrell, 1942) and disengagement theories (Marshall, 1994) discouraged seniors' social involvement, while activity theories (Bengtson, 1969) and continuity theories encouraged their involvement. This following section introduces the literature on social gerontology theories in the context of employment, particularly entrepreneurship related employment.

3.1. Theories against seniors' involvement in the labor force

3.1.1. Role theory

The role theory is one of the earliest theories explaining how individuals adjust to aging (Cottrell, 1942). According to this theory, individuals play a variety of social roles that vary with their ages[31] or stages of life. At each stage in life, the roles reflect social being and offer the basis of their self-concept. Age norms control the roles that individuals play and they operate informally in society. For example, older people can be refused employment due to the assumption that their older age makes them less productive and difficult to train, compared to their younger counterparts, for a new position. The age norm is also often an individual's measure of the appropriateness of their behavior. In this context, Hagestad and Neugarten (1985) noted that social clocks became internalized and age norms operated to keep people on the time track. The age norm is conveyed by socialization and thus, most people in the U.S. society have age-normative expectations of the roles. According to this theory, older people are expected to withdraw from the labor force based on societal norms and consequently, take on the role of retirement. The change of roles sometimes also equates with role disconti-nuity. That may be why some newly retired seniors feel bored and experi-ence a dramatic decline in life satisfaction.

3.1.2. Disengagement theory

The disengagement theory looks at the social system, rather than just individuals, as an explanation for successful adjustment to aging (Hooyman and Kiyak, 2005). According to this theory, older people expe-rience reduced activity levels and tend to interact less frequently with oth-ers. This situation leads them to seek more passive roles and become preoccupied with their inner lives. Disengagement is thus viewed as adap-tive behavior that justifies older people's loss of occupational roles. This theory challenges the assumption of activity theory[32] and views older age as a separate period of life, not as an extension of middle age.

Achenbaum and Bengtson (1994) claimed that disengagement theory was the first real comprehensive, explicit, and multidisciplinary theory on social gerontology, but it had many limitations. The disengagement theory, although attempting to explain both system- and individual-level changes with one grand theory, has not found empirical supports (Achenbaum and Bengtson, 1994). With better health and increased longevity, a growing number of seniors remain in the labor force. Similar to previous theories, disengagement theory also fails to account for variations in individual

preferences, personality, socio-cultural settings, and environmental opportunities as factors influencing older people's life (Achenbaum and
Bengtson, 1994; Estes and Associates, 2000; Marshall, 1994). As Hooyman
and Kiyak (2005) have noted, it cannot be assumed that older people's withdrawal from useful roles is necessarily good for society or for older people.
For example, policies to encourage retirement that have been implemented
in the past resulted in the loss of older workers' skills and knowledge in the
workplace. This is an increasingly critical issue, especially during periods
of employees' skill shortages along with an aging workforce.

3.2. Theories in support of seniors' involvement into labor force

3.2.1. Activity theory

The activity theory views aging to a large degree as an extension of the
middle age. According to this theory, the more active an older person is,
the greater their life satisfaction, positive self-concept, and adjustment to
the aging process can be (Bengtson, 1969). Activity theory thus encourages the integration of seniors into society. Therefore, seniors who stay in
the labor force and keep productive as entrepreneurs (with more responsibilities and control than wage-and-salary employment) are expected to
increase older people's positive self-concept. Hooyman and Kiyak (2005)
also showed evidence that a person's experience with the aging process
was more positive if they remained engaged in the workplace.

Activity theory, however, fails to consider other variables, such as personality, lifestyle, and socioeconomic status, when addressing the relationship between activity level and well being, as Covey (1981) indicates.
The level of older people's activeness is not the only factor determining
their positive self-concept. Other factors may play an important role.

3.2.2. Continuity theory

The continuity theory focuses on the social-psychological theories of
adaptation. Similar to activity theory, continuity theory purports that
individuals tend to maintain a consistent pattern of behavior as they
age and their life satisfaction is determined by how consistent their

current activities or lifestyles are with their lifetime experiences (Atchley, 1972; Neugarten *et al.*, 1968). This theory is consistent with the empirical finding that seniors with previous entrepreneurial experience or experience in white-collar manager occupations are more likely to venture into entre-preneurship around the retirement age (Fuch, 1982). Like many other gerontology theories, however, continuity theory overlooks the role of external social and environmental factors during the process of aging.

3.3. *Other related gerontology theories*

The aforementioned theories fail to adequately address the socio-cultural contexts of the aging process. The following three theoretical perspectives place more emphasis on the macro-level and structural analysis.

3.3.1. *Interactionist theory*

The interactionist theory interprets the person-environment transaction process and emphasizes the dynamic interaction between older individu-als and the social environment (Hooyman and Kiyak, 2005). The theory purports that the dynamic social world shapes older people's perceptions, decisions, behavior, etc., and older individuals also change the ongoing social environment (including policies, culture, social biases, economic environment, etc). Over time, older people's occupational choices are expected to change. Various socioeconomic factors interact with an older individual's experience in terms of aging and affect their decisions regard-ing employment and entrepreneurship.

3.3.2. *Political economy of aging*

Political economy of aging theory emphasizes the socioeconomic and political constraints that shape older people's experience. According to this theory, socioeconomic class is a structural barrier to older people's access to social resources; more dominant groups perpetuate class inequalities (Olson, 1982; Minkler and Estes, 1984; Overbo and Minkler, 1993). In a capitalized society, the socioeconomic and political constraints that are socially constructed play an important role in older individuals' employment decisions.

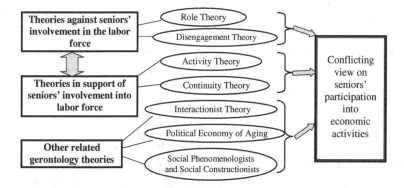

Figure 5.2 Social Gerontology Theories

3.3.3. *Social phenomenologists and social constructionists*

The social phenomenologists and social constructionist theory also address the socioeconomic environment as an important source shaping older individuals' attitudes and behavior. This theory argues that individual behavior shaped by social definitions and social structures produces a "reality" (Ray, 1996), or a fact and environment, which in turn structures individuals' lives (Bengtson *et al.*, 1997). The following chart (Figure 5.2) summarizes the above social gerontology theories.

4. Utility Theories: Entrepreneurship and Seniors' Utility

Utility Theory has been used to characterize seniors' decisions regarding retirement versus leisure. This theory assumes that senior's attempt to maximize utility:

$$\text{Max } U \text{ (work, leisure).}$$

Budget constraints come into play. Choices regarding consumption (C_i) are subject to income (Y_i), the amount of which is typically based on total hours a person works (H), social welfare benefits, and other types of income. Seniors choose their hours of work (H) to maximize their utility that is subject to the income constraint (Y_i), i.e.,

$$U(C_i, H), \quad \text{where } C_i = Y_i.$$

There are some tradeoffs that are important to consider. On the one hand, working more can generate more income, which can allow for more consumption. On the other hand, some seniors would like to maintain a certain (often less than full time) number of hours of work after retirement to improve their life satisfaction (Research from CED, 1999; Hooyman and Kiyak, 2005; Smith, 2006; AARP, n.d.).

According to Evans and Jovanovic (1989), Holtz-Eakin *et al.* (1994a), and Bruce *et al.* (2000), an elderly person's income was comprised of three parts: salary or wage (assuming this person was a wage-and-salary employee), asset income, and benefits through work — e.g., transfer income. Wage income is traditionally measured by wage rate (W) the hours worked (h). Personal asset income is based on the assets (A) a person has and the interest rate (r), or the rate of return they can get on their assets. The benefits include public and private pension and welfare benefits. Therefore, the total income for an elderly wage-and-salary employee becomes

$$Y_i^w = W_i * h_i + r * (A_i - K_i) + B_i^w, \qquad (5.1)$$

where

i: subscript for individuals;
w: superscript representing wage-and-salary employment;
Y: total income;
W: wage rate;
h: hours worked;
r: returns from personal assets;
A: personal assets;
K: capital;
B: public and private pension and welfare benefits.

If an elderly person is an entrepreneur but not a wage-and-salary employee, his or her income is composed of the following three parts: income as an entrepreneur, asset income, and benefits through work. Entrepreneurs' income is measured by the ability of the entrepreneur (θ), and a production function [$f(.)$] that depends on the capital (K) invested in the business and hours the entrepreneur worked for his or her business (h). A reason for characterizing an entrepreneur's income in a different way from a wage-and-salary employee is that an entrepreneur's wage rate is not always transparent. Entrepreneurial ability (θ), the initial amount of capital invested in the business, and hours worked by the self-employer or entrepreneur are all important for their contribution to gross receipts. For a career wage-and-salary employee, θ is unknown; but as a self-employer, θ is revealed (Bruce *et al.*, 2000). The entrepreneur's asset income is still subject to his or her assets (A) and market interest rate (r) and the benefits still include public and private pension and welfare benefits. Therefore, an elderly entrepreneur's income becomes

$$Y_i^e = \theta * f(K_i) * h_i e + r * (A_i - K_i) + B_i^e, \qquad (5.2)$$

where

i: subscript for individuals;

e: superscript representing self-employment or entrepreneurship;

Y: total income;

θ: individual's ability as an entrepreneur;

$f(.)$:   production function depending on the capital (K) invested in the business;

K: capital;

e: random component reflecting business prospects (e.g., business cycles);

h: hours worked as an entrepreneur;

r: returns from personal assets;

A: personal assets;

B: public and private pension and welfare benefits.

Different from the above two models (Model 5.1 and 5.2) that characterize an elderly person's income, Zhang (2007a) and (2007d) modify and extend those two models in the following ways. First, Zhang combines Equation (5.1) and Equation (5.2), given the fact that some people have a wage-and-salary job and simultaneously are entrepreneurs.

Second, Zhang specifies a person's entrepreneurial ability as a factor of education and knowledge (R), previous work-related skills and experience (S), social networks (N), and other personal abilities as an entrepreneur (P). Previous studies show that all of these factors are key factors of being an entrepreneur and running a business. For example, Blanchflower *et al.* (2001), van der Sluis and van Praag (2004), and Berkovec and Stern (1991) all emphasized the importance of education in being an entrepreneur; Fuchs (1982) mentioned the importance of previous self-employment experience and Lazear (2002) addressed the importance of having broad skills for a person's entrepreneurial propensity. While social networks are being recognized as an important factor in business activities, there is evidence that seniors have more established business ties and social networks, compared to the young (Collison, 2003). Other personal entrepreneurial abilities (P) are included to capture the abilities not reflected by R, S, and N. The reason to specify individuals' entrepreneurial abilities is to reduce the difficulty of measurement and to reflect the individual perspectives in the "knowledge economy". Last, the extended model also considers venture capital as a source for the startup investment by including a venture capital (V) in the production function $[f(.)]$. Models (5.1) and (5.2) assume startup investment capital comes only from the business owner, or self-employer. However, for startups that do not have access to capital markets or have limited capital funds, venture capital becomes significant.

The extended model uses H to represent total working hours, h for hours worked as an entrepreneur, and $H-h$ for hours worked as a wage-and-salary employee. In this fashion, entrepreneurs who are also wage-and-salary employees of another firm will be included in this extended model as well[33].

The extended utility model divides an elderly person's total income into entrepreneurs' business income or entrepreneurship income[34], wage-and-salary income, asset income, and various public and private pension, retirement plans, and welfare benefits. If an elderly person is retired, the entrepreneur's business income and wage-and-salary income would be 0; if an elderly person is only a wage-and-salary employee, the entrepreneur's business income would be 0; if an elderly person is only an entrepreneur, his or her wage-and-salary income would be 0; if an elderly person is both an entrepreneur and a wage-and-salary employee of another employer, he or she will have both entrepreneurship income and wage-and-salary income. Assuming rationality on the part of senior citizens, the model characterizes an elderly person's income as follows:

$$Y_i^{w,e} = g\,\overbrace{(R_i,S_i,N_i,P_i)}^{}*\underbrace{f\,(K_i+V_i)}_{}*\underbrace{h_i e}_{} + \overbrace{W_i*(H_i-h_i)}^{}$$

$$\text{Entrepreneurship Income} \qquad \text{Wage-and-salary Income}$$

$$+ r*\underbrace{(A_i-K_i)}_{\text{Assets}} + \underbrace{B_i^{w,e}}_{\text{Benefits}}. \qquad (5.3)$$

i: subscript for individuals (or a person's different time periods);
w: superscript representing wage-and-salary employment;
e: superscript representing entrepreneurship;
Y: total income;
g(.):   function for individual entrepreneurial ability;
R: education and knowledge;
S: previous work-related skills and experience;
N: social networks;
P: other personal/individual entrepreneurial attributes;
f(.):   production function that depends upon the capital (*K,V*) invested in the business;
A: personal assets;
K: self-funded capital (normally sourcing from personal assets);
V: venture capital;
h: hours worked as an entrepreneur;
e: random component reflecting business environment/prospects, e.g. business cycles;
W: wage rate;
H: total personal working hours;
r: returns from personal assets;
B: public and private pension and welfare benefits.

People choose their total hours of work (*H*) and allocate hours for occupational choices to maximize their utility that is subject to the income constraint:

$$U(C_i, H_i, h_i), \quad C_i = Y_i. \tag{5.4}$$

For wage-and-salary employees, $h_i = 0$; therefore,

$$Y_i^w = W_i * (H_i - h_i) + r * (A_i - K_i) + B_i^w. \tag{5.5}$$

For self-employers/entrepreneurs, $h_i = H_i$; therefore,

$$Y_i^e = g(R_i, S_i, N_i, P_i) * f(K_i + V_i) * h_i e + r * (A_i - K_i) + B_i^e. \tag{5.6}$$

This utility model explains seniors' participation in entrepreneurship. In the "knowledge economy", seniors' skills, working experience, and social networks, i.e. R_i, S_i, N_i, P_i respectively, are important and can be reflected in their income. Education and knowledge, skills, previous working experience, and social networks are particularly important in the "knowledge economy" (Atkinson and Court, 1998; Jin and Stough, 1998).

American economist Thurow (1975) had observed an interesting salary phenomenon: the *seniority principle*. As introduced in Chapter 2, during the first stage of a workers' career (normally at younger age), their earnings are lower than their productivity levels, and however, during the second stage of workers' careers, their earnings are higher than their productivity. This observation may explain why some employers do not favor employing seniors. The high wage rate (*W*) for hiring seniors is possibly lower than their productivity contribution to employers' profits. This situation sometimes forces seniors to accept a lower wage or salary rate or to become entrepreneurs.

Entrepreneurs' working hours, in contrast to those associated with wage-and-salary jobs, are more flexible, i.e., *h* is more flexible than *H-h*.

The working hour flexibility offered by entrepreneurship caters to many seniors' needs to tend to their own health and that of their significant others. This flexibility provides an incentive for seniors to choose entrepreneurship over wage-and-salary employment. Bruce *et al.* (2000) suggested that self-employment (or being an entrepreneur) was a "bridge job" for seniors to gradually withdraw from the labor force; however, it could also be argued that self-employment was not just a "bridge job" for seniors. The enhanced life satisfaction it brings matters (AARP, n.d.).

For seniors who have retired but need additional income beyond their assets (*A*) and benefits (*B*), they have to either become a wage-and-salary employee or an entrepreneur to obtain additional income. There are at least two forces preventing seniors from becoming a wage-and-salary employee: (1) age discrimination in workplace (Rix, 2004) and (2) private sector pension penalizing policies for working beyond a particular age that reduces benefits (B_i^w) (Bruce *et al.*, 2000). Hence, self-employment, or being an entrepreneur, becomes an option for obtaining additional income. For seniors who do not have to work after the retirement age or those who have enough income (including asset income) to retire, job satisfaction could be the key for them to choose self-employment, rather than wage-and-salary employment.

For personal assets (*A*), older people tend to have more wealth accumulation than younger cohorts, which means they have more capital (*K*) to invest into a startup. Holtz-Eakin *et al.* (1994a, 1994b) had noted the significance of liquidity constraints in entrepreneurial activities.

When $h_i = H_i - h_i$ and *ceteris paribus*, if more income can be generated from being an entrepreneur than being a wage-and-salary employee, i.e., $g(R_i, S_i, N_i, P_i) * f(K_i + V_i) * e > W_i$, seniors who are entrepreneurs (or self-employed seniors) will gain a higher utility level than those who live on wage-and-salary jobs. Even if they might gain less income from self-employed jobs than from potential wage-and-salary jobs, self-employment might still be seniors' option due to additional utility sourcing from more self-control and time-flexibility.

5. Regional Economic Development Theories

Neoclassic growth theory assumed a closed economy; endogenous growth theory and human capital theory introduced above do not necessarily emphasize the regional disparity and dynamics of economic development. However, location does matter. Distance decay is a key concept in regional development theories. It delineates the fact that socioeconomic interactions between two locations decline with the increase of the distance in between. This term explains an important pattern in which knowledge spills over. With a longer distance, knowledge spills over to a smaller extent. As a necessary addition to the above economic theories, this section will thus briefly introduce three basic regional development theories that would help to set up theoretical background for later spatial analysis of this book.

5.1. *Central place theory*

According to King (1985), Walter Christaller (1933) and August Lôsch (1940) both described regional development as core-periphery structure with hierarchies. The core, or the central place, is normally an urban area with a large population and higher density than peripheral areas that are more distant from the center. With this view, the core is the controlling center of the economy with agglomeration advantages of economic activities; whereas the peripheries are economically less developed.

Central place theory[35] offers an initial regional development model through integrating a region with several levels of hierarchies for cores and peripheries. As for the weakness of central place theory, firstly, Mayer (1968) criticized Lôsch (1940)'s central place theory as a highly idealized and stylized theory with few empirical possibilities. However, this critique occurred four decades ago. Secondly, central place theory was developed in 1940s and emphasized the development of central places. The periphery's development only depends on top-down or spillover development effect from the central place. This situation puts the peripheries into passive economic development situations.

5.2. *Growth pole theory*

Perroux (1955) and Hirschman (1958) developed the theory of growth pole as that the development in hinterland areas was fueled by expanding metropolitan centers and investment trickled out from the growth pole or growth center to the hinterland through linkages. The concept of a growth pole refers to the center of the economic growth within a regional context and with a certain concentration or agglomeration of economic activities in an abstract space. Nelson (1993) defined growth center (or pole) as an urban or extended metropolitan area, which is opposite to hinterland, the area outside the urban. Through agglomeration, the resources are sucked into the center, which enlarges the difference between the peripheries and growth center and thus forms a polarizing effect. Nelson (1993) referred polarizing effect as a process that expanded metropolitan centers and fueled the development in hinterland regions. Development-from-above school purports that growth center can stimulate growth of other linked areas by inducing their actions and eventually push the regional develop-ment. The pressure point is to redistribute growth to underdeveloped areas (hinterlands or peripheral areas) through trickling down effects. Nelson (1993) defined the trickling down effect as a process of deconcentration from centers to hinterlands and from core to peripheral regions.

Growth pole theory has promoted many regions' development (such as many metropolitan regions in the United States). It is designed to integrate a region's economy through hierarchy between the pole and hinterland and emphasizes the trickling down effect from the pole. However, it has also been criticized as the mechanism causing disparities in a region. With the theory's favorable assumptions, Gore (1984) and Lipton (1977) were suspicious of effect of growth pole theory. Also, case study keeps chal-lenging this theory. With limited trickling down effect but evident polar-ization effect, some scholars (Myrdal, 1957; Stohr and Todtling, 1977) contributed this theory as a cause of regional inequality.

5.3. *Endogenous growth theory in regional science*

Endogenous growth theory has been previously introduced in this chapter. This subsection emphasizes the regional science perspective of this theory. Endogenous growth theory developed by Arrow (1962), Romer (1986), and Lucas (1988), emphasizes that internally driven development in a region based on high value-added knowledge can bring competitive advantage. In this case, knowledge-based economy and locally based producer services, such as developing technology and institutional framework, drive the region's development. According to endogenous growth theory, producer services become dominant source of jobs in many places and are in most cases components of manufacturing, e.g. sales, soft cost, and architecture.

Endogenous growth theory was developed in 1990s and reflected the economic and technological changes in recent decades and catered for the need of developing producer services. This theory emphasizes the significance and great catalyzing role of high value-added knowledge and product services in regional development. However, this theory emphasizes developing locally based services, which leads to self-sufficient status. In such an open market economy world, even developing locally based services need to look at non-local service market and need to export for growth and development. Moreover, knowledge-based economy is difficult to track, model, and measure. In addition, producer services, compared with manufacturing, are much more difficult to export (though it is still possible), which may bring a big disadvantage for a region to grow. The security of knowledge-based and service-based economy is more difficult to ensure. Emphasizing knowledge-based economy may result in the lack of manufacturing engineers with emphasis of producer services.

6. Conclusion on Theories

The "footloose" "knowledge economy" appears to be more conducive for seniors' participation in the economy as entrepreneurs and their participation can have positive impacts on the economy. This economy is less physically demanding and seniors' cumulative knowledge and experience become a critically valuable capital in this economy. Models of growth in the "knowledge economy" should include a variety of factors, including not only the more traditional capital and labor, but also human capital, knowledge capital, entrepreneurial capital, and technology. While the concept of entrepreneurship capital is drawing more and more attention, the effect of elderly entrepreneurship as a factor that contributes to economic growth has been only minimally discussed in the literature. Additionally, the importance of location and its related pattern of knowledge spillovers is another missing component in elderly entrepreneurship research. The analysis in this book brings together various elements of growth theories, gerontology theories, and even regional development theories, with an underlying assumption of utility optimization.

Summary

- In the "knowledge economy", seniors' cumulative job-specific skills, management skills, and social and business ties provide unique advantages to drive economic growth.
- None of the growth theories and models, nor human capital theories, has stressed seniors' human capital or entrepreneurship capital. The economic growth predicted by the neoclassic growth theory does not integrate knowledge and typically falls short of the actual growth observed. New growth theory does not shed much light on how knowledge spills over and assumes that knowledge spillovers are automatic, costless, and unconstrained by spatial factors. A model that incorporates entrepreneurship capital into the neoclassical production function did not control for the regional economic scale effects, neither was spatial autocorrelation controlled.
- Social gerontology theories in general have conflicting views on seniors' participations into economic activities. Among them, the role theory and the disengagement theory discourage and the active theory and the continuity theory encourage seniors to be

involved in continued employment. The interactionist theory, political economy of aging, social phenomenologists and social constructionists, treat environment, political economy, or socioeconomic environment as an important source shaping older individuals' attitudes and behavior.

- Using the utility maximization function, seniors' income can be composed of entrepreneurship income (that relies on individuals' motivation, efforts, skills and capital), wage-and-salary job income (that relies on working hours), assets, and benefits. This model can help explain seniors' occupational choice.
- Regional economic theories, such as central place theory, growth pole theory, and endogenous growth theory, indicates that location matters to economic development.

End notes

19   The "knowledge economy" is also often referred as "knowledge-based economy" or "new economy".

20   In 1980, only 66.3% population aged over 15 obtained a high school diploma; in 1990, this figure jumped to 74.4%; in 2000, this figure further increased to 78.5; in 2004, 79.5% of U.S. population aged over 15 had graduated from high school, according to the U.S. Census data on population estimation.

21   People whose jobs are based on knowledge, or knowledge-driven.

22   This production function states that output Y depends on the capital stock K and the labor force L, $Y = f(K, L)$.

23   When the economy starts with less than the steady-state level of capital, the level of investment exceeds the amount of depreciation, and the capital stock will rise with output until it reaches the steady state; when the economy starts with the capital above the steady-state level, investment is less than depreciation, and the capital stock will fall to the steady-state level. The steady state represents the long-run equilibrium of the economy where investment equals depreciation, and there is no pressure for the capital stock to either increase or decrease (Mankiw, 2005).

24 That is based on knowledge, skills, or human capital.

25 Because technology is treated as an endogenous variable, the new growth theory is also called "endogenous growth theory".

26 $Y = AK$, where Y is output, K is the capital stock, and A is a constant measuring the amount of output produced for each unit of capital.

27 Though sometimes the positive externality is challenged because of enhanced exclusiveness of knowledge capital through patent, trademarks, and copyrights.

28 The early new growth theory treats knowledge as absolutely non-excludable and thus ignored property rights protection. The later revisions change this knowledge assumption to partially non-excludable or non-rival.

29 Becker defined those elements as "human capital" because they were related to human attributes and could not be separated from individuals' financial and physical assets (Becker, 1993). Becker (1992) also suggested that migration, marriage, divorce, family size, and formation of habits could affect human capital.

30 Particularly on-the-job training.

31 Mostly chronological ages, sometimes biological or psychological ages.

32 The activity theory will be introduced in the following section.

33 In the dataset this study uses Public Use Microdata Samples (PUMS) which does not allow the joint-status as a self-employer and wage-and-salary employee from another firm. In this case, this distinction does not display an advantage; but if another dataset is available, this model will be superior to previous ones.

34 In this case, self-employment income includes entrepreneurship income.

35 Earlier than growth pole theory, central place theory helps understand growth pole theory.

PART 5

ENTREPRENEURSHIP OF SENIORS?

CHAPTER 6

AGE AND ENTREPRENEURSHIP

Entrepreneurship has been conventionally detached from older age and has been often assumed to be the privilege of the young. Younger people are often believed to be more likely to generate new ideas and more likely to take risks; whereas seniors who have reached retirement ages are traditionally unassociated with business adventure. In the United States, some Americans unfortunately do not give a very positive attitude toward seniors and the process of aging becomes a sort of taboo for those people. When talking about entrepreneurship, magazines and newspaper typically focus on young entrepreneurs: being young becomes an asset and the fact of being young itself possesses a natural marketing power to attract venture capital and social attention. Some venture capital even aims at young college students and there are numerous college student business plan competitions. However, have any of these efforts focused on seniors? Although population aging has been a heatedly discussed social concern, seniors are basically addressed to be a social burden that causes problems. In some rare occasions, seniors are recognized as contributors to the economy, normally due to their contribution to consumption that stimulates the economy. Very little literature addresses seniors as a valuable source of human capital to the economy and to entrepreneurship.

In many places, it is not unusual to see seniors who have reached retirement ages still standing at the leading edge of the socioeconomic activities. Some of them have their own businesses and some are executives of firms or organizations. Some of them have even tried to retire, but boredom after withdrawing from their beloved career where they have devoted heart and soul for decades has irresistibly brought them back. Some of them are just so valuable in a field that people working in this specific field cannot help frequently turning to them. In the Washington D.C. metropolitan area, many well-educated and highly-skilled seniors run their own consulting businesses where they can continue their career that they have been loving for a long time and where they also have more control over their own schedules. Being an entrepreneur becomes an attractive choice for those seniors who are still healthy with limited family responsibilities, possess skills, love their careers, and want more flexibility, control, and freedom. In the "knowledge economy" and with a better health condition than before, becoming an entrepreneur becomes more possible than before for seniors.

In the "knowledge economy", is age a factor affecting the propensity for entrepreneurship? Are seniors who have reached retirement age less likely to be entrepreneurs, compared to the younger ones? This chapter examines how the age of an individual affects their propensity to be an entrepreneur and whether seniors are more likely than the young to make this occupational choice.

As indicated in Chapters 4 and 5, previous literature projects a vague shadow on the relationship between age and entrepreneurship (or self-employment). A conventional view holds that seniors are not as entrepreneurial as the young and seniors are less likely to start a new firm. The global research on entrepreneurship by the GEM (2001, 2004) noted that people aged 55–64 tend to be less entrepreneurial than the younger working-age groups because seniors have a lower scale of TEA opportunities, TEA necessity, the quantity of nascent firms and entrepreneurship prevalence. Johnson (1978) and Miller (1984) justified this conventional view by a risk factor — they purported that younger workers, compared to older workers, would tend to try riskier occupations first.

The opposite view on the relationship between age and entrepreneurship purports that seniors have a higher self-employment or a higher entrepreneurial propensity. An empirical study in the United States and Canada indicated the existence of a higher self-employment rate among seniors than among the younger cohorts (Reardon, 1997). Blanchflower *et al.*

(2001) also found in their cross-country study a higher proportion of seniors than of younger people was actually self-employed, though a higher proportion of younger people preferred to be self-employed. The stronger preference for self-employment among the young could be due to several reasons including psychological ones.

There also exists a neutral view on the relationship between age and entrepreneurship. Evans and Leighton (1989) suggested that the probability of switching to self-employment was roughly independent of age. To be more specific, the fraction of the self-employed labor force increases with age until the early 40s and then remains constant until the retirement years.

In terms of theories, social gerontology theories do not make a clear conclusion whether seniors should be involved in the entrepreneurial activity or not. Role theory and disengagement theories discourage seniors to be involved in active economic activities and entrepreneurship because seniors, as well as other cohorts, should accept their age characteristics and adjust to the role of their corresponding age. This stream of theories believes that learning how to adjust people's behavior to the social role of that age, seniors can get more happiness. On the other hand, active theory and continuity theory purport a more active life for seniors. This stream of theories believes that happiness in the late life comes from active retirement life and continues to do what they are used to do before.

This chapter attempts to reveal the mystery of the relationship between age and entrepreneurship as well as self-employment. Specifically, three questions are investigated: first, whether individuals older than the average retirement age (62 currently in the United States) are more likely than younger people to be self-employed[36]; second, whether those seniors' self-employment tends to be more concentrated in the knowledge-based sectors than younger individuals' self-employment; third, whether elderly individuals who are aged 62 and above but still stay in the labor force are more likely than their younger counterparts to become entrepreneurs.

The analysis presented in this book uses some specific definitions for the "knowledge economy", the elderly, and entrepreneurship. As a quick review, the **knowledge economy** is measured by employment in the "creative class" (Florida, 2004). The **elderly** are defined as those aged 62 and above. In the United States, 62 is the average retirement age (Gendell, 2001) and the initial eligibility age for Social Security. The younger cohort is defined as individuals between the ages of 16 and 61, considering the fact that 16 is the starting age for labor force participation. **Entrepreneurship** is defined by unincorporated and incorporated self-employment rates in knowledge-based occupations.

1. Age and Self-Employment

Descriptive statistics were generated using the U.S. Census 2000 *Public Use Microdata Samples* (PUMS) 1-percent sample data[37]. Some of the advantages of this data are that it has detailed information broken down by age going all the ways up to age 90, the information can be extracted for different geographic units — State, County, Public Use Microdata Sample Areas (PUMA), MSA, PMSA, and Consolidated Metropolitan Statistical Areas (CMSA)[38], it contains detailed socio-economic information, and it has a large sample size. The PUMS sample contains over 2.8 million individuals, 1.66 million employed people and 0.44 million seniors. The data it offers is much more detailed and information-rich than some of the other large-scale datasets that have been used for the study of seniors, such as HRS.

While the PUMS 1-percent sample has only one-fifth of the observations that the 5-percent sample has, it still offers a large quantity of observations. Each observation in the PUMS database contains a weight that can be used to estimate the frequency of a particular characteristic in the entire population. It should be noted though, that the estimates derived from the U.S. Census sample files are expected to differ from the 100-percent figures because they are subject to sampling and non-sampling errors. The U.S. Census Bureau has taken several measures, however, to control for sampling and non-sampling errors.

The descriptive statistics reveal that the self-employment rate for seniors is higher than that of their younger counterparts. Specifically, the data shows that 19% of the elderly (62+) in the labor force are self-employed, as compared to 9% for their younger cohort (16–61)[39] in 2000. This is illustrated in Figures 6.1 and 6.2.

When examining self-employment rates relative to the entire population rather than just the labor force, seniors' self-employment rate is only

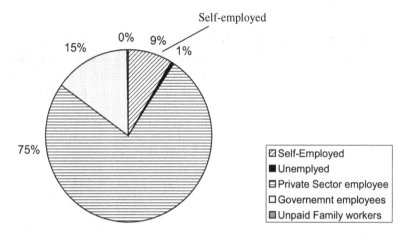

Figure 6.1 Percentages of Younger Workers by Employment Type in 2000

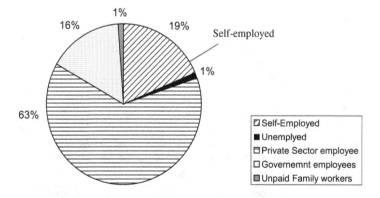

Figure 6.2 Percentages of Older Workers by Employment Type in 2000

slightly lower than the rate associated with the young. The details of the data to support this finding are given in Appendix 6.1. The labor force participation rate for seniors is much lower than that of the younger cohorts, perhaps due to differences between the two age groups in health, family responsibilities, and life goals. The lower labor force participation rate among seniors helps to explain why seniors have a lower self-employment rate in the entire population but a higher self-employment rate in the labor force than the young.

While the numbers show that the rate of self-employment in the labor force is much higher among seniors, the finding could be misleading due to the selection of the cut-off age. This possibility is explored by investigating the rates along a continuum of ages. Figure 6.3 displays the

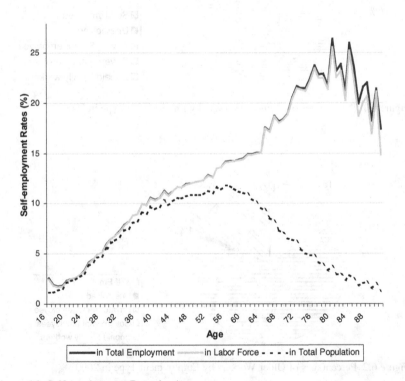

Figure 6.3 Self-employment Rates by Age

self-employment rates in the population as a whole, in the labor force, and in the employed population. The raw data for this figure is provided in Appendices 6.2 and 6.3[40]. The top two curves of this figure show that self-employment rates in the labor force and in employment both increase with age since the age of 20, though there is some fluctuation in this trend for the oldest cohorts (over 88). This implies that older people who partici-pate in the labor force tend to have a higher self-employment rate than the younger ones and that the self-employment rates generally increase with age except for oldest age cohorts (starting from late 80s). The bottom curve, which shows the proportion of self-employment in the population, displays a nearly normal distribution with peak around the ages 52 to 62. The discrepancies between self-employment rates in the labor force and self-employment rates in the population reveal that many seniors do not participate in the labor force. Once they participate in the labor force, they are more likely to be self-employed than the younger workers.

The rates associated with wage and salary employment look much differ-ent from those associated with self-employment, particularly when com-paring seniors to younger individuals. In fact, the pattern of wage and salary employment rates in the labor force is nearly opposite to that of self-employment rates. Figure 6.4 shows that the wage-and-salary employment rates in the labor force (shown as the top curve) begins to decrease around the age of 20 or so. The raw data for this figure is pre-sented in Appendices 6.2 and 6.5. In conclusion, seniors have higher self-employment rates, but lower wage-and-salary employment rates than the younger employed individuals.

It also appears that seniors over 70 face higher unemployment[41] rates than the younger cohorts. Figure 6.4 shows that the unemployment rates in labor force (indicated by the bottom dashed curve) begins to increase around the age of 70. This possibly partially relates to age discrimination.

2. Elderly Self-Employment in the "Knowledge Economy"

As indicated earlier, the "knowledge economy" offers more opportunities to the elderly than the "Fordist economy". In the "knowledge economy",

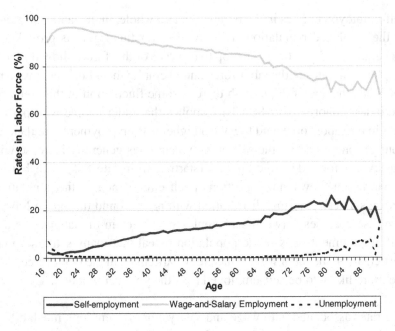

Figure 6.4 Self-employment Rates versus Wage-and-salary Employment Rates in the Labor Force by Age

knowledge and human capital, which are characterized by such factors as experience, information, skills, education attainment, social network, and health (Becker, 1986, 1990, 1992, 1993), have become a central element for economic growth in the "knowledge economy". Seniors possess many of these above human capital factors through their cumulative working experience. Seniors tend to possess a higher level of management skills, mentoring, a mature social network, and job-specific skills. The types of jobs that define the "knowledge economy" also tend to be less physically and location demanding than the manufacturing based "Fordist economy". The smaller physical and location limitations make it more possible for elders to be more involved in the labor force. The "footloose" characteristic, i.e. the location freedom, facilitated by information technology reduces the limitation of older people's mobility, which further enhances older people's human capital in the "knowledge economy". As indicated previously, this book defines the "knowledge economy" through creative class occupations. *Creative class*, as introduced earlier, was a concept Florida (2004), uses to describe the characteristics of our current economy and is explained as a key indicator of growth.

Of those seniors who are self-employed, a majority is in the knowledge-based occupations (or creative class); this is in contrast to the young, who as a whole is primarily employed in non-knowledge-based sectors. This finding is illustrated in Figures 6.5 and 6.6 (see data table in Appendix 6.5).

Seniors also have higher self-employment rates than the young for each of the major occupational sectors that falls under the classification of knowledge-based sectors (or the categories of creative class) and for non-knowledge-based sectors as a whole. This is illustrated in Figure 6.7, which compares side-by-side the self-employment rates of seniors and younger individuals in the labor force by occupational category. The self-employment rates associated with seniors more than double that of younger individuals for all of the knowledge-based (or creative class occupations), except the sector *Arts & Entertainment* [Standard Occupational Code (SOC) = 27].

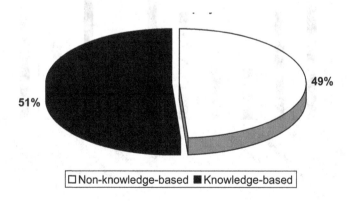

Figure 6.5 Proportion of Knowledge-based versus Non-knowledge-based Self-employment among Seniors in 2000[42]

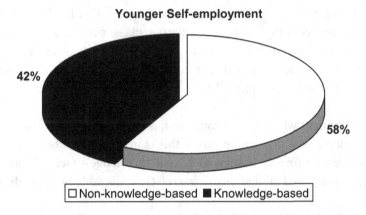

Figure 6.6 Proportion of Knowledge-based versus Non-knowledge-based Self-employment among Younger Cohorts in 2000[43]

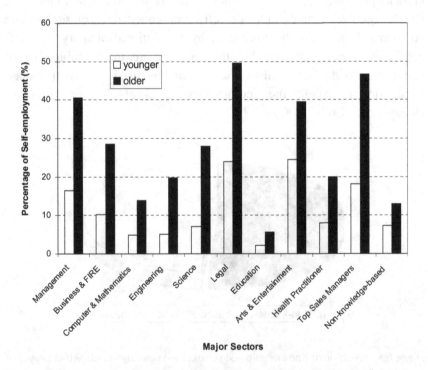

Figure 6.7 Self-employment Rate by Major Sectors, Older versus Younger Workers in 2000

The distribution of self-employed seniors across the knowledge-based occupations and non-knowledge-based professions as a whole highlights a slightly different pattern in relation to the respective distribution for the young. Figure 6.8 shows the percentage breakdown by occupational class for seniors and non-seniors. When viewed in this manner, seniors' self-employment is more specialized in the knowledge-based occupations, compared to that of the younger cohorts. The exceptions are the two sectors — *Computer & Mathematics* (SOC = 15) and *Arts & Entertainment* (SOC = 27). Both groups show similar concentration in *Legal, Education, and Health Practitioner* occupations, but seniors' self-employment is evidently more concentrated than their younger counterparts in most knowledge

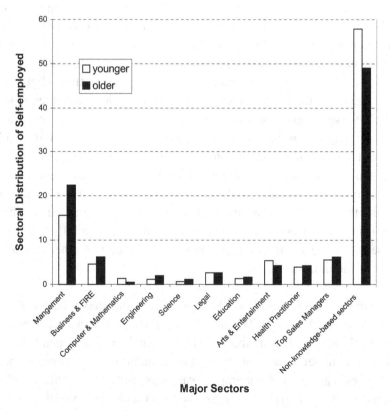

Major Sectors

Figure 6.8 Sectoral Distribution of Older versus Younger Self-employed in 2000

sectors — *Management, Business and Finance, Architecture and Engineering, Physical and Social Science,* and *High-level Sales Management.* Younger entrepreneurs accordingly tend to concentrate more than seniors in the non-knowledge-based economy.

The picture is somewhat different when looking at wage-and-salary employment. For this type of employment status, the elderly are more concentrated than their younger cohorts in non-knowledge-based occupations. This is illustrated in Figure 6.9.

3. Age and Entrepreneurship

The following of the chapter focuses on self-employment only in the knowledge-based sectors, i.e., entrepreneurship. Considering the innovation and knowledge components in the nature of entrepreneurship, entrepreneurship is defined in this book as knowledge-based self-employment instead of self-employment in all economic sectors. The previous section was presented through descriptive statistics both self-employment rates and knowledge-based self-employment rates among seniors versus among the younger cohorts. It is obvious that, compared to the younger working cohorts, seniors not only have a higher self-employment rate in the labor force, but also have a much higher knowledge-based self-employment rate. Based on those data, seniors are expected more likely to be entrepreneurs than younger working people. To test this hypothesis, a binomial logit model is estimated in Zhang (2007a) to more rigorously explore how someone's age influences their propensity to be an entrepreneur, controlling for certain other characteristics of the individual.

This binomial logit model was based on the utility maximization theory introduced in Chapter 5. The model was estimated using the 1-percent sample of individuals from the 2000 PUMS database. The dependent variable in the model is the probability that an individual is an entrepreneur, given their age, other demographic variables, and socio-economic characteristics. Age is specified in the model as a dummy variable, where

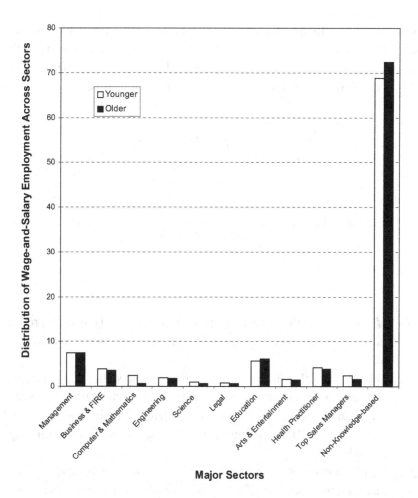

Figure 6.9 Sectoral Wage-and-salary Employment, Older versus Younger Workers, 2000

"1" indicates a senior (age 62 or over) and "0" for younger people of working ages (age 16–61). The model controls for a number of characteristics specific to the individuals that are consistent with other models that have been developed in previous literature to examine seniors' occupational choices. Those control factors affecting seniors' entrepreneurial propensity include health conditions (Quinn, 1980), educational levels (Berkovec and Stern, 1991), wealth (Bruce *et al.*, 2000; Parker and Rougaier, 2004), and other demographic characteristics (such as race, gender, marriage status, and citizenship). The statistical details of this model estimation and the details of the variable measurement and descriptions are explained in Zhang (2007a). The specification of the binomial model is:

$$\ln\left[\frac{P_i}{1-P_i}\right] = \alpha_0 + \phi Age_i + \sum \beta_m X_m,$$

or

$$P(Y_i = 1 \mid Age, X_m) = \frac{1}{1+\exp(-\alpha_0 - \phi Age_i - \sum \beta_m X_m)}, \qquad (6.1)$$

where

$P(Y = 1, Age, X_m)$ is the probability that an individual i is an entrepreneur given their age, other demographic and socio-economic characteristics;

Y_i is a binary variable with value "1" indicating the status of an entrepreneur and "0" indicating the status of a wage-and-salary employee;

Age_i is a binary variable with value "1" referring to individuals of age 62 or greater and "0" referring to those under 62 and of working age (16–61);

$\sum \beta_m X_m$ measures m other factors that are related to the individuals. Those factors have been identified in the literature to influence the probability that an individual will be an entrepreneur. Those factors include income, property value, educational level, disability status, gender, marital status, citizenship, and race. Among them, disability status is used as a proxy for health conditions. Appendix 6.6 displays all of the variables in the model and their sources of data.

The estimated results of the above model offer some interesting findings. The results indicate that there is a statistically significant ($p = 0.0000$) and positive relationship between being a senior and being an entrepreneur, controlling for other demographic and socioeconomic characteristics of the person. More specifically, seniors are more likely than younger individuals to be entrepreneurs. The coefficient on *being a senior* is 0.83 (shown in Appendix 6.7). This means that the log of the odds of someone being an entrepreneur increases by 0.83 if they are aged 62 or over (rather than within the age range of 16–61), controlling for other characteristics of the individual. In fact, this variable has the strongest impact on entrepreneurial propensity out of all of the dummy variables in the model.

All of the other characteristics of an individual that are specified in the model were found to be important determinants of entrepreneurship. Human capital is found to associate with entrepreneurial propensity. One human capital indicator, education attainment, has a positive effect on the likelihood of being an entrepreneur. Additional levels of education an individual has achieved enhance the log of the odds for this person to participate in the labor force as entrepreneur. Another human capital indicator, health condition, is also found to relate to entrepreneurial propensity. This chapter uses employment disability status as a proxy for health conditions. Individuals with employment disabilities were found to be more likely to be entrepreneurs, a finding which on the face may appear to be somewhat counterintuitive. Individuals with disabilities face barriers to entry into wage-and-salary employment due to discriminatory attitudes on the part of employers, and consequently, self-employment may be a more attractive option for them. Disability may face discrimination in wage-and-salary workplace, which could increase an individual's chance to choose entrepreneurship as an outlet of a career. Further, a person's employment disability may make them more strong-willed and independent, which allows them to excel in an entrepreneurial setting.

Gender, the immigration status, marital circumstances, and race of an individual were also found to be important determinants of entrepreneurship. Being a male has a strong association with an individual's chance to be an entrepreneur. Newer immigrants are more likely to be entrepreneurs[44], but the impact of this factor is relatively small[45]. In comparison to those who are separated, the widowed, the divorced, and the married are more likely to be entrepreneurs and singles less likely. Of all of these categories, being single appears to matter the most. The coefficient on this dummy variable, while negative, is much larger than those that are associated with the other marriage status categories. Being white, Asian or being of mixed descent, compared to people of other races, increases one's odds of being an entrepreneur. On the other hand, those who are Black are less likely to be entrepreneurial.

Those with money are more likely to be entrepreneurs. The coefficients on both of the wealth indicators, i.e., household income and property value, are significant ($p = 0.0000$) and positive. The coefficient on property value is big[46], but the coefficient on household income is small[47]. This situation indicates that property value has a strong association with an individual's entrepreneurial propensity while a person's household income has a weak effect, controlling for other factors. Wealth and income provide an individual with the financial capital that is often necessary to start a business and so it is not surprising to find out that those with more assets are more likely to be entrepreneurial.

The responsibility of taking care of grandchildren has a negative impact on the likelihood that someone is an entrepreneur and this is largely a function of the duration of care taking. More specifically, the longer a person has had the responsibilities of taking care of grandchildren, the less likely they are to be entrepreneurs. Taking care of grandchildren for a longer period normally means detaching from the labor force and foregoing the development of new work-related skills and network building, which makes it eventually more difficult for them to start a business.

4. Conclusion

The analysis summarized in this chapter indicates that there is a correlation between someone's age and their propensity for entrepreneurship as well as the self-employment rate. The descriptive statistics highlight several points. Older individuals have a higher self-employment rate than their younger cohorts and seniors' self-employment tends to concentrate in the knowledge-based sectors. The self-employment rate for seniors is higher than that for those in younger age groups and this is consistent across all occupations. Compared with younger self-employment, elderly self-employment tends to concentrate in knowledge-based sectors, with the exception of those occupations in the sectors of Computer and Mathematics, and Arts and Entertainment.

A binomial logit model shows that seniors in the labor force are more likely to be entrepreneurs than the young. To be more specific, being of age 62 or over increases the log of the odds by 0.83 for someone to be an entrepreneur, controlling for other demographic and socioeconomic characteristics of the individual. The factor *being a senior* has a stronger impact than all other dummy variables in the model. All of the other characteristics of an individual that are specified in the model were found to be important determinants of entrepreneurial propensity. Individuals with higher education attainment, with employment disabilities, being male, of the race of White and Asian, having the responsibility for grandchildren for a shorter period of time, and owning a higher property value are found more likely to be an entrepreneur.

Summary

- Based on PUMS data, older individuals have a higher self-employment rate than their younger cohorts and seniors' self-employment tends to concentrate in the knowledge-based sectors.
- The binomial logit model developed in this chapter shows that seniors in the labor force are more likely to be entrepreneurs than the young, controlling for other demographic and socioeconomic characteristics of individuals.
- Age has a stronger impact than all other demographic dummy variables in this model.
- Education attainment has a positive effect on the likelihood of being an entrepreneur.

- Interestingly, individuals with employment disabilities were found to be more likely to be entrepreneurs. Individuals with disabilities possibly face various barriers to entry into wage-and-salary employment, and self-employment may be a more attractive option for them. Further, a person's employment disability may make them more strong-willed and thus independent, which allows them to excel in an entrepreneurial setting.
- Being a male has a strong association with an individual's chance to be an entrepreneur.
- Newer immigrants are more likely to be entrepreneurs, but the impact of this factor is relatively small.
- In comparison to those who are separated, the widowed, the divorced, and the married are more likely to be entrepreneurs and singles less likely.
- Being a white, an Asian or of a mixed descent, compared to people of other races, increases one's odds of being an entrepreneur. Those who are African Americans are less likely to be entrepreneurs.
- Those with money are more likely to be entrepreneurs, though the impact from income is weak. Wealth provides an individual with the financial capital to start a business. There is a double-sided effect of income. More household income can provide more capital to their businesses, but the need to obtain more income also motivates many people to become entrepreneurs.

End notes

[36]　Observations of the very old ages (in the upper 80s or 90s) would possibly be dropped due to their different behavior patterns from others.

[37]　Instead of PUMS 5-percent samples and previously used HRS data. HRS only offers age information till 57 and PUMS 5-percent does not offer as flexible geographic identification information.

[38]　The flexible geographic identification (state and metro area) of PUMS 1-percent samples makes it more possible to integrate data from other sources.

[39]　Though the older cohort has a higher proportion of people who are not employed or not in the labor force.

40   Appendix 6.2 presents the counts of people for each variable, while Appendices 6.4, 6.5, and 6.6 present the rates or percentages in Figures 6.3, 6.4 and 6.5 respectively.

41   Unemployment is part of the labor force, like various employments.

42   Data table for this figure presentation is displayed in Appendix 6.5.

43   Data table for this figure presentation is displayed in Appendix 6.5.

44   The variable *Year to U.S.* is measured by the year an individual came to the United States. For a newly immigrated person, the value of this variable (e.g. 2000, 1999, 1998, etc.) is larger.

45   The impact of immigration factor is 0.000055 according to Appendix 6.7 and Zhang (2007a).

46   The coefficient on property value is 0.046 according to Appendix 6.7 and Zhang (2007a).

47   The coefficient on household income is 0.0000025 according to Appendix 6.7 and Zhang (2007a).

CHAPTER 7

SOCIAL AND POLICY FACTORS FOR ELDERLY ENTREPRENEURSHIP

This chapter extends the analysis of the previous chapter and explores social and policy factors as possible determinants for an elderly person's decision to be an entrepreneur. The previous literature has indicated that the socio-cultural environment of an individual is an important driving factor for entrepreneurship. Those socio-cultural factors that have been identified to be important include business environment and cultural norms (Giannetti and Simonov, 2004), tax policy (Long, 1982; Blau, 1987; Schuetze, 2000), research and development (R&D) expenditures (Keuschnigg and Nielsen, 2001; Daly et al., 2004), and immigration policy (Borjas and Bronars, 1989). To date, the literature has only minimally addressed the role of age in this relationship. Most studies have mainly focused on the cohorts younger than the average retirement age 62; seniors aged 62 and above are not particularly focused yet.

Previous chapter has found out that seniors who have reached average retirement age and are still active in the labor force are more likely than their younger counterparts to be self-employed and to be entrepreneurs. This finding seems opposite to the conventional wisdom. Hence, it would be interesting to investigate what factors contribute to the higher entrepreneurial propensity from seniors, or what factors affect those seniors' entrepreneurial propensity.

Age seems to be a relevant factor to entrepreneurship and self-employment, as Chapter 6 has suggested; however, there must be many other socio-economic factors as well as demographic factors that contribute to seniors' entrepreneurial propensity. Although the topic of entrepreneurship in general has received extensive scholarly attention, aging and retirement issues are relatively limitedly addressed in the entrepreneurship literature. Among related previous literature, those addressing seniors' occupational choices have touched the factors that may be related to seniors' entrepreneurial propensity.

Quinn (1980) believed self-employment to be a "bridge job" between full engagement in the labor force and retirement. He used two waves of RHS (Data from the 1969 and 1971 interviews of the RHS) on 836 white married men aged 58–63 in 1969, and identified a few important factors that are related to seniors' entrepreneurial propensity. Health status and Social Security benefits are found to be associated with higher withdrawal rates from the labor force, according to this study. Moreover, Quinn also found that lack of flexibility in hours worked and psychological and financial traumas of sudden retirement in wage-and-salary work places result in the comparative attraction from entrepreneurship and lower labor force withdrawal among senior entrepreneurs, compared to their wage-and-salary counterparts.

A few other studies use the same data source, RHS, to examine factors that are related to seniors' occupational choices. Fuchs (1982) found that seniors with previous self-employment experience or white-collar quasi-entrepreneurial occupations, such as managers and executives, tended to create ventures before retirement. This finding might partially explain the entrepreneurial propensity among the elderly. Seniors, with more working experience and particularly even previous leadership experiences, are more likely to be leaders, managers, and executives of a firm or organization and could also be more likely to be entrepreneurs.

Other seniors' occupational choice studies discussed the impact of health, education, gender, earnings and wealth, and family circumstances on seniors' entrepreneurial propensity. Berkovec and Stern (1991) noted a few factors that increase the probability of older men's retirement: bad health, age, and lack of education. However, the authors further noted that job-specific differences were an important source of unobserved heterogeneity. Bruce *et al.* (2000) based on 1992 and 1996 HRS data, suggested that there was little impact of older workers' health insurance status and coverage on their self-employment propensity. Using cross-country comparative time-series and micro-data from the OECD countries, Blanchflower (2000) found that self-employment rates rose with age, were higher among men, had nonlinear patterns with education, and varied across countries. Parker and Rougaier (2004), relying on a sample of 200 self-employed people from the British Retirement Survey (1988, 1989, and 1994), found that greater actual and potential earnings were associated with a declined retirement probability among the self-employed, and that gender, health or family circumstances did not appear to affect self-employment retirement decisions.

Although seniors' occupational choice literature has touched the factors related to their self-employment and entrepreneurial propensity, those factors are basically focused at individual levels. In the non-age-specific entrepreneurship literature, institutional factors, as well as a few other individual factors, are addressed to relate to entrepreneurial propensity. Those institutional factors include immigration policy (Borjas and Bronars, 1989), retirement policies (Quinn, 1980), and tax policy (Long, 1982; Blau, 1987; Schuetze, 2000). For example, Schuetze (2000) compared self-employment patterns and trends in Canada with those in the United States and noted that the self-employment rate increased with tax rates in primary jobs but not as much in secondary jobs. Schuetze suggested that this was possibly a tax-sheltering effect that made the self-employed more likely underreport.

Knowledge capital is found a critical factor not just in seniors' occupation choice literature, but also in the non-age-specific entrepreneurship literature. Equally prevalently noted in the literature is physical capital. Evans and Leighton (1989) and Evans and Jovanovic (1989) found that entrepreneurs faced liquidity constraints that were expressed in the literature as family assets. This study was based on the U.S. micro data from the National Longitudinal Survey of Young Men for 1966–1981 and the CPS data for 1968–1987. Blanchflower *et al.* (2001) noted that in Europe old workers and men with more education were more likely to be self-employed. This study used a survey of self-employment development in eighty countries. Lazear (2002) further investigated the importance of practical knowledge by indicating that people with many and broad skills were more likely to be self-employed than others.

In sum, the non-age-specific entrepreneurship literature has addressed several key contributing factors that are related to entrepreneurship: the availability of assets, tax policy, education/knowledge and skills, immigration policies, and demographic factors. Health and family circumstances have been identified in the literature on seniors' occupational choice. However, the nature of a social environment that spurs elderly entrepreneurship has been minimally researched, compared to individual factors. Moreover, the literature on seniors typically addresses only young seniors (aged up to 59 in those studies) and those who are even older are not yet addressed. In fact, the cohorts that are older than average retirement age are particularly meaningful to the calculation of aging-resulted fiscal and labor issues. The labor force participation of those seniors who are aged over the average retirement age (62) is the focus of this book. This chapter, therefore, focuses on exploring a few key social/policy factors, as well as individual factors, that affect seniors' entrepreneurial propensity after age 61.

The social and policy factors that are considered in this chapter as determinants of entrepreneurial propensity include cultural openness and diversity, tax rates, and R&D environment. Cultural openness and diversity is expected to have impact on seniors' entrepreneurial propensity because it is an important element of business environment where entrepreneurship occurs. Cultural openness and diversity have been argued to spur more creative and innovation (Florida, 2004), which motivates entrepreneurship. Tax rates are included in this chapter to follow previous entrepreneurship literature (Long, 1982; Blau, 1987; Schuetze, 2000). R&D environment supports and further spurs innovation and makes it more possible to channel innovation into the markets. R&D investment has been addressed in previous literature to directly relate to entrepreneurship (Acs and Audretsch, 1990).

The individual factors to be tested in this chapter basically follow those used in the previous chapter. When focused only on seniors after retirement age and tested with social/policy factors, it is worth investigating the association of those individual factors with elderly entrepreneurial propensity. Additionally, adding those individual level factors helps to control heterogeneity across individuals when the effects of social/policy factors are observed.

A binomial logit model is estimated to test two hypotheses, controlling for individual level heterogeneity. First, it is expected that policies that encourage R&D and cultural openness and diversity increase the probability that a senior is an entrepreneur. Second, tax rates are anticipated to have a negative impact on this likelihood.

1. Binomial Logit Model

A binomial logit model can capture the probability that a senior is an entrepreneur, given the cultural openness and diversity, R&D environment in the MSA or Primary Metropolitan Statistic Areas (PMSA) in which they live, tax rates they face in their state of residence, and other socio-economic characteristics specific to the individual. Zhang (2007b) explored a binomial logit model to test the factors affecting seniors' entrepreneurial propensity. The independent variables that are used in the model are consistent with the factors that have been used in previous empirical studies on entrepreneurship and occupational choice[48]. Unlike the logit model in the previous chapter, this model is estimated for only individuals who are seniors and therefore does not explicitly capture the age effect through a dummy variable.

The model is specified as follows:

Binomial Logit Model:

$$\ln\left[\frac{P_i}{1 - P_i}\right] = \alpha_0 + \phi_1 T_i + \phi_2 R_i + \phi_3 S_i + \sum \beta_m X_{im},$$

or

$$P(Y_i = 1 | T_i, R_i, S_i, X_{im}) = \frac{1}{1 + \exp\left(-\alpha_0 - \phi_1 T_i - \phi_2 R_i - \phi_3 S_i - \sum \beta_m X_{im}\right)}$$

$$(7.1)$$

Y_i: a binary variable for elderly (age 62 and above) entrepreneurship (1 indicates an entrepreneur and 0 a wage-and-salary employee);

T_i: state tax rate;

R_i: R&D expenditures in MSA/PMSA;

S_i: MSA/PMSA social tolerance index that measures cultural openness;

$\sum \beta_m X_{im}$:   other m demographic and socioeconomic characteristics of the individual i, e.g., household income to represent wealth, educational attainment, disability status as a proxy for health, the year that a person came to the U.S. to indicate immigration status, gender, marital status[49], and race[50].

Appendix 7.1 summaries the variables used in this model. The social factors that measure entrepreneurial milieu come from various sources. The *social tolerance index* that is used in the model to measure cultural openness and diversity comes from Florida (2005)[51] and is summarized at the PMSA/MSA level. This *social tolerance index* by Florida (2005) includes four dimensions of diversity and tolerance: inclusion of immigrants, integration of different races, tolerance toward homosexuality, and concentration of arts and entertainment professionals[52]. The variable *R&D environment* is used to measure the innovation and human capital milieu of a PMSA/MSA. Data for this variable comes from the National Science Foundation (NSF). The data on taxes considers both *corporate income taxes* and *personal income taxes* and is summarized at the state level. The employment data comes from the Public Use Microdata Samples (PUMS).

The independent variables that are used to characterize each individual include wealth, human capital (include health and education attainment), responsibility for grandchildren, and other demographic factors. Previous literature has indicated the importance of liquidity constraints as a factor that drives an individual to be an entrepreneur or to be self-employed. Liquidity constraints, or wealth, in most cases, are believed to depend on family and household wealth, rather than individual income. Therefore, *household income* is used in the model to measure wealth. The demographic variables include gender (using dummy variable *Male*), race (using dummy variables *White, Black, Asian, Native, mixed*[53]), marital status (using dummy variables *married, widowed, divorced, single*[54]), and immigration status (measured by the year that a person arrived at the United States and using the variable *year to U.S.*). Health, as a part of human capital, is mentioned in previous literature and also hypothesized in this study to be an important determinant of a senior's employment choice; therefore, the dummy variable *disability*[55] is used to proxy the health status of an elderly person[56]. The variable *education attainment* is used to measure another important dimension of human capital and is expected to have a positive impact of a senior's choice of employment status. For the elderly, their responsibilities associated with grandchildren could hamper their motivation to participate into the labor force. Therefore, the Zhang (2007b) model includes a variable, *responsibility for grandchildren,* to test whether this is a factor and if so, how strong is this factor.

More detailed measurement issues are discussed in Zhang (2007b). For example, considering the fact that the social and policy variables that have been selected for the model are at different geographic levels, either at the MSA/PMSA level or at the state level, whereas the variables measuring demographic and socioeconomic characteristics are at the level of the individuals, Zhang (2007b) has assigned the values of social and policy variables to individuals who reside in the corresponding states or PMSA/MSA. This is done through PUMS geographic identifiers. All of the PUMS data is for the year 2000 and the social and policy variables in the model are for previous years, i.e., the 1990s.

2. Estimation Results

The estimated Zhang (2007b) model shows that there is a significant ($p = 0.000$) relationship between a senior's propensity to be an entrepreneur and R&D policies, tax rates and social tolerance or diversity. According to the Pseudo R-squared, the social, political and individual level variables in the model explain collectively about 12% of elderly people's probability of being entrepreneurship. Although the R-squared is relatively small, it is, like the model in the previous chapter, consistent with the models that have been estimated in the previous literature. The regression results are reported in Table 7.1.

Social cultural openness and diversity (measured by *Social tolerance index*) displays a significant ($p = 0.000$) and positive impact on a senior's probability to be an entrepreneur. The coefficient on this variable is 0.26, which means that as the social tolerance of an individual's place of residence increases by one unit according to the measured scale, the log of the odds of that person being an entrepreneur increases by 0.26, *ceteris paribus*. In other words, the more cultural and racially tolerant a society is, the more likely it is for seniors to become entrepreneurs, controlling for other factors. A tolerant cultural and diversity has been argued to motivate higher creativity, according to Florida (2005). Creativity, defined by Florida (2005), is an important aspect of the knowledge-based economy and creativity and the knowledge base have been found to foster entrepreneurship. Therefore, it is not surprising to find that this relationship also holds for seniors specifically.

R&D expenditures were also found to have a significant ($p = 0.000$) and positive impact on the log of the odds that a senior is an entrepreneur. The coefficient on this variable is 0.002, which means that as the rate of R&D expenditure in the gross product of the metropolitan area where a senior resides increases by 0.1%, the log of odds of a senior to be an entrepreneur improves by 0.002, controlling for other factors. R&D expenditures have been shown empirically in previous literature to have a positive association with entrepreneurship and have been used as a proxy for entrepreneurship (Acs and Audretsch, 1990). Therefore, it is not surprising to find a positive association in this book as well. However, it appears that this relationship is weak in this model, a finding that slightly diverges from what has been found in previous literature on entrepreneurship literature in general. This would deserve further investigation.

Table 7.1 Regression Results

Y = log of odds for being an elderly entrepreneur	Coef.	Std. Err	Z	P > |z|
Social Factors				
Social tolerance index	**0.2550756**	0.0095349	26.75	0.000
R&D environment (1/1000)	*0.0022658*	0.000115	19.7	0.000
Corporate Tax rate	**−0.0129941**	0.002012	−6.46	0.000
Individual income & employment tax rate	**−0.0365517**	0.0007407	−49.35	0.000
Human capital				
Disability	−0.0075608	0.0034728	−2.18	0.029
Education attainment	0.1972315	0.0005657	348.68	0.000
Wealth				
Household income	3.35E-06	1.48E-08	226.39	0.000
Demographic characteristics				
Married	0.1999258	0.0147296	13.57	0.000
Widowed	0.2702245	0.0152492	17.72	0.000
Divorced	0.075352	0.0153418	4.91	0.000
Single	−0.17412	0.0164703	−10.57	0.000
White	1.101366	0.0229923	47.9	0.000
Black	0.0890868	0.0242143	3.68	0.000
Native	0.3848818	0.0450633	8.54	0.000
Asian	0.8265104	0.0238976	34.59	0.000
Mixed	0.7920302	0.0271795	29.14	0.000
Male	0.8524927	0.0034441	247.53	0.000
Responsibility for grandchildren				
Responsibility for Grandchildren	−0.1171071	0.0038462	−30.45	0.000
Immigration status				
Year to U.S.	−0.0000128	2.38E-06	−5.37	0.000
Constant	−6.132059	0.0306118	−200.32	0.000
Number of obs		6979586		
Log likelihood		−1771738.3		
LR chi2(19)		469122.58		
Prob > chi2		0.0000		
Pseudo R2		0.1169		

Tax rates were found to have a negative impact on a senior's entrepreneurial propensity. This was found to be the case for both corporate tax rates and individual income and employment tax rates; both variables were highly significant ($p = 0.000$). The coefficient on corporate tax rate is -0.01, which means that a 1% increase in the ratio of corporate tax revenue to the gross state product decreases the log of odds of an elderly person being an entrepreneur by 0.01, *ceteris paribus*. The coefficient on individual income and employment income tax rate is -0.04, which means that for a 1% increase in the ratio of individual income and employment income tax revenue to the gross state product, the log of odds for an elderly person to be an entrepreneur decreases by 0.04.

The variables that were used in the model to characterize human capital — i.e., disability status (as a proxy for health condition) and education level, were also found to be significant ($p = 0.029$ for disability status and $p = 0.000$ for education attainment). Poor health, indicated by the presence of a disability, was found to have slight negative impact on a senior's probability of being an entrepreneur. This makes sense. Individuals with poorer health or with some disability are less likely to be physically or even mentally capable of independent work, which may affect their motivation and ability to start and manage a business. However, it should be noted that for some physically and mentally challenged people, their disability makes them more strong-willed and this could increase their motivation to be independent and thus become an entrepreneur. Compared with the findings in the previous chapter, disability displays an inconsistent result.

In the previous chapter, being with employment disability slightly increases an individual's chance to be an entrepreneurial; however, for seniors, this chapter empirically indicates that being with disability decreases a senior's entrepreneurial propensity. This might relate to the factor that health offers a very important precondition for seniors' social activities. Although being disabled might not necessarily reduce entrepreneurial propensity for a younger person, it seems to reduce seniors' entrepreneurial propensity.

Another key human capital indicator, education attainment, has a positive, significant ($p = 0.000$) impact on entrepreneurial propensity. This is consistent with the findings of previous literature on entrepreneurship.

Other individual-level characteristics were also found to be significant. The coefficient on wealth (household income) in this model is positive and significant ($p = 0.000$), though the impact of this variable on entrepreneurial propensity appears to be weak (0.00000335), compared to social factors, the human capital factors, and demographic factors of an individual. One possible reason for this finding could be the double-sided effect of wealth. On the one hand, more household income can provide the elderly with more capital to start a business or invest further in their current business. On the other hand, many elderly could become self-employed because of the need to obtain more income.

Seniors are also found to be more likely to be entrepreneurs if they are male, married or widowed (compared to those who are separated), and of white, Asian, Native, or mixed races (compared to those of other races). Seniors who have never married tend not to be entrepreneurs, compared to people who are separated. It is not surprising that males are more likely to be entrepreneurs than women, considering the social expectation and more opportunities generally males have been exposed to. The influence of race on entrepreneurship is consistent with the fact that whites and Asians are generally better equipped with knowledge capital, social capital, and other resources, compared to people of other races. The reason that elderly persons of mixed race tends to be entrepreneurs could be related to diversity, which gives an advantage.

Seniors who have taken care of grandchildren for a longer period of time were found to be less likely to become entrepreneurs. A longer time span of responsibility for grandchildren tends to detach seniors for a longer period from the labor force and from learning new skills, which makes it more difficult for them to ultimately return to the labor force.

The effect of immigration status is weak (-0.0000128), compared with most of the other socio-economic variables, though the sign associated with the coefficient on this variable is what was expected. Seniors who have just arrived at the United States have a higher difficulty in acculturation than people who have been in the country for a longer time. Since social capital is important for business development, newer immigrants may generally have a higher difficulty to start and manage a business. For seniors who have been in this country for a long time, staying in this country longer does not necessary mean a higher level of acculturation. There is a diminishing marginal effect for their learning curve.

Elderly immigrants generally differ from younger immigrants in terms of their immigration purposes. The immigration status effect of seniors seems inconsistent with the finding from the previous chapter that tests on the determinants for entrepreneurial propensity in general, not just for seniors. In the previous chapter, immigrants who have been in the United States for a longer period of time tend to be less likely to be entrepreneurs, though the coefficient on this fact is weak as well. Younger immigrants normally tend to come with some career ambition and therefore their immigration most often relate to jobs. For seniors who are relatively new to the United States, the chance for them to start a business might not be high. Most of these newly immigrated seniors are perhaps either dependent on their family members or they are not coming to the United States with much career ambition.

3. Discussion and Future Research Directions

Similar to many other empirical studies, this Zhang (2007b) logit model test has a few limitations that need to be noted. First, a better dataset would worth exploring for a hierarchical model to work well in this analysis. The independent variables used in this model are at different scales: individual, MSA/PMSA, and state. To integrate the variables at the three different scales into one model, this model applies the geographically aggregate value for a specific variable to all individuals residing in that geographic unit. This method shares the rationale of using a regional dummy variable. However, if data were available, a hierarchical model would be ideal to investigate a model with variables at different scales. A hierarchical model can single out the variable impact from the impact of geographic proximity along the geographic hierarchy. The reason that a hierarchical model is not used in this chapter is the lack of data at all the three scales. Instead, the data is only available at one of the three scales. If data at all the three scales (individual, MSA, and state) were available, a hierarchical model would have been conducted. This would not only introduce more observations, but more importantly, the dynamics along the geographic hierarchy would be captured as well. Therefore, exploring other data possibilities could be a direction for future research on this topic.

Second, the time span of the variable, *Social Tolerance Index*, is worth further investigation. In this chapter, *Social Tolerance Index* measures culture openness and racial diversity across MSA/PMSA during 1990s. Using the values during 1990s can help capture the lagged effect on the output that is measured in 2000. This is similar to the rationale of measuring the tax variables by the value in 1999. There is an assumption that social cultural phenomenon in 1990s, instead of in 1980s or only in 1999, would have a significant impact on seniors' entrepreneurial propensity in 2000. The reason this is not investigated is that no other related data measuring social cultural tolerance is found when this analysis is conducted. Hence, future study could explore a better data set and investigate the best time span for this variable.

Third, there might be a few other model specification issues. The pseudo R-squared for this model is small (0.117), the number of independent variables might display a "kitchen sink effect", and there might be other variables for a better model specification. The small pseudo R-squared is not a big concern considering two facts: it is similar to the R-squared in previous studies using micro data sets like HRS; the very large samples size (69 million observations after applying PUMS sampling weights) introduces more variances across observations and thus makes a smaller R-squared expected. However, this situation reduces the explanation power of this model and could still be suspected to be a source of omitted variables. On the other hand, the model might not be efficient enough due to possible multicollinearity or lack of being parsimonious. Totally 19 independent variables are used in this model.

Although correlations between the independent variables are not high enough to suspect multicollinearity, the large sample size with more complex variance could obfuscate the multicollinearity possibility. Additionally, the current logit model does not use any nonlinear forms for independent variables. To improve the model fit, other possible model specifications including various non-linearity forms might be worth exploring.

4. Conclusion

Social factors, such as culture openness and racial/ethnic diversity and tax policy have significant impact on elderly persons' chance to be an entrepreneur. A higher tolerance level of a society or a lower corporate and personal income tax rate is associated with higher probability for an elderly person to be an entrepreneur, controlling for other factors. Hence, with a policy milieu that stimulates more cultural openness, tolerance, and diversity could help improve a higher level of elderly entrepreneurship. Lower corporate income and individual income and employment tax rates could help to reduce hurdles for elderly persons to be entrepreneurs. Among individual factors, based on this empirical study, improving seniors' education attainment, promoting marriages, and reducing seniors' involuntary responsibility for their grandchildren would help increase elderly people's chance to be entrepreneurs. Policies should also focus on promoting female and minority seniors' entrepreneurial propensity.

Summary

- The model in this chapter finds out that the more cultural and racially tolerant a society is, the more likely it is for seniors to become entrepreneurs, controlling for other factors.
- R&D expenditures were also found to have a positive impact on the log of the odds that a senior is an entrepreneur.

- The corporate and the individual income tax rates were found to have negative impacts on a senior's entrepreneurial propensity.
- Poor health, indicated by the presence of a disability, was found to have slight negative impact on a senior's probability of being an entrepreneur. Although being disabled might not necessarily reduce entrepreneurial propensity for a younger person, it seems to reduce seniors' entrepreneurial propensity.
- Education attainment has a positive impact on entrepreneurial propensity.
- The impact of income on seniors' entrepreneurial propensity in this model is positive but appears to be relatively weak.
- Seniors are also found to be more likely to be entrepreneurs if they are male, married or widowed (compared to those who are separated), and of a white, an Asian, Native, or a mixed races (compared to those of other races).
- Seniors who have taken care of grandchildren for a longer period of time were found to be less likely to become entrepreneurs. A longer time span of responsibility for grandchildren tends to detach seniors for a longer period from the labor force and from learning new skills, which makes it more difficult for them to ultimately return to the labor force.
- The effect of immigration status is relatively weak. Many newly immigrated seniors do not come to the United States with much career ambition. For seniors who have been in this country for a long time, staying in this country longer does not necessary mean a higher level of acculturation. There is a diminishing marginal effect for their learning curve.
- Policy to promote elderly entrepreneurship therefore should focus on stimulating more cultural openness, social tolerance and diversity, requesting lower income tax rates (particularly for seniors), and reducing seniors' involuntary responsibility for their grandchildren. Policies should also focus on promoting female and minority seniors' entrepreneurial propensity.

End notes

48   The related literature is introduced in Chapter 2. Zhang (2007b) described in details those variables.

49   For marital status, dummy variables are generated and the number of separated couples is omitted.

50   For race, dummy variables are generated and the number of persons of other races is omitted.

51   This dataset is obtained with permission under the help of Kevin M. Stolarick.

52   Florida (2005) used four distinct indices to measure those four dimension: the Melting Pot Index (measuring the concentration of foreign-born people), the Racial Integration Index (referring to racial integration, the Gay Index (measuring the tolerance toward homosexuality), and the Bohemian Index (referring to the relative concentration of artists, musicians, and entertainers).

53   *Other race* is the omitted item for comparisons with those above race variables.

54   Being *separated* is the omitted item for comparisons with those marital status dummy variables.

55   In Zhang (2007b), disability is measured by general disability, including employment disability. Different from the previous chapter where all-age individuals are investigated and employment disability would be more relevant to employment status, this chapter only addresses seniors. Considering the fact that many seniors are not in the labor force, employment disability would not be as good as general disability to measure their health situation.

56   PUMS does not offer detailed information on an individual's health status. Although Health and Retirement Studies (HRS) offers much detailed information on seniors' health, this dataset lacks information for senior aged over 59 and thus cannot serve the purpose of this study. Therefore, this study ends up using PUMS disability information to proxy health status of seniors.

PART 6

REGIONAL DYNAMICS OF ELDERLY ENTREPRENEURSHIP

CHAPTER 8

REGIONAL DISTRIBUTION OF ELDERLY ENTREPRENEURSHIP

Previous two chapters revealed existence and prevalence of elderly entrepreneurship and explored the factors related to elderly entrepreneurship. Then the question is whether elderly entrepreneurship can enhance regional and local economic growth. Controlling for the relative economic homogeneity, the following two chapters focus on exploring the economic power of elderly entrepreneurship at the U.S. regional level. Before investigating the regional economic impacts of elderly entrepreneurship, this chapter explores the regional distribution of elderly entrepreneurship and attempts to examine whether elderly entrepreneurship distributes with a regional clustering pattern. If a regional clustering pattern exists, it means that regional socioeconomic environment affects the development of elderly entrepreneurship and it will be necessary to consider spatial autocorrelation when building the model to test regional economic impacts.

This chapter explores the regional disparities of elderly entrepreneurship through metropolitan areas. As indicated earlier, this book defines entrepreneurship as self-employment in knowledge-based sectors. Most knowledge-based sectors are concentrated in metropolitan areas; metropolitan areas are often-used units for studies of regional industry mix and economic patterns. MSA and Primary Metropolitan Statistics Areas (PMSA) are therefore used as the units of analysis in this chapter. This chapter uses descriptive statistics as the methodology to analyze regional disparities of elderly entrepreneurship.

1. Regional Disparities and Clustering

To investigate the existence of regional disparities of elderly entrepreneurship, the most direct way is to map the levels of the elderly entrepreneurship across a scope of areas. To control for the population and economic size of the area, proportion of elderly entrepreneurs relative to the area's economy is examined. To be more specific, the level of entrepreneurship is measured through knowledge-based self-employment rate relative to the area's employment size.

Shown in Figure 8.1, there exists disparities across the metropolitan areas for elderly self-employment rate among elderly employment. The elderly self-employment rates range from 10.6% to 25.1%. The disparities across the metropolitan areas also occur to knowledge-based elderly self-employment rate, i.e. elderly entrepreneurship. This is shown in Figure 8.2.

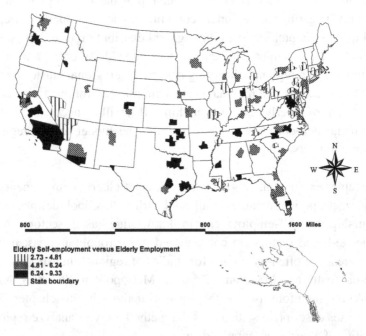

Figure 8.1 Elderly Self-employment Rate in Elderly Employment in MSA/PMSA in 2000
Source: U.S. Census Bureau PUMS.

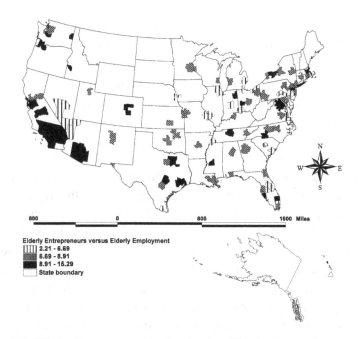

Figure 8.2 Elderly Entrepreneurship Levels (i.e. Elderly Knowledge-based Self-employment in Elderly Employment) in MSA/PMSA in 2000
Source: U.S. Census Bureau PUMS.

Beyond areal disparities, slight clustering phenomenon can also be vaguely identified in Figures 8.1 and 8.2. Adjacent metropolitan areas tend to show similar patterns and several clusters can be identified, such as the West Coast, the Mid South Area, the Great Lake Area, and the Northeast Area. This clustering pattern is basically consistent with the U.S. Census nine regional divisions (shown in Appendix 8.1). Elderly entrepreneurship levels distribute with a clustering pattern by the census region divisions and with disparities between those nine regions. This suggests that regional socioeconomic environment possibly matters to the level of elderly entrepreneurship. The next section thus examines the relationship between elderly entrepreneurship and the regional economic environment.

2. Entrepreneurial Environment and Elderly Entrepreneurship

To examine the impact of regional economic environment on elderly entrepreneurship, this section uses scatter plots to intuitively plot the relationship between elderly entrepreneurship and a few regional economic indices. Then trend lines based on the scattered dots are added. Considering the close relationship between self-employment and entrepreneurship, as defined in this book, the relationship between elderly self-employment rate and non-age specific self-employment rate is also investigated.

The regional economic indices that may be related to elderly entrepreneurship[57] include non-age-specific entrepreneurship level and the regional knowledge environment. Considering the fact that regional non-age-specific entrepreneurial level could offer the entrepreneurial atmosphere and other resources to elderly entrepreneurship, the relationship between regional non-age-specific entrepreneurship level and elderly entrepreneurship level is plotted. Entrepreneurship level, as defined in previous chapters, is represented by the percentage of knowledge-based self-employment in the total employment. Considering this specific definition of entrepreneurship and the fact that regional knowledge base may offer necessary knowledge capital facilitating entrepreneurship, the scale of regional "knowledge economy" is also used to plot with elderly self-employment and entrepreneurship levels. The scale of regional "knowledge economy" or the size of knowledge base is measured by the percentage of knowledge-based employment in the total regional employment.

To simplify the relationship, linear trend lines are assumed. Non-linear trend lines were tried originally; since no major visual difference between non-linear trend lines and linear trend lines was identified in the preliminary analysis, only linear ones are shown in this chapter to simplify the visualization.

Since the disparities and clustering patterns are identified across the Census nine Regional Divisions, the following sections of this chapter uses the Census nine Regional Divisions to define regions. The basic unit of analysis is still the metropolitan areas, i.e., MSA and PMSA. The MSA and PMSA are put in the scope of each Regional Division in the following comparisons.

2.1. Elderly self-employment rate versus regional non-age-specific self-employment rate

Before examining the entrepreneurship level, this section starts with examining self-employment rates. Figures 8.3 and 8.4 display the elderly self-employment rate of a region through the Y-axis and the non-age-specific self-employment rate of that region through the X-axis. Each scattered dot represents a metropolitan area. Figure 8.4 generates the trend lines for the corresponding scattered dots in Figure 8.3 by regions. As can be easily identified from Figures 8.3 and 8.4, most of those plots show an upward trend, except for the West South Central region. The upward trend indicates that local self-employment level is positively related to elderly self-employment level across the metropolitan areas.

Comparing across the nine regions, dots representing the East North Central metropolitan areas tend to concentrate the most and thus display

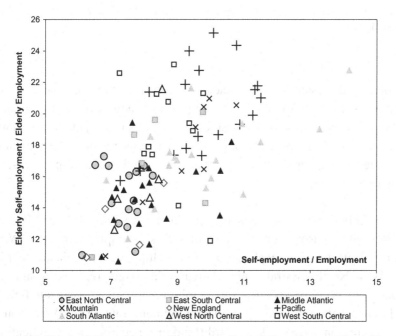

Figure 8.3 Elderly Self-employment Rate versus Total Self-employment Rate (Scatter Plots)

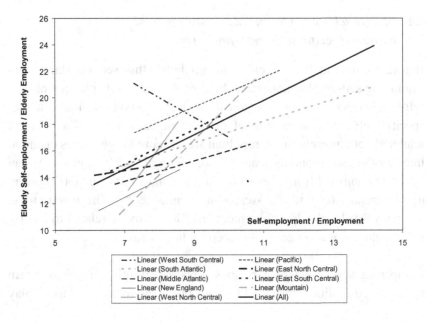

Figure 8.4 Elderly Self-employment Rate versus Total Self-employment Rate (Trend Lines)

a condensed cluster. Figure 8.4 adds trend lines to the above scatter plot figure (Figure 8.3). The line graph (Figure 8.4) shows even a clearer clustering effect of East North Central region. For this region, the line is shortest, meaning that this metropolitan areas in this region have the most homogeneous elderly self-employment rates and non-age-specific self-employment rate.

The different slopes of each line in Figure 8.4 indicate the different self-employment rate elasticity of elderly self-employment rate. West North Central region displays the biggest slope, which indicates that in the West North Central region versus other eight regions, a smaller change in non-age-specific self-employment rate is associated with a larger change in elderly self-employment rate. The West South Central region shows a downward trend or a negative slope, indicating a negative relationship between this region's self-employment rate and elderly self-employment rate. In another word, in the West South Central region, a higher self-employment rate of a metropolitan area is associated with a lower elderly self-employment rate. Compared to the all-region average trend line [shown as the dark solid line, with the legend "Linear (All)"], Mountain and West North Central regions have a larger positive self-employment rate elasticity of elderly self-employment.

2.2. *Elderly entrepreneurship level versus regional entrepreneurship level*

Figures 8.5 and 8.6 illustrate the relationship between elderly entrepreneurship and non-age-specific entrepreneurship (or knowledge-based self-employment). In these two figures, the Y-axis illustrates the percentage of elderly entrepreneurs among elderly employment, and the X-axis illustrates the percentage of non-age-specific entrepreneurs among total

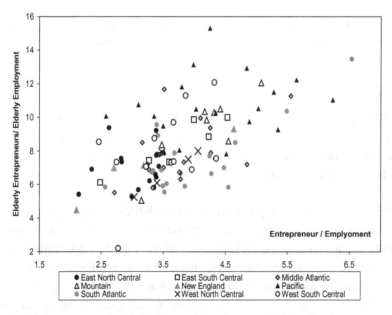

Figure 8.5 Percentage of Elderly Entrepreneurs among Elderly Employment versus Percentage of Non-age specific Entrepreneurs among the Total Employment

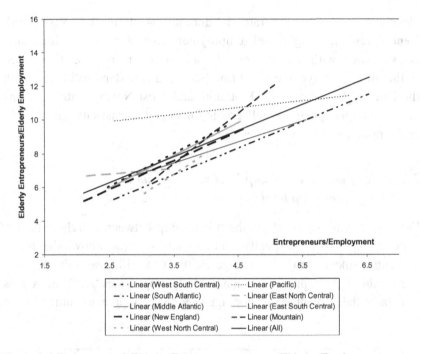

Figure 8.6 Percentage of Elderly Entrepreneurs among Elderly Employment versus Percentage of Non-age Specific Entrepreneurs among the Total Employment (Trend Lines)

employment. The scale of X-axes in Figures 8.5 and 8.6 is smaller than that of Y-axis. This situation indicates that the entrepreneurship level relative to the labor force is smaller than the elderly entrepreneurship level relative to the elderly labor force.

In Figure 8.5, the dots representing the East North Central region tend to concentrate at the bottom left corner, while dots representing other regions tend to scatter. This situation indicates that the East North Central metropolitan areas tend to have a homogeneously low entrepreneurship levels and low elderly entrepreneurship levels, compared to other eight regions. The concentrated dots reveal homogeneity in entrepreneurship and elderly entrepreneurship environment across metropolitan areas of the East North Central region.

Similar to the East North Central region, dots representing the West North Central regional tend to cluster as well, though they tend to be in the middle part along the X-axis and in the lowest section along the Y-axis. This situation indicates that the West North Central metropolitan areas tend to share similar entrepreneurship levels and elderly entrepreneurship levels and that this region tend to have medium level of entrepreneurship but low level of elderly entrepreneurship, compared with other regions.

Entrepreneurship levels and elderly entrepreneurship levels across metropolitan areas inside other regions tend to be more heterogeneous, compared to the East North Central and the West North Central regions. Dots for those seven regions tend to scatter along both axes.

To further explore the relationship between a region's general entrepreneurial atmosphere (i.e. a region's non-age-specific entrepreneurship level) and its elderly entrepreneurship level, trend lines based on Figure 8.5 would provide a clearer clue. Figure 8.6 displays those trend lines.

Generally speaking, a region's entrepreneurship level is associated with its elderly entrepreneurship level. The trend line representing the nine-region average (shown as the dark thick long black line) is upward diagonal, indicating an overall positive relationship between elderly entrepreneurship levels and corresponding non-age-specific entrepreneurship levels for the nine regions. The trend lines representing individual regions all have a positive slope, though some of the lines are almost flat. This situation indicates an overall positive relationship with disparities between a region's entrepreneurship level and the same region's elderly entrepreneurship level.

However, in the East North Central region and the Pacific region, there does not seem to have an elastic relationship between their general entrepreneurship levels and the corresponding elderly entrepreneurship levels. In Figure 8.6, the trend lines representing those two regions have relatively small slopes. For the East North Central region, the trend line is almost flat. The small slope indicates that a big change in the non-age-specific entrepreneurship level of a region is in association with a very minimal change in elderly entrepreneurship. The trend lines representing the Mountain region and the West Central region have evidently bigger slope than other regions. The bigger slope indicates that each one unit of change in non-age-specific entrepreneurship in those two regions is associated with a bigger change in their elderly entrepreneurship.

Other five regions tend to have similar relationships between their non-age-specific entrepreneurship and elderly entrepreneurship. The trend lines for the rest five regions have similar slopes to the trend line representing the nine-region average (seen as the dark thick solid black long line).

The lengths of those trend lines differ from one other. This indicates the heterogeneity of the entrepreneurship or elderly entrepreneurship levels across the metropolitan areas in the nine regions. For example, in the East North Central region, the short flat trend line indicates a big homogeneity in entrepreneurship levels and a much bigger homogeneity in elderly entrepreneurship levels across the metropolitan areas in this region. In the South Atlantic region, the long diagonal trend line indicates a large heterogeneity in both entrepreneurship and elderly entrepreneurship levels across its metropolitan areas.

2.3. *Elderly entrepreneurship level versus the scale of regional knowledge economy*

However, the scale of regional knowledge economy (i.e., the size of regional knowledge base) does not seem to necessarily associate with elderly entrepreneurship in general. Shown in Figure 8.7, the scatter plots that represent the relationship between the sizes of knowledge base in the regional economies display a messy pattern without a clear trend. The dots spread along the two axes.

The scales of the Y-axis are generally much bigger than the scales of the X-axis for both Figures 8.7 and 8.8, indicating that the rate of knowledge-based

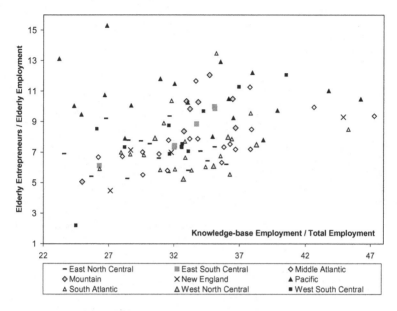

Figure 8.7 Elderly Entrepreneurship versus Knowledge Environment

employment in employment is much higher than the rate of elderly entrepreneurship among elderly workforce.

In Figure 8.8, most slopes of the trend lines show a small value. Considering the scale of the Y-axis is much smaller than that of the X-axis, the minimal slopes greatly over-show the actual slopes. Therefore, local knowledge economy structure seems to barely have any relationship with elderly entrepreneurship across the metropolitan areas in most of the nine regions and the knowledge economy elasticity of elderly entrepreneurship is very low. The Mountain, the West South Central, and the East South Central Regions have relatively stronger positive slopes. But considering the fact that the scale of the X-axis is much bigger than that of the Y-axis, even those three slopes would be largely discounted if using the same scale for both axes. The trend lines for the East North Central and the Pacific regions even show a slightly downward trend, indicating a slightly negative relationship between the

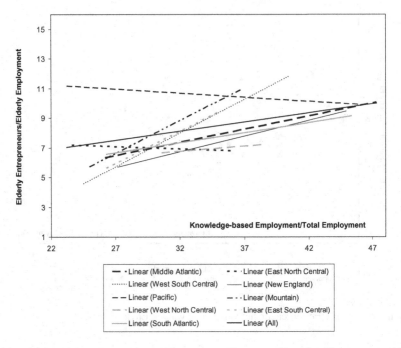

Figure 8.8 Elderly Entrepreneurship versus Non-age Specific Entrepreneurship (Trend Lines)

two regions' elderly entrepreneurship level and the sizes of knowledge bases in their economies. However, considering the much bigger scale of the X-axis than the scale of the Y-axis, those slightly negative relationships cannot be seriously considered as an evidence for negative relationships between their elderly entrepreneurship levels and regional knowledge bases.

2.4. *Elderly self-employment rate versus elderly entrepreneurship level*

Considering the fact that self-employment is directly related to entrepreneurship by definition, it would be interesting to compare the regional influence on elderly self-employment versus on elderly entrepreneurship. This subsection therefore compares the relationship between regional non-age-specific self-employment rate and elderly self-employment rate to the relationship between regional non-age-specific entrepreneurship and elderly entrepreneurship. To make this comparison possible, Figures 8.9 and 8.10 are adapted from Figures 8.4 and 8.6 respectively to the same scales for easier comparisons.

As shown in Figures 8.9 and 8.10 (or Figures 8.4 and 8.6), the scales of the Y-axis are generally much bigger than the scales of the X-axis, indicating that elderly self-employment rate is higher than non-age-specific

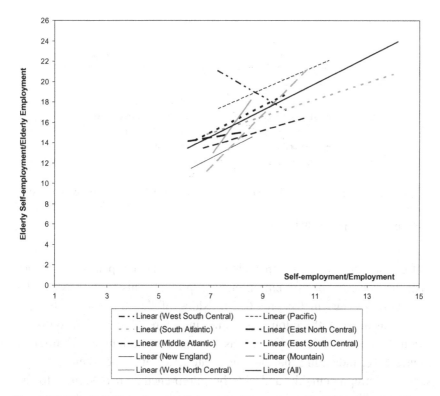

Figure 8.9 Elderly Self-employment Rate versus Non-age specific Self-employment Rate. [This figure is adapted from Figure 8.4]

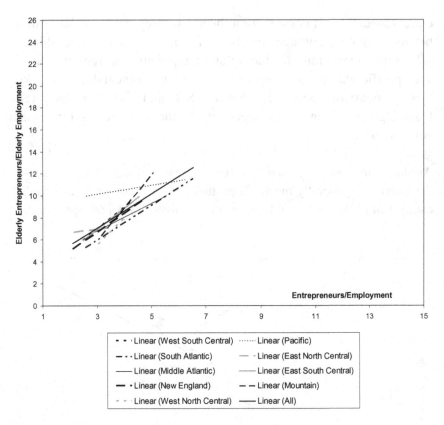

Figure 8.10 Elderly Entrepreneurship versus Non-age Specific Entrepreneurship (Trend Lines).
[This figure is adapted from Figure 8.6]

self-employment rate and that elderly entrepreneurship level is higher than the non-age-specific entrepreneurship level. This finding is consistent with findings in Chapter 6. The slope of the nine-region average (shown as the dark thick long solid line) in Figure 8.9 is similar to that of the nine-region average (shown as the dark thick long solid line) in Figure 8.10, indicating that the aggregate association between non-age-specific entrepreneurship and elderly entrepreneurship is similar to the association between non-age-specific self-employment rate on elderly self-employment rate. The spreads of trend lines in Figure 8.9 are larger than that of Figure 8.10, indicating that the disparities of self-employment rates inside each region are generally larger than that of entrepreneurship levels. The position of the lines in Figure 8.10 is generally lower and is situated typically on the left, compared with the trend lines in Figure 8.9. This situation is consistent with the fact that entrepreneurship is a subset of self-employment, based on the definition if entrepreneurship in this book.

Specific to each region, there are more details. The Pacific Region has a high elderly entrepreneurship level and a high elderly self-employment rate; but, shown as the slopes, the association between non-age-specific self-employment rate and elderly self-employment rate is much higher than the association between non-age-specific entrepreneurship and elderly entrepreneurship.

The East North Central Region tends to have a lower self-employment rate, elderly self-employment rate, entrepreneurship, and elderly entrepreneurship, compared with most other regions, shown as the positions of this region's trend lines. Also, the self-employment rate of the East North Central Region does not seem to have an evident association with elderly self-employment rate (shown as the unclear slopes). This weak relationship is also shown for this region's entrepreneurship levels.

The New England Region has a low elderly self-employment rate, but its elderly entrepreneurship level is not as low. This region also displays low non-age-specific self-employment rate and low non-age-specific entrepreneurship level, compared to most other regions.

The situation of the South Atlantic Region is different from that of the New England Region. Although its elderly self-employment rate is close to the average level, its elderly entrepreneurship level is the lowest among all regions.

For the West North Central Region, the association between regional self-employment rate and elderly self-employment rate is higher than the association between its regional entrepreneurship and elderly entrepreneurship. This is shown as a bigger slope in Figure 8.9 than Figure 8.10 for this region.

The Middle Atlantic Region has the opposite situation to that of West North Central Region. The Middle Atlantic Region has a stronger association between entrepreneurship and elderly entrepreneurship than the association between self-employment rate and elderly self-employment rate.

Surprisingly, the West South Central Region shows a negative slope in Figure 8.9, but not in Figure 8.10. This situation indicates that in this region, elderly self-employers compete with younger self-employers; however, this is not the case between its older and younger entrepreneurs.

The Mountain Region shows consistently large slopes. This situation indicates that a small change in this region's non-age specific self-employment rate is associated with a large change in its elderly self-employment rate; a small change in this region's non-age specific entrepreneurship level is associated with a large change in its elderly entrepreneurship level.

For disparities inside a region (shown as the spreads of each trend line), metropolitan areas in the East North Central, the West North Central, and the New England regions tend to have a more similar level for their self-employment rates and entrepreneurship levels, compared with other regions; while metropolitan areas of the South Atlantic and the Pacific regions tend to show larger disparities across their metropolitan areas. The Mountain region exhibits a large disparity for its self-employment and elderly self-employment rates, but relatively smaller disparity for its entrepreneurship and elderly entrepreneurship levels.

2.5. *Elderly entrepreneurship and regional economy in individual regions*

For the relationship between elderly entrepreneurship and regional economy, the slopes, lengths, and positions of the trend lines in Figures 8.6

and 8.8 display rich information. The higher slope indicates a larger X-axis variables elasticity of Y-axis variables. If it is an upward trend, there is a positive relationship; if it is a downward trend, there is a negative relationship. The length of a trend line indicates the level of heterogeneity for a variable across metropolitan areas in a region: the longer, the higher heterogeneity is existent. The position of a trend line indicates the value of the variables: the lower position indicates a lower value of the Y-axis variable and the left position indicates a lower value of the X-axis variable. The following paragraphs details the implications of each region based on Figures 8.6 and 8.8.

The Pacific region has a low non-age-specific entrepreneurship elasticity of elderly entrepreneurship. This region has a very heterogeneous entrepreneurship level and knowledge base concentration across its metropolitan areas. It has a high level of elderly entrepreneurship. Its elderly entrepreneurship level tends to be negatively related to its scale of knowledge economy, though this negative association is weak.

The Mountain region has the strongest entrepreneurship elasticity of elderly entrepreneurship and it has a relatively strong knowledge base elasticity of elderly entrepreneurship, compared with other eight regions. The disparity levels of elderly entrepreneurship, entrepreneurship in general, and knowledge base across its metropolitan areas are about the nine-region average.

The West North Central region has a high entrepreneurship elasticity of elderly entrepreneurship. This region's elderly entrepreneurship, entrepreneurship in general, and knowledge base are most homogeneous across its metropolitan areas. This region has a relatively low level of elderly entrepreneurship, compared to other eight regions. The relationship between elderly entrepreneurship and its knowledge base is minimal.

The West South Central region has a strong entrepreneurship elasticity of elderly entrepreneurship. The diagonal short-medium length of the trend line in Figure 8.6 indicates a low-medium level of disparity for both elderly entrepreneurship and entrepreneurship across West South Central metropolitan areas. The influence of this region's economic knowledge base on its elderly entrepreneurship level is slightly stronger than the national average level, though still not very strong. The disparity level (or heterogeneity level) of the economic knowledge base across its metropolitan areas is relatively high.

The East North Central region has the lowest entrepreneurship elasticity of elderly entrepreneurship. This region has the highest homogeneity level for its elderly entrepreneurship and entrepreneurship in general across its metropolitan areas. It has the lowest level of entrepreneurship and knowledge base and the medium-low level elderly entrepreneurship among all the nine regions. The relationship between elderly entrepreneurship and this region's knowledge base is very weak and negative. This region has a medium level of disparity for its knowledge base concentration.

The East South Central region has a slightly above-average entrepreneurship elasticity of elderly entrepreneurship and relatively strong knowledge base elasticity of elderly entrepreneurship. The disparity level of elderly entrepreneurship, entrepreneurship, and knowledge base is about the nine-regional average level. This region has a medium level of non-age-specific entrepreneurship and knowledge base.

The New England region has a medium level of entrepreneurship elasticity of elderly entrepreneurship and a medium level of heterogeneity for both elderly entrepreneurship and entrepreneurship. As for the relationship between elderly entrepreneurship and regional knowledge base, this region has a slightly stronger elasticity of elderly entrepreneurship than the nine-region average. The heterogeneity level of knowledge base across its metropolitan areas is high. This region has a medium-low level of elderly entrepreneurship, compared to other eight regions.

The entrepreneurship elasticity of elderly entrepreneurship for the Middle Atlantic region is slightly stronger than national average for all the nine regions. The disparity level for its elderly entrepreneurship and entrepreneurship is about the medium level among the nine regions. The knowledge base elasticity of its elderly entrepreneurship is slightly higher than the nine-region average. The disparity level of the knowledge base is high across Middle Atlantic metropolitan areas.

The South Atlanta region has a medium level of entrepreneurship elasticity of elderly entrepreneurship. This region's trend line in Figure 8.6 is the longest and diagonal line, indicating a big heterogeneity level of both elderly entrepreneurship level and non-age-specific entrepreneurship level across South Atlanta metropolitan areas. The knowledge base elasticity of elderly entrepreneurship is about the national average level and the scale of knowledge base in the economy has a big disparity across its metropolitan areas.

2.6. *Linearity assumption*

The above findings are based on the assumption that there exists linear relationships between regional entrepreneurship and elderly entrepreneurship and between regional elderly entrepreneurship and knowledge base concentration level. However, whether it is reasonable to assume such a linear relationship is worth investigating.

Table 8.1 presents the significance test results of Pearson correlation coefficients between the aforementioned Y-axis variables and the X-axis variables in Figures 8.7 and 8.8. It turns out that the relationships for the nine regions' aggregate variables are linear with significant Pearson correlation coefficients. Down to each individual region, the linearity does not hold for all regions.

Several typical types of non-linear relationships, such as logarithmic, power, and exponential relationships, were tried for Figures 8.7 through 8.10 in the preliminary studies of this chapter. As a result, those non-linear trend curves display very similar images to the assumed linear trend lines. Therefore, the assumed linearity is still reasonable for the visualization purpose.

Table 8.1 Pearson Correlation between X-variables and Y-variables

Division	Elderly Self-employment Rate in Elderly Employment versus Self-employment in Employment		Elderly Entrepreneurship Level versus Entrepreneurship Level		Elderly Entrepreneurship level versus Knowledge Environment		Elderly Self-employment Rate in Elderly Population versus Self-employment rate in Population	
	Corr	p	Corr	p	Corr	p	Corr	p
all	0.5690*	0	0.5868*	0	0.2727*	0.0047	0.5587*	0
1 New England	0.6439	0.3561	0.9483	0.0517	0.8689	0.1311	0.9069	0.093
2 Mid Atlanta	0.3981	0.0914	0.4877*	0.0342	0.5339*	0.0185	0.6594*	0.002
3 South Atlanta	0.5975*	0.0088	0.7159*	0.0008	0.2865	0.249	0.2057	0.413
4 East North Central	0.1224	0.664	0.1069	0.7044	-0.0844	0.7649	0.485	0.067
5 East South Central	0.4774	0.3383	0.9206*	0.0092	0.9212*	0.0091	0.4582	0.361
6 West North Central	0.7252	0.1656	0.8271	0.084	0.1707	0.7837	0.6279	0.257
7 West South Central	-0.3577	0.2537	0.4785	0.1156	0.7974*	0.0019	0.4574	0.135
8 Mountain	0.9211*	0.0012	0.8608*	0.0061	0.7701*	0.0254	0.8655*	0.006
9 Pacific	0.5109*	0.0254	0.202	0.4069	-0.1949	0.424	0.5566*	0.013

3. Regional Industry Mix and Regional Elderly Entrepreneurship Disparities

After identifying the regional disparities of elderly entrepreneurship across the nine regions, this chapter explores the possible regional economic reasons behind the disparities. Industry mix is a key indicator of regional economic structure. This section, therefore, examines the relationship between regional industry mix and elderly entrepreneurship disparities. To analyze regional industry mix, this chapter calculates location quotients (LQ), a simple and direct way to present regional industry mix.

Combining Table 8.2 with Figures 8.3 through 8.6, regions with low LQs in the sectors of agriculture and mining tend to have a low elderly self-employment rate (e.g. the New England, Mid Atlantic, East North Central, and even West North Central regions). The Mountain region is an exception with a high elasticity between its non-age-specific self-employment rate and elderly self-employment rate. Regions with high agriculture LQ tend to have a high elderly self-employment rate (e.g. the Pacific region).

Strong retail and government sectors tend to associate with a high entrepreneurship elasticity of elderly entrepreneurship (e.g. in the Mountain, West North Central, East South Central, and West South Central regions). Take the Mountain region as an example, the relatively strong retail trade, FIRE, services, and government sectors might be a reason leading to the high regional non-age-specific entrepreneurship elasticity of elderly entrepreneurship.

Strong knowledge-based sectors [e.g., services, Finance, Insurance, and Real Estate (FIRE), government, and retail trade] and manufacturing is possibly related to a strong self-employment rate elasticity of elderly self-employment rates (e.g. the West North Central, East South Central, and New England regions). For the East South Central region, although it has a strong manufacturing sector, its weak agriculture and mining reduce its potential strong self-employment rate elasticity of elderly self-employment rate to the average level. For the West South Central region, although

Table 8.2 Location Quotients by Regions and Major Sectors

Location Quotients	New England	Mid Atlantic	South Atlantic	East North Central	East South Central	West North Central	West South Central	Mountain	Pacific
100 Agriculture	0.93	0.67	1.05	0.73	0.9	0.93	0.99	1.14	1.56
200 Mining	0.16	0.33	0.86	0.51	1.03	0.79	4.09	2.03	0.47
300 Construction	0.92	0.84	1.12	0.92	1.09	0.97	1.14	1.27	0.94
400 Manufacture	1.03	0.85	0.96	1.42	1.33	1.09	0.86	0.63	0.9
500 Transport	0.78	1.02	1.01	0.94	1.11	1.1	1.15	0.98	0.94
610 Whole sale trade	0.95	1.01	0.98	1.04	0.95	1.07	1.01	0.88	1.01
620 Retail trade	0.98	0.92	1.04	1.03	1.04	1.05	1.02	1.04	0.96
700 FIRE	1.08	1.13	0.9	0.94	0.78	0.95	0.94	1.15	1.05
800 Service	1.12	1.11	0.97	0.94	0.86	0.93	0.92	1.01	1.05
900 Government	0.85	1.00	1.07	0.88	1.08	1.02	1.08	1.04	1.01

there is a very strong mining, its young people concentrated sectors, e.g. construction, transportation, and even retail trade are also strong, which might generate competition between elderly and younger self-employment and therefore result in a relatively high elderly self-employment rate but a negative relationship (shown as a negative slope) between elderly self-employment rate and self-employment rate.

However, the above arguments in this section are only speculations and they need to be further tested for their validity and reliability. Considering the fact that those arguments are only based on the aggregate data from nine regions and thus with limited quantity of observations, the findings in this section that is based on this small sample (number of observation is equal to nine for those arguments) cannot be called as evidence.

4. Conclusion

There exist regional disparities for elderly entrepreneurship development across the nine census regional divisions. Regional non-age specific entrepreneurship generally has a positive relationship with elderly entrepreneurship, though the strength of the elasticity differs across regions.

The regional disparities of elderly entrepreneurship and the impact of regional entrepreneurial environment on elderly entrepreneurship may relate to regional industry mix. Strong knowledge-based concentrations in a region tend to associate with higher regional non-age-specific entrepreneurship elasticity of elderly entrepreneurship. However, to evidence these trends, further empirical tests are necessary in future studies.

To promote elderly entrepreneurship, developing regional entrepreneurship and regional knowledge based economy might be helpful. Improving regional non-age specific entrepreneurship would help enhance elderly entrepreneurship. According to regional industry mix analysis, strengthening knowledge-based sectors might increase the sensitivity of elderly entrepreneurship to regional non-age-specific entrepreneurship, assuming the sample size and its findings are valid enough. Further empirical tests exploring the relationship between regional industry mix and elderly entrepreneurship would be meaningful.

Summary

- There exist regional disparities for elderly entrepreneurship development across the nine census regional divisions.
- Regional non-age specific entrepreneurship generally has a positive relationship with elderly entrepreneurship, though the strength of the elasticity differs across regions.
- The regional disparities of elderly entrepreneurship and the impact of regional entrepreneurial environment on elderly entrepreneurship may relate to regional industry mix. Strong knowledge-based concentrations in a region tend to associate with higher regional non-age-specific entrepreneurship elasticity of elderly entrepreneurship. However, to evidence these trends, further empirical tests are necessary in future studies.
- According to regional industry mix analysis, strengthening knowledge-based sectors might increase the sensitivity of elderly entrepreneurship to regional non-age-specific entrepreneurship, assuming the sample size and its findings are valid enough.

End notes

[57]   Please note that entrepreneurship in this book is defined as knowledge-based self-employment rate.

[58]   This figure is adapted from Figure 8.4.

[59]   This figure is adapted from Figure 8.6.

CHAPTER 9

THE IMPACT OF ELDERLY ENTREPRENEURSHIP ON METROPOLITAN ECONOMIC GROWTH

Entrepreneurship has been argued to be one of the major factors, like physical capital and labor, to drive regional economic growth (Audretsch and Keilbach, 2004), but whether elderly entrepreneurship is a significant factor, like entrepreneurship in general, that drives regional economy to grow is unknown. Considering the fact that seniors' pursuits differ from their younger counterparts, the economic role of elderly entrepreneurship could differ from that of the young. Many people believe that seniors are not as motivated as the young to try new creations and new methods and that seniors tend to stay with what they have been familiar with for many decades. If it were the case, elderly venture creation might not really generate much Schumpeter's "creative disruption" (1950) that leads to economic growth. If this assumption and argument were correct, elderly entrepreneurship would not be expected to generate as much positive impacts as younger entrepreneurship or entrepreneurship in general on economic growth.

However, there exists counter-argument. In the "knowledge economy", seniors have cumulated job skills, many years' working experience, established business ties, etc. All these contribute to knowledge capital that is a key drive for the growth of the "knowledge economy". Those special knowledge capital components make seniors very valuable in the "knowledge economy". Chapter 6 has found out that elderly self-employment tends to concentrate in knowledge-based sectors, compared to younger people's self-employment. This situation evidences the argument that the "knowledge economy" offers a cultivating setting for seniors' entrepreneurship.

In this case, it is expected in this book that elderly entrepreneurship has a positive impact on regional economic growth.

Although growth theories have been popular in general economic literature, it is not until recent decades that the economic role of entrepreneurship begins to be recognized and emphasized. Neoclassic economic theories recognized labor and physical capital as the two key factors driving economic growth. This set of theories seems to interpret well industrial economy (or Fordist economy) and even agricultural economy, but it leaves a big "Solow residual" unexplained in empirical studies. Also, this set of theories, though with several attempts, does not explain well technological shifts. Technological conditions are set to be given in this set of theories.

When the Fordist economy began to transfer to the "knowledge economy", economists observe the rising importance of knowledge, information, and innovation. Cultivated and also pushed by the information technology, the role of knowledge, information, and human capital began to be formally integrated in the growth model. Here comes the new growth theory which adds a non-rival (or partially rival) quasi public good, knowledge capital, to physical capital and labor as key economic growth drivers. This new element, compared with the traditional two factors, labor and physical capital, has a special property — non-diminishing returns to scale. Therefore, knowledge capital not only explains economic growth, but also helps to explain why the economy could keep growing. Technological conditions are integrated inside the new growth theory models as a changing factor that drives economic growth. Therefore, the new growth theories are also called endogenous growth theories.

Yet, new growth theories are not the end of the story. In addition to lacking a mature widely accepted model for this set of theories, new growth theories still do not explain well where knowledge comes from. Not all knowledge is usable. There exists a knowledge filtering effect. In this case, location theories join the growth theories to explain the distance decaying effect of knowledge. Regional economic growth thus catches more academic attention. Entrepreneurship, though it has been popular in mostly microeconomic and organization theories, has eventually been observed to join knowledge capital to become a factor for economic growth. The special role of entrepreneurship in regional economic growth can be partially explained by its knowledge filtering effect. Entrepreneurship, through its innovation or "creative destruction", either creates something new by applying and spreading new knowledge or reallocates resources by promoting knowledge spillovers.

If entrepreneurship in general can be an important factor that contributes to the economic growth, how about elderly entrepreneurship? Does elderly entrepreneurship contribute to the regional economic growth as well? If so, does the contribution from elderly entrepreneurship is as large as that from entrepreneurship in general, or even larger? Chapter 6 has shown that the elderly are more likely to be self-employed and seniors' self-employment tends to concentrate in knowledge-based sectors. Seniors are also more likely to be entrepreneurs, as both Chapter 6 and Zhang (2007a) indicate. In the meantime, the "knowledge economy", as mentioned previously in this chapter, possibly offers a better socioeconomic environment for the elderly to participate in economic activities. In this case, if entrepreneurship in general contributes to economic growth, elderly entrepreneurship is expected to generate positive externalities to the economic growth as well.

Additionally, developing elderly entrepreneurship might not only just contribute to economic growth as non-age-specific entrepreneurship does, more elderly entrepreneurship might also involve more seniors' participation in economic activities. Increased labor participation from seniors will absorb and make better use of seniors' knowledge capital, brainpower, social ties, their mentoring function, and other various forms of seniors' human capital. This situation would be particularly meaningful in an aging society because more economic participants could help mitigate the aging related labor and fiscal crises, settle a wealthier society in general, and create a more reliable late life. Mitigating the labor and fiscal crises will help to sustain social programs that help seniors. More opportunities for seniors' economic activity participation could not only generate more income and wealth for seniors, but could also fulfill many seniors' career ambition and thus improve their life satisfaction. Elderly entrepreneurship, thus, could possibly generate additional contribution to regional economic growth in a magnitude that younger people's entrepreneurship cannot achieve.

It is in this special social background — an aging population and the "knowledge economy" — that elderly entrepreneurship becomes particularly meaningful and is expected to generate special positive contribution to economic growth. This chapter focuses on the economic contribution of elderly entrepreneurship at the metropolitan area level and addresses whether elderly entrepreneurship has a positive impact on economic growth across a heterogeneous set of metropolitan areas. It extends the Solow growth model formulated by Audretsch and Keilbach (2004) to test two hypotheses. First, elderly entrepreneurship is expected to have a positive and important role in fostering regional economic growth. Second, elderly entrepreneurship is hypothesized to have even a stronger impact on regional economic growth than entrepreneurship from younger working age people.

1. Extensions of the A-Spatial Audretsch and Keilbach (2004) Model

To examine the impact from the elderly self-employment on regional economic growth, the Audretsch and Keilbach (2004) extension to Solow's (1957) growth model is used in this chapter to extend and incorporate senior entrepreneurship as an input to production. Solow's model is formulated as a Cobb–Douglas production function and takes the following form:

$$Y = A(t)K^{\beta}L^{1-\beta},$$ (9.1)

where, Y is output, K represents physical capital, L is labor, and $A(t)$ technical change through time t.

Audretsch and Keilbach (2004) incorporate entrepreneurship into the model in the following way:

$$Y_i = \alpha^{\beta_0} K_i{}^{\beta_1} L_i{}^{\beta_2} R_i{}^{\beta_3} E_i{}^{\beta_4} e_i{}^{\varepsilon}, \qquad (9.2)$$

where R_i represents the knowledge capital of region i, E_i represents entrepreneurship capital in the region, α represents the constant, and all of the other variables follow from the basic Solow model. Audretsch and Keilbach (2004) measured the economic growth of a region (Y_i) by its Gross Value Added, corrected for the purchases of goods and services, VAT, and shipping costs. Physical capital (K_i) in their model is characterized by capital stock in the manufacturing and labor (L_i) by total employment. Knowledge capital (R_i) is defined by the number of public and private sector employees engaged in research and development. The number of start-ups relative to population is used to measure entrepreneurship (E_i).

The regression model that corresponds to the Cobb-Douglas function is:

$$\log Y = \beta_0 \log \alpha + \beta_1 \log K + \beta_2 \log L + \beta_3 \log R + \beta_4 \log E + v_i, \qquad (9.3)$$

Y: economic growth output, measured by Gross Value Added corrected for purchases of goods and services, VAT, and shipping costs;

K: physical capital stock in the manufacturing sector in Audretsch and Keilbach (2004);

L: labor, measured by the size of employment;

R: knowledge capital, measured by the number of employees engaged in R&D in the public and private sectors;

E: entrepreneurship capital, measured by the number of startups relative to the regional population size.

1.1. *Extension I: The per labor model*

Some limitations of the Audretsch and Keilbach (2004) model are that it does not control for agglomeration effects (or scale economy effects) or correct for multicollinearity[60]. To control for the influence of economic scales and to mitigate multicollinearity, standardizing the variables to per–labor equivalents would help because the size of the regional economy would not be a confounding factor affecting independent variables in the regression form[61]. Solow (1957) formulated the following per labor model:

$$\frac{Y}{L} = A(t)\left(\frac{K}{L}\right)^{\beta}, \tag{9.4}$$

which is transformed from the base Solow production function, $Y = A(t)K^{\beta}L^{1-\beta}$ by dividing an L for both sides.

Adding entrepreneurship to the model and assuming constant returns to scale for capital and labor, i.e., $\beta_1 + \beta_2 = 1$ in equation (9.2), the per labor version of their growth model is generated by dividing an L through for both sides of the equation (9.2). The resulting per labor entrepreneurship model becomes:

$$\frac{Y_i}{L} = \alpha^{\beta_0}\left(\frac{K_i}{L}\right)^{\beta_1} R_i{}^{\beta_3} E_i{}^{\beta_4} e_i{}^{\varepsilon}, \quad \text{where } \beta_1 + \beta_2 = 1. \tag{9.5}$$

The corresponding regression model is:

$$\log\left(\frac{Y_i}{L}\right) = \beta_0 \log\alpha + \beta_1 \log\left(\frac{K_i}{L}\right) + \beta_3 \log R_i + \beta_4 \log E_i + v_i. \tag{9.6}$$

This model assumes that the total of coefficients for capital and labor is set to be 1. To be more specific, this model assumes constant returns to scale for capital stock and labor and constant elasticity of substitution.

The above per labor entrepreneurship growth model is used to explore the role of entrepreneurship in the regional economic growth. To incorporate elderly entrepreneurship in this a-spatial model, a sensitivity analysis is also performed.

1.2. Extension II: Sensitivity analysis

Equation (9.6) is used to conduct a sensitivity analysis that compares the effects of senior entrepreneurship, younger entrepreneurship, and entrepreneurship as a whole on regional economic growth. The sensitivity analysis uses three related regression models. Model (9.7) tests the impact of entrepreneurship from all ages as a whole on regional growth, model (9.8) measures the impact of only elderly entrepreneurship, and the third one [model (9.9)] models the effect from the younger and older entrepreneurship simultaneously as separate factors. Through a comparison of the coefficients, the analysis explores the sensitivity of elderly self-employment on the regional growth. The equations are specified as follows:

$$\log\left(\frac{Y}{L}\right) = \beta_0 \log \alpha + \beta_1 * \log\left(\frac{K}{L}\right) + \beta_3 * \log R + \beta_4 * \log E + v_i, \quad (9.7)$$

$$\log\left(\frac{Y}{L}\right) = \beta_0' \log \alpha' + \beta_1' * \log\left(\frac{K}{L}\right) + \beta_3' * \log R$$
$$+ \beta_4' * \log(\text{elderly } E) + v_i', \quad (9.8)$$

$$\log\left(\frac{Y}{L}\right) = \beta_0'' \log \alpha'' + \beta_1'' * \log\left(\frac{K}{L}\right) + \beta_3'' * \log R$$
$$+ \beta_4'' * \log(\text{elderly } E) + \beta_5'' * \log(\text{younger } E) + v_i''. \quad (9.9)$$

In the above models, positive coefficients for capital intensity (β_1, β_1', β_1'') are expected, according to the neoclassical growth theory posited by Solow (1957). Positive coefficients on knowledge capital (β_3, β_3', β_3'') are expected to be consistent with the endogenous growth theory posited by Romer (1986). The coefficient β_4 in model (9.7) is expected to be positive to reflect the positive role of entrepreneurship on economic growth. If β_4' in model (9.8) is significant and positive, it indicates that elderly entrepreneurship has a favorable impact on the regional economic growth, controlling for other factors. In model (9.9), if β_4'' is positive and is bigger than β_5'' and both coefficients are statistically significant, it indicates that elderly entrepreneurship has a stronger impact on economic growth than that associated with the young, *ceteris paribus.*

1.3. Extensions III: The spatial model

Knowledge spillovers are known to be subject to spatial constraints. The new growth theory does not characterize clearly how spillovers occur and assumes that knowledge spillovers occur automatically without constraints, such as those imposed by geographic distance. Knowledge is not automatically transmitted, as Arrow (1962) noted. Instead, there is a filter that extracts economically useful information from knowledge (Acs *et al.*, 2004). Knowledge spillovers, and the entrepreneurship capital that comes through the knowledge filtering process, are often spatially localized (Glaeser *et al.*, 1992). With a higher level of proximity, knowledge can be transferred from transmitter to a receiver with more ease. Empirical evidence also shows that knowledge spillovers are subject to legal, geographic, and cost constraints (Jaffe *et al.*, 1993; Anselin *et al.*, 1997, 2000).

The growth model is extended in this section to capture spatial effects. Spatial auto correlation tests are used to detect the role of space. To conduct a spatial auto correlation test, a spatial distance weight matrix is used as the adjacency matrix and to calculate the Moran's I statistics. Appendix 9.5 presents the Moran's I statistics for this specific test. More details of generating spatial weight matrix are introduced in Zhang (2007c).

The spatial auto correlation tests are used to investigate spatial dependence and heteroskedasticity and the results are used to help define what the appropriate spatial model specification should be for the per labor elderly entrepreneurship growth model. The general spatial lag and error models are as follows:

Spatial Lag Model:

$$y = \rho W y + X \beta + \varepsilon, \qquad (9.10)$$

y: dependent variable
X: independent (explanatory) variables

β: regression coefficients
ε: random error term
ρ: spatial auto-regressive coefficient
Wy: spatially lagged dependent variable

Spatial Error Model:

$$y = X\beta + \varepsilon, \quad \text{where } \varepsilon = \lambda W \varepsilon + \xi, \tag{9.11}$$

y: dependent variable
X: independent (explanatory) variables
β: regression coefficients
ε: random error term
ρ: spatial autoregressive coefficient
$W\varepsilon$: spatial lagged error term with spatial weight matrix W
ξ: normal distribution with mean 0 and variance σ^2.

After running spatial diagnostics tests, either spatial lag or spatial error model will be selected. For example, assuming spatial lag models will be more appropriate than spatial error models, transforming models (9.7), (9.8), and (9.9) to spatial lag formulations results in the following:

$$\log\left(\frac{Y}{L}\right) = \rho W \log\left(\frac{Y}{L}\right) + \beta_0 \log\alpha + \beta_1 * \log\left(\frac{K}{L}\right) + \beta_3 * \log R$$
$$+ \beta_4 * \log E + v_i, \tag{9.12}$$

$$\log\left(\frac{Y}{L}\right) = \rho W \log\left(\frac{Y}{L}\right) + \beta_0' \log\alpha' + \beta_1' * \log\left(\frac{K}{L}\right)$$
$$+ \beta_3' * \log R + \beta_4' * \log(\text{elderly } E) + v_i', \tag{9.13}$$

$$\log\left(\frac{Y}{L}\right) = \rho W \log\left(\frac{Y}{L}\right) + \beta_0'' \log\alpha'' + \beta_1'' * \log\left(\frac{K}{L}\right) + \beta_3'' * \log R$$
$$+ \beta_4'' * \log(\text{elderly } E) + \beta_5'' * \log(\text{younger } E) + v_i''. \tag{9.14}$$

where $\rho W \log(Y/L)$ captures the spatially lagged effects.

2. Empirical Evidence

Zhang (2007c) used Primary Metropolitan Statistic Areas (PMSA) or Metropolitan Statistics Areas (MSA) as the geographic unit of analysis and empirically estimated the above spatial per labor model with sensitivity analysis. The reasons for selecting PMSA and MSA as units of analysis for this study, in addition to data availability, include: First, the PMSA/MSA offers a certain level of homogeneity in employment and commuting patterns; the economic characteristics inside this geographic scale are much more homogeneous than those at the state level (Glaeser *et al.*, 1995). Second, cities are the significant source of innovation due to the great diversity of knowledge (Jacob, 1969). Third, the unit has been often used in many other sub-national studies on regional development. Other sub-national units, states, counties or Combined Metropolitan Statistical Areas (CMSA), are not as appropriate as PMSA and MSA. One problem associated with using states as the geographic unit of analysis for economic studies is that the boundaries are arbitrary and are based on political definitions. The county level data are not often available for many detailed variables. The CMSA was viewed too large as a geographic area for economic analysis because it has too much heterogeneity.

The data sources used in Zhang (2007c) study is Public Use Micro Samples (PUMS) 2000 data, the BEA 2000 data, and the ACS 2005 data. Appendices 9.2 and 9.8 describe the variables. The details on how to extract data and use them to measure the variables in the above models are introduced in Zhang (2007c). To make it brief, the **physical capital** variable (K) is measured through the per labor value of fixed assets (private and public sectors) at the PMSA/MSA level[62]. The **labor** variable (L) is measured by the total employment at the PMSA/MSA level, including wage and salary employees and the self-employed. In the per labor entrepreneurship model, the labor variable is divided by the **capital stock variable** (K) across PMSA/MSA.

The **entrepreneurship capital** variable (E) is measured by the percentage of incorporated and unincorporated self-employers who belong to the knowledge-based sectors relative to the total population at the

PMSA/MSA level[63]. The **knowledge capital** variable (*R*) is measured by the number of people who have attained postgraduate education. Although Bachelor's degree holders are often used as a measure for knowledge capital, it is believed here that postgraduate education has a stronger impact on R&D than Bachelor's level education attainment. The **output** variable (*Y*) is measured by the median personal income of a PMSA/MSA.

The estimation results in Zhang (2007c) confirm that a spatial lag model is an appropriate formulation for Models (9.13), (9.14), and (9.15) and the spatial dependence factor, the spatial lags for each model, were found to be highly significant (all $ps \leq 0.01$, as shown in Table 9.1). This indicates that the regional growth in a MSA/PMSA is influenced by the regional growth of the first-order nearest metropolitan areas (i.e., MSA and PMSA), according to the distance threshold, controlling for the other variables in the model. Table 9.1 presents the spatial lag models estimation results.

Elderly entrepreneurship is found to have a significant [$p = 0.000$ in both Models (9.14) and (9.15)] and positive impact on regional growth. Younger entrepreneurship, on the other hand, is now found to be insignificant [$p = 0.797$ and $t = -0.26$ in Model (9.15)] and the effects of this factor on regional growth are negative. It should be noted that entrepreneurship for all age groups as a whole is significant [$p = 0.009$ and $t = 2.62$ in Model (9.13)]. The estimation results along with the levels of significance for each of the co-efficients are presented in Table 9.1.

For every 1% increase in the proportion of elderly entrepreneurs in any given MSA/PMSA elderly population, there is a corresponding 0.13% increase in median personal income for that area, *ceteris paribus*. This impact is lagged by five years. The technical details on why a five-year lag is selected are explained in Zhang (2007c). Compared with the other traditional factors that drive regional economic growth — i.e., physical capital and knowledge capital, elderly entrepreneurship was found to have a stronger impact. *Ceteris paribus*, each additional 1% increase in per capita physical capital generates a 0.10% increase in median personal income in a metropolitan area, while each additional 1% increase in

Table 9.1 Regression Results and Diagnostic Tests for Spatial Lag Model by MLE

			Dependent variable: Economic output — 2005 Median personal income	

		Spatial Lag Models (MLE) parameters		
	Independent variables	Model (9.13)	Model (9.14)	Model (9.15)
K	Per labor capital	0.2043691***	0.1036223**	0.1034293**
		(4.16)	(2.5)	(2.5)
R (#)	# Attained postgraduate	0.0517804***	0.0666594***	0.0677358***
	education	(3.62)	(5.58)	(5.35)
E (%)	% Entrepreneur among	0.1111273***		
	population	(2.62)		
	% Elderly Entrepreneur		**0.1263556***	**0.1293551***
	among elderly		**(3.7)**	**(3.58)**
	% Young Entrepreneur among			**−0.0138458**
	young working-age people			**(−0.26)**
	Rho	0.4036052***	0.3590498***	0.3563363***
		(3.16)	(2.79)	(2.76)
	Constant	3.474251**	5.003107***	4.983334***
		(2.54)	(3.53)	(3.51)
	Observations	90	90	90
	Log likelihood	**77.154915**	**80.260636**	**80.293583**
	Variance ratio	0.444	0.486	0.487
	Squared corr.	0.484	0.514	0.514
	Sigma	0.10	0.10	0.10
Wald test of rho = 0: chi2(1) =		**9.991 [0.002]**	**7.788 [0.005]**	**7.609 [0.006]**
Likelihood ratio test of				
rho = 0: chi2(1) =		**8.452 [0.004]**	**6.831 [0.009]**	**6.679 [0.010]**
Lagrange multiplier test of				
rho = 0: chi2(1) =		**9.760 [0.002]**	**7.930 [0.005]**	**7.686 [0.006]**
Acceptable range for rho:		−1.169 < rho < 1.000		
Weight matrix type		Distance-based (inverse distance,		
		row standardized)		
Distance band		0.0 < d ≤ 5.5		

Notes: Numbers in round parentheses are *t* statistics.
*: significant with 90% confidence interval.
**: significant with 95% confidence interval.
***: significant with 99% confidence interval.
Source: Zhang (2007c)

postgraduate education attainment generates a 0.07% increase in metropolitan median personal income.

Elderly entrepreneurship is also found to have a stronger impact on regional economic growth than that associated with entrepreneurship across all age groups, and much stronger than that from younger entrepreneurs. Controlling for other factors, for every 1% increase in the proportion of all-age entrepreneurs in a given metropolitan population, there is a 0.11% increase in median personal income for that MSA/PMSA; the increase in the proportion of younger entrepreneurs in a given metropolitan younger population has an insignificant negative effect on the corresponding MSA/PMSA median income.

Based on the regression diagnostics, the log likelihood is strong, which helps to confirm that the spatial lag model is a better fit than the spatial error model. However, the residual map (see Appendix 9.1) after applying the spatial model still displays a substantial level of clustering. This situation indicates the presence of some regional spatial auto correlation. The Northeast cluster around New York, the upper Great Lakes, and the Nevada–California area display high clusters; the south central area has a low cluster. High clusters mean over prediction of the model and low clusters means under prediction. Therefore, there might still exist some model mis-specification issues. Future research to investigate the potential model mis-specification issues would be worthwhile.

3. Conclusion

Elderly entrepreneurship has a statistically positive impact on economic growth. This impact is even stronger than other two factors that are traditionally considered to drive economic growth — physical capital and knowledge capital. Compared with other entrepreneurship, elderly entrepreneurship shows a stronger impact on economic growth than entrepreneurship as a whole and definitely stronger than entrepreneurship of younger people (which displays an insignificant and negative effect on economic growth).

The per labor entrepreneurship spatial lag model with sensitivity analysis turns out to have a good model fit. It is superior to the original entrepreneurship growth model by Audretsch and Keilbach (2004) in that it avoids multicollinearity problem, spatial dependence and heterogeneity, that the measure of knowledge capital by postgraduate education attainment avoids the redundancy with the measure of labor, and that this model singles the elderly entrepreneurship out and compares it with other types of entrepreneurship.

There may be better ways to measure knowledge capital that should be explored in future research. The Zhang (2007c) models measure knowledge capital through education attainment. However, knowledge capital does not just come from formal education at school. Tacit knowledge and job-specific skills are also valuable assets that contribute to the economy. However, tacit knowledge and skills are generally intangible and difficult to measure and that is why educational attainment is used as an indicator of knowledge capital in this book. Future efforts should focus on finding ways to measure the intangible aspects of knowledge and explore their impacts on regional economic growth.

Alternative measures of regional economic growth are also worth pursuing. Zhang (2007c) uses median regional income to measure regional economic output. In fact, Gross Regional Product (GRP)[64] would be a better measure. However, GRP data are not directly available. Calculating GRP (or GMP in this case) using population or personal income weight, as many other studies have done, would invalidate the tests because it would generate the same variation in physical capital across the observations. Personal income weight is used to generate physical capital at the regional level. Further discovery on a better measurement of GRP could be helpful for a more effective test. The measure of economic output is not the best, but it seems an available and feasible choice.

The "Solow residual" has not been fully interpreted yet. Although the addition of entrepreneur capital and knowledge capital to the model improves the explanatory power of the Solow endogenous growth model, there may be other important factors that are worth exploring and including in the model. As the result of this test shows, the constant is much bigger than any coefficients.

This study still follows previous literature on using Cobb Douglas entrepreneurship growth model with both the assumption of constant elasticity of substitution between capital and labor and the assumption of constant return to scales for capital and labor combined (but increasing returns for the total of all inputs — capital, labor, knowledge, and entrepreneurship are allowed). Therefore, further research might explore alternative formulations of the model, like a translog production function, which relax such strong assumptions.

Summary

- Elderly entrepreneurship, as well as entrepreneurship for all age groups as a whole, has a statistically significant and positive impact on economic growth.
- According to this modified growth model with spatial analysis, for every 1% increase in the proportion of elderly entrepreneurs in any given MSA/PMSA elderly population in 2000, there is a corresponding 0.13% increase in median personal income for that area in 2005, controlling for all other factors.
- Compared with other entrepreneurship, elderly entrepreneurship shows a stronger impact on economic growth than entrepreneurship as a whole and definitely stronger than entrepreneurship of younger people (which displays an insignificant and negative effect on economic growth).
- This economic growth impact from elderly entrepreneurship is even stronger than that from knowledge capital.
- The per-labor entrepreneurship spatial lag model extended with sensitivity analysis turns out to have a good model fit and it is superior to the previous entrepreneurship growth model in that it avoids multicollinearity problem and spatial dependence and heterogeneity, that the measure of knowledge capital by postgraduate

education attainment avoids the redundancy with the measure of labor, and that this model singles the elderly entrepreneurship out and compares it with other types of entrepreneurship.

End notes

[60] Appendix 9.3 shows high correlations between variables using the Audretch and Keilbach (2004) model using the U.S. data. The data sources and measurement for each variable will be introduced in more details in the following text.

[61] Appendices 9.4 and 9.3 contrast the correlation coefficients for per capita model to that of Audretsch and Keilbach (2004) model.

[62] This process follows Garofalo and Yamarik (2002). Details of this process are introduced in Zhang (2007c).

[63] Although Audretsch and Keilbach (2004) used the number of new start-ups to measure entrepreneurship, data on start-ups by the age of business owners was not available. Self-employment has been mentioned as the best-available measurement of senior entrepreneurship (Evans and Leighton, 1989; Blanchflower *et al.*, 2001); this revised definition that uses seniors' self-employment in knowledge-based sector would be even better and closer to the knowledge concept of entrepreneurship, compared to the measure that uses self-employment in general. One concern in using self-employment data as a measure of entrepreneurship is that, while knowledge base and innovation are the key components that make the concept of entrepreneurship appealing, self-employed businesses are not necessarily innovative and many are low-tech personal or family-owned businesses that fall into the class of self-employed businesses. To address this, only knowledge-based self-employment is considered in the measure of entrepreneurship. Creative class, although focused more on creativity rather than innovation and knowledge, is a decent proxy for knowledge-based occupations. Knowledge-based self-employment or analytic self-employer class is used specifically to characterize entrepreneurship. Another problem of using self-employment as a measure for entrepreneurship is that, in many cases, self-employment is characterized as a sole proprietorship or partnership and incorporated business

owners are typically not included. To avoid this problem, the data used for self-employment includes incorporated self-employment as well as unincorporated self-employment. In addition, measuring entrepreneurship by self-employment avoids problems of two other commonly used measures. The use of R&D expenditures tends to underestimate small-business entrepreneurship (Acs and Audretsch, 1990) and the measure by startups (Audretsch and Keilbach, 2004) does not necessarily capture the innovation component of entrepreneurship either. The model considers only the static value of PMSA/MSA knowledge-based self-employment rate (or quantity), which may not accurately characterize establishment of the new startups by the elderly. However, data on elderly (aged 62 and above) startups was not available. Using the regional growth rate of elderly knowledge-based self-employment was once considered to be an avenue for measuring the establishment of new businesses by the elderly; but regional growth in elderly knowledge-based self-employment does not necessarily reflect the actual levels of elderly startups. Business death and migration contribute partially to the change of self-employment level 63. Therefore, the model uses a cross-sectional static measure of entrepreneurship. This static measure is consistent with the notion of the production-function-based growth model.

[64] Or in this case, Gross Metropolitan Product, considering the fact that the unit of investigation is PMSA/MSA.

PART 7

ELDERLY ENTREPRENEURSHIP
TO MITIGATE LABOR AND FISCAL CRISES

CHAPTER 10

THE LABOR AND SOCIAL SECURITY IMPACTS
OF ELDERLY ENTREPRENEURSHIP

This chapter examines the fiscal and labor impacts of elderly entrepreneurship. The large and growing retiree cohort is argued to drain the Social Security fund and result in a labor shortage (Peterson, 1999). With an increasingly large retirement population and a shrinking share for working population, each working-age person will have to support more and more retirees to meet the social demands, under the same or very similar technological and policy conditions (i.e., with the average retirement age staying at 62). This situation would not just mean an increasingly large demand for working people to support, but also a rising threat for an unreliable retirement life. The baby boomer generation makes this situation even worse.

This threat from an increasingly large retiree population includes a rising demand for the Social Security fund pay benefits. With a shrinking share of working people in the population but a rising demand for the Social Security fund pay benefits, the Social Security fund contribution that is based on payroll tax also relatively declines. This relatively declining Social Security fund contribution would eventually not be able to meet the increasing demand of the Social Security fund pay benefits and the Social Security system would face bankruptcy.

The potential labor shortage, the enlarging threat against guaranteed Social Security benefits, and growing social demands would result in an increasingly fierce competition for social resources and therefore a less and less reliable retirement life, if no major technological shift and policy enhancement were realized. After contributing heart and soul to social wealth for most of their life, seniors deserve a decent peaceful and reliable late life after they decide to withdraw from the labor force. Therefore, something needs to be done to mitigate the prognostic labor shortage and Social Security fund bankruptcy and to enhance seniors' late life.

Although various policy options have been proposed, they all have their own limitations, as previous chapters have indicated. In the meantime, involving more seniors in the labor force, particularly on a voluntary basis, is expected to largely help to balance the social resource supply and consumption demand. A possible approach to increase seniors' voluntary labor force participation is through entrepreneurship. Entrepreneurship could offer seniors more flexibility for their time and location arrangement, could provide them with more control of their own life, and could give them a large platform to make use of their own skills and fulfill their own ambitions. Many seniors, after years' working experience, have cumulated rich skill sets that not only provide expertise in certain aspects, but also build trustworthy social networks; many of them also have had management and executive experience. Given enough policy motivation, those seniors who want to continue their career ambitions and excitements or those seniors who need more financial supports would very possibly join the labor force as entrepreneurs.

Elderly entrepreneurs not just directly participate in the labor force and contribute to the payroll tax and Social Security fund contribution, but also help foster an economic environment that is more elderly friendly. This is particularly important for an aging society. Elderly entrepreneurs are possibly more likely to accept elderly employees than the younger entrepreneurs. For example, it is natural and easy for them to turn to their old colleagues/bosses, long-term friends, and business partners who are mostly likely within the similar age ranges and share similar interests. Also, more active elderly entrepreneurs could help to improve social image of an active late life and indirectly motivate more seniors to join the labor force or to be more active in the society. Eventually, elderly entrepreneurship could help mitigate the potential labor shortage and Social Security crisis that is resulted from population aging under current technical and policy conditions.

In this situation, whether elderly entrepreneurship can help to mitigate the potential Social Security crisis and labor shortage becomes a fundamental and important research question. Although entrepreneurship as a whole has been discussed for its role in creating jobs (Acs and Armington, 2003), it has not been well addressed for elderly entrepreneurship specifically. Also, creating jobs does not necessarily imply expanding the labor force size. Further, the impact of elderly entrepreneurship on the Social Security fund has yet to be examined.

1. Hypotheses

This chapter tests three hypotheses. First, it is hypothesized that a higher level of elderly entrepreneurship is associated with a larger labor force. Second, elderly entrepreneurship has a direct and positive association with the Social Security fund contribution. Third, through the jobs that elderly entrepreneurship creates and seniors' continued participation in the workforce, elderly entrepreneurs have an indirect and positive association with the Social Security fund contribution.

Elderly entrepreneurship is not just expected to create jobs, but also expected to expand the labor force size. Previous literature indicates that entrepreneurship and self-employment play a significant role in job creation (Picot and Manser, 1999; Acs and Armington, 2003; Van Stel and Storey, 2004; Burke and Fitzroy, 2006). The same relationship is expected to hold for elderly entrepreneurship as well. Elderly entrepreneurship is hypothesized to contribute to enlarging the labor force size for three reasons. First, seniors' participation as entrepreneurs in the labor force contributes directly to the job pool. Second, entrepreneurial activities create wage-and-salary jobs in the economy (see Acs and Armington, 2003). Third, elderly entrepreneurs retire more gradually than elderly wage-and-salary employees (Quinn, 1980) and thus retain in the labor force for a longer period.

There are many reasons to believe that elderly entrepreneurship contributes positively to the Social Security fund. Since Social Security pay benefits are funded by taxes imposed on wages and salaries of employees and entrepreneurs, the size of the labor force directly contributes to the size of Social Security fund. Steuerle (2005) testified in the U.S. House of Representatives that there is, in fact, a positive relationship between the labor force and the Social Security fund. Elderly entrepreneurship is hypothesized to have a positive impact on the Social Security fund through its contribution to the labor force. Elderly entrepreneurs are also expected to directly contribute to the Social Security fund, and this contribution would not be as much if they chose to participate in wage-and-salary jobs instead. Elderly entrepreneurs pay 100% of their Social Security taxes, while wage-and-salary employees pay only 50%.

2. Methodology

A path analysis model is used to verify and quantify the direct and indirect effects of senior entrepreneurship on the labor force and the Social Security fund. The effect of elderly entrepreneurship on Social Security fund has not been directly tested; neither is there any model from the literature or previous studies that can be followed. The analysis is therefore intended to be exploratory and to provide a base from which further research in this area can build.

Path analysis was selected as the methodology to test the above hypotheses because it is able to capture correlation when there are chain effects between variables. The method decomposes correlations into different components. Path analysis is a type of multiple regression analysis that is used to test hypothetical causal models, where single indicators are specified for each of the variables in the model. Although a path analysis model does not necessarily imply the causal property of the output or consequence of the technique (Everitt and Dunn, 1991), it is a widely accepted technique to test causal assumptions.

2.1. Specification of the base path analysis model

The conceptual specification of the path model captures the relationships between the variables that have been hypothesized to ultimately affect the Social Security fund. Figure 10.1 illustrates the model. Brackets between variables indicate the expected signs of the path coefficients in the model. To be more specific, elderly entrepreneurship is hypothesized in this model to affect wage-and-salary employment and then indirectly affect the labor force (or total employment[65]); eventually, through the impact on the total employment, elderly entrepreneurship affects the Social Security fund contribution. In the meantime, the direct impacts from elderly entrepreneurship on the total employment and the Social Security fund are also modeled. All the path coefficients are expected to be positive due to the logic that is introduced above.

The path model is based on several assumptions, as most path analysis models: (1) All relations in the model are linear and additive; (2) The residuals or error terms are uncorrelated with each other or with the variables in the model; (3) The causal flow is one-way; (4) The variables are measured without error for perfect reliability.

A Pearson's correlation coefficient matrix was first generated between each pair of variables that are hypothesized to have causal relationships in the model. To estimate and compare the direct and indirect effects between variables, standardized beta path coefficients (ranging from

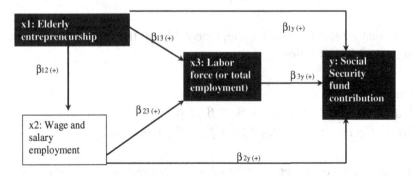

Figure 10.1 Hypothetical Path Analysis Model

−1.0 to +1.0) were estimated using linear regressions. The regression models for the path model include the following:

Wage-salary employment
$$= \beta_1 + \beta_{12} * \text{Elderly entrepreneurship} + \varepsilon_1; \tag{10.1}$$

Labor force (or total employment)
$$= \beta_2 + \beta_{13} * \text{Elderly entrepreneurship}$$
$$+ \beta_{23} * \text{Wage-and-salary employment} + \varepsilon_2; \tag{10.2}$$

$$\text{The Social Security fund} = \beta_3 + \beta_{1y} * \text{Elderly entrepreneurship}$$
$$+ \beta_{2y} * \text{Wage-and-salary employment}$$
$$+ \beta_{3y} * \text{Labor force} + \varepsilon_3. \tag{10.3}$$

The total direct and indirect effects were extracted and calculated from the path coefficients. The total effect between any pair of variables in the model is comprised of a compound effect that comes from the direct path effect between the pair of variables and an indirect effect calculated as the product of path coefficients via other variables. The direct, indirect, and total effects of elderly entrepreneurship on the labor force (or total employment) is thus calculated as follows:

Direct effect   : β_{13}
Indirect effect : $\beta_{12} * \beta_{23}$
Total effect   : $\beta_{13} + \beta_{12} * \beta_{23}$

The total effects of elderly entrepreneurship on the Social Security fund are calculated as follows.

Direct effect   : β_{1y}
Indirect effect : $\beta_{12} * \beta_{2y} + \beta_{13} * \beta_{3y} + \beta_{12} * \beta_{23} * \beta_{3y}$
Total effect   : $\beta_{1y} + \beta_{12} * \beta_{2y} + \beta_{13} * \beta_{3y} + \beta_{12} * \beta_{23} * \beta_{3y}$

The total effects are then compared to the corresponding bivariate correlation coefficients to measure the goodness of fit of the model.

2.2. *Spatial extensions*

Tests to detect whether there is spatial autocorrelation or spatial dependence in the underlying data is necessary to be conducted because the observations in the sample are geographically based and the units of analysis (states) are contiguous with each other. Both spatial lag and spatial error models were considered to diagnose and capture the potential spatial autocorrelation. A spatial lag model explains variation in the dependent variable as a linear combination of contiguous or neighboring units and shows up as an endogenous variable through the spatial lag vector Wy. Spatial error model exhibits spatial autocorrelation in the disturbances through a spatial error term $W\varepsilon$. Spatial models are usually estimated using Maximum Likelihood Estimations. Equations (10.a) and (10.b)[66] represent the general spatial lag and spatial error models, as introduced in Chapter 9.

2.3. *Data sources and base variables*

Four base variables would be needed for the analysis: elderly entrepreneurship, wage-and-salary employment, labor force (or total employment), and the Social Security fund contribution. Two datasets are used to estimate this path model: the U.S. Census 2000 *Public Use Microdata Samples* (PUMS) 1-percent sample data[67] and Social Security trust fund data for each state in the United States. Data on the labor force (or total employment), elderly entrepreneurship, and wage-and-salary employment comes from PUMS through the recoding of the variable "class of workers". Data to calculate the Social Security fund contribution for each state comes from the Social Security Administration (SSA). This data, which refers to Old age, Survivors, and Disability Insurance (OASDI), captures the benefits associated with retirement, widows and survivors, and disability income. All variables are of the value of year 2000. The units of analysis are states. The variables and their sources of data are summarized in Table 10.1. This chapter did not use Health and Retirement Study (HRS) data because HRS only offers age information till 57 or 59 for the latest data.

Table 10.1   Summary of Variables

For path analysis model (state level)				
Variable	Description	Type	Sources	Scale
# of Elderly entrepreneurs	Number of elderly knowledge-based (or creative class) self-employment; recoded from variable occupation (SOC), "class of workers" and age in PUMS dataset.	Numerical	PUMS	State
Wage-and-salary employment share among total employment	Wage-and-salary employment/total employment; recoded from variable "class of workers" in PUMS dataset.	Numerical	PUMS	State
Log (employment)	Log (Total employment); recoded from variable "class of workers" in PUMS dataset.	Numerical	PUMS	State
Log (Social Security Contribution)	Log (Social Security Contribution).	Numerical	SSA	State

2.4. *Description of base variables*

Figures 10.2 through 10.5 map the base variables this analysis relies on. As shown in Figure 10.2, the state that has the largest amount of the Social Security contribution is California. Followed by big states, such as Taxes, Florida, or labor-intensive heavy industrial states, such as Pennsylvania and states around the Great Lakes. States that have the least amount of the Social Security contribution tend to be either small states (such as Vermont and New Hampshire) or states that have low population density (such as Alaska, Montana, and Wyoming) and thus a smaller employment size. This makes sense because the total amount of the Social Security fund contribution heavily depends on the employment size.

As expected and also as explained above, the Social Security contribution amount has a very high correlation with employment size; Figure 10.3, total employment map, is very similar to Figure 10.2, the Social Security fund

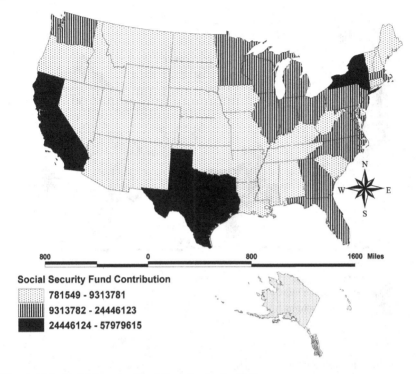

Social Security Fund Contribution
- 781549 - 9313781
- 9313782 - 24446123
- 24446124 - 57979615

Figure 10.2 Social Security Fund Contribution by U.S.
Source: U.S. Social Security Administration.

contribution map. The minor discrepancies (see Michigan and New Jersey) possibly lie in the monetary salary levels. States with the same employment size but a higher monetary salary level tend to have a larger Social Security contribution amount. Again, larger states or labor-intensive industrial states tend to have a larger employment size, while smaller states or states with a lower population density tend to have a smaller employment size.

Figure 10.4 displays the map for wage-and-salary employment sizes by states. Interestingly, this figure has the same distribution pattern as Figure 10.3. There are two reasons for this: first, wage-and-salary employment is the absolute majority among the total employment; second, Figures 10.3 and 10.4 are both maps based on a 5-level scale. If using a more detailed scale, the maps of the two variables might show some differences.

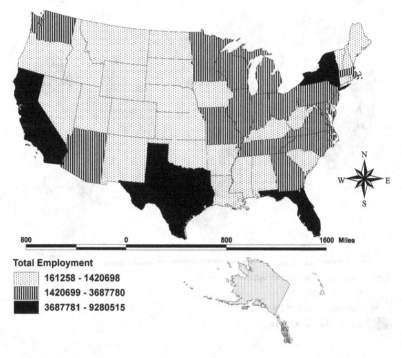

Total Employment
- 161258 - 1420698
- 1420699 - 3687780
- 3687781 - 9280515

Figure 10.3 Total Employment by U.S.
Source: U.S. Census Bureau PUMS.

Figure 10.5 displays the distribution pattern of elderly entrepreneurs by state. Figure 10.5, though different from Figures 10.2 through 10.4, still display a high level of similarity with the previous three figures. This situation indicates that the four variables are highly correlated. The difference between Figure 10.5 and previous three figures is that the Great Lake states and Pennsylvania show a lighter color scale in Figure 10.5. A major reason could be the industry characteristics. Pennsylvania and the Great Lake states are labor-intensive heavy industry states. Heavy industries tend to calibrate large factories where most employees are workers. Most workers tend to have limited exposure to entrepreneurial experience and environment, which limit their motivation and opportunity to become entrepreneurs. Therefore, even if those states have decent sizes of population as well as labor force,

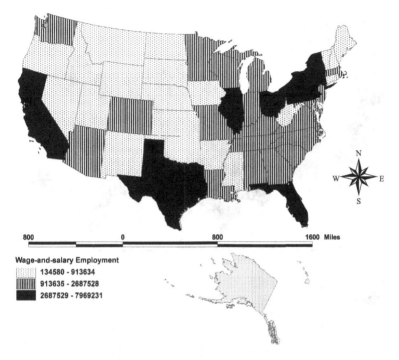

Figure 10.4 Wage-and-salary Employment by U.S.
Source: U.S. Census Bureau PUMS.

their entrepreneurship might not be high. This could also be the case for elderly entrepreneurship.

2.5. Variable measurements

As the above figures (Figures 10.2 through 10.5) show, there seem to exist high correlations between the four base variables. The population size of a state could easily relate to the values of the four base variables that are used for the above maps. To avoid multicollinearity issues in regressions and also considering the different value scales of those variable, the variables are all measured in different formats to capture various forms of marginal change. The details on how the variables are measured are presented in Zhang (2007d). Table 10.1 summarizes the variable

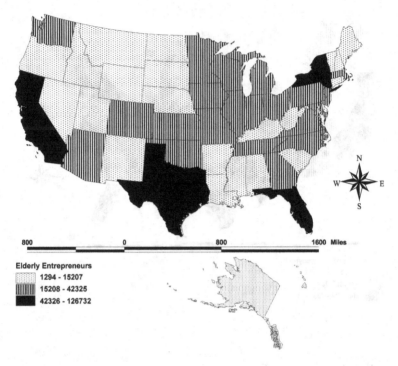

Figure 10.5 Elderly Entrepreneurship by U.S.
Source: U.S. Census Bureau PUMS.

measurements and data sources. Appendix 10.1 describes all the variables used in this analysis.

3. Empirical Evidence

The Pearson correlation coefficient matrix (see Table 10.2) provides information on the strength of linear relationship between pairs of variables in the path model. As shown in this table, all the correlation coefficients are statistically significant. The correlation between the level of elderly entrepreneurship and the state employment indicator (in log transformed value) is 0.7854, which is strong. The correlation between elderly entrepreneurship and the Social Security fund contribution (in log

Table 10.2 Pearson Correlation Matrix

		Log (Social Security Contribution)	Log (Employment)	% Wage- and-salary employment among total employment	# of Elderly entrepreneurs
Log (Social	Corr.	1	—	—	—
Security	Sig. (p)	—	—	—	—
Contribution)	Obs.	51	—	—	—
Log	Corr.	0.9913	1	—	—
(Employment)	Sig. (p)	0.0000	—	—	—
	Obs.	51	51	—	—
% Wage-and-salary	Corr.	0.4605	0.4151	1	—
employment	Sig. (p)	0.0007	0.0025	—	—
among total	Obs.	51	51	51	—
employment					
# of Elderly	Corr.	**0.7768**	**0.7854**	0.0906	1
entrepreneurs	Sig. (p)	0.0000	0.0000	0.5273	—
	Obs.	51	51	51	51

transformed value) is similarly strong, as indicated by the correlation coefficient, 0.7768. These strong correlation coefficients indicate that the elderly entrepreneurship level of a state is evidently related to the state employment indicator (or labor force indicator) and the Social Security fund contribution.

Figure 10.6 presents the estimated path coefficients (standardized beta regression coefficients). The detailed regression analysis [including those of linear ordinary least square (OLS) regressions as well as those of spatial regression] are presented in Zhang (2007d). Appendices 10.2 through 10.5 present the regression estimation results. Each of the regression model was first estimated using Ordinary Least Squares (OLS). Diagnostics test were performed to detect multicollinearity, heteroskedasticity, and spatial autocorrelation (through the global Moran's I test).

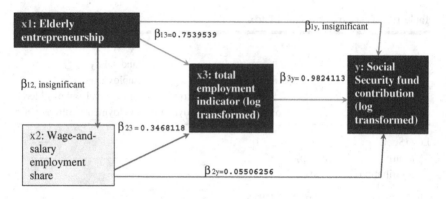

Figure 10.6 Path Analysis Model Estimation Results

All regressions estimate standardized coefficients and the path coefficients (shown in Figure 10.6) use the standardized coefficients of the best models.

Based on the structure of path analysis model, the total impacts of elderly entrepreneurship on the size of total state employment and on the Social Security fund contribution are calculated as follows. Please note that the insignificant standardized regression coefficients are not used to calculate the direct or indirect effects.

Calculation of Total Effect of Elderly Entrepreneurship on the Size of Total Employment

Direct effect   : β_{13}
Indirect effect : $\beta_{12} * \beta_{23}$
Total effect   : $\beta_{13} + \beta_{12} * \beta_{23}$
$$= 0.7539539$$

The total effect (0.7540) is close to the correlation coefficient (0.7854) between elderly entrepreneurship and total employment.[68] This could indicate that this part of the model provides an acceptable or good fit and it helps to reemphasize that there is a strong relationship between elderly entrepreneurship and the size of total employment.

Similarly, the total effect of elderly entrepreneurship on the Social Security fund contribution is calculated as:

Calculation of Total Effect of Elderly Entrepreneurship on Social Security Fund Contribution

Direct effect $\quad:\quad \beta_{1y}$

Indirect effect $\quad:\quad \beta_{12} * \beta_{2y} + \beta_{13} * \beta_{3y} + \beta_{12} * \beta_{23} * \beta_{3y}$

Total effect $\quad:\quad \beta_{1y} + \beta_{12} * \beta_{2y} + \beta_{13} * \beta_{3y} + \beta_{12} * \beta_{23} * \beta_{3y}$

$\qquad\qquad\qquad = 0.7539539 * 0.9824113$

$\qquad\qquad\qquad = 0.74069283103907$

This total effect (0.7407) is also close to the correlation coefficient (0.7768). This could suggest that this path analysis model that tests the relationship between elderly entrepreneurship and the Social Security fund contribution also offers an acceptable fit.

However, the path through wage-and-salary employment does not seem to be viable for either the labor or Social Security effects. The direct effect from elderly entrepreneurship on the Social Security fund contribution is also insignificant. Further model specification might deserve to be explored to improve the model. Since path analysis is based on linear regressions and the Pearson correlation matrix is linear as well, there is possibility that a linear model transformed from some nonlinearity might make the model even better.

In general, the strong associations between elderly entrepreneurship and total employment and between elderly entrepreneurship and the Social Security fund contribution are evident. This can be seen either from the Pearson correlation coefficients, the total path analysis model effects (as described above), or the standardized regression coefficient [e.g. in the case of labor effect of elderly entrepreneurship, as tested in Zhang (2007d)].

Additionally, this path analysis model reveals the role of space in the function of labor and the Social Security fund contribution. Zhang

(2007d) identified a significant spatial error vector in the regression that measures the impacts on Social Security contribution and a spatial lag vector in the regression that measures the impacts on the share of wage-and-salary employment. This suggests that the neighboring states' wage-and-salary employment shares have a statistically highly significant effect on a state's wage-and-salary employment share, *ceteris paribus*. This displays a regional economic spillover effect.

4. Limitations of This Study

This chapter uses a simple path analysis model and it is intended to be exploratory. With limited information on other variables that could be relevant and included in the model, the concept of the model is kept simple. Further model developments should build on the following limitations of this model.

First, this path analysis model only uses limited variables in the regressions. For example, the path from elderly entrepreneurship ($x1$ in Figure 10.1) to the total employment ($x3$ in Figure 10.1) only uses one additional explanatory variable, wage-and-salary employment share. This might generate the problem of missing some important variables and leave a large part of the residual unexplained. Although the regression diagnostics [details are on shown in Zhang (2007d)] do not necessarily detect omitted variable problem, this does not necessary justify or guarantee all important variables are explained through this regression. In fact, the Pearson correlation coefficients (between elderly entrepreneurship and total employment size and between elderly entrepreneurship and the Social Security fund contribution) are bigger than the total labor and Social Security effects respectively. This situation is a hint that some variables are unexplained in this path analysis model. Future efforts to explore a possibly better model integrating additional important variables might be necessary.

Second, using a path analysis, the tested association between elderly entrepreneurship and labor force size or between elderly entrepreneurship and the Social Security fund contribution might not necessarily to be causal. Although the arrow directions in path models reflect hypotheses of causations, path analysis ultimately models the correlations, which could be two directional (Everitt and Dunn, 1991). Therefore, total effects in a successful path analysis model between variables are supposed to be similar to the correlation coefficients. In this chapter, path analysis statistically identifies the association between elderly entrepreneurship and labor force size and between elderly entrepreneurship and the Social Security fund contribution, but not necessarily identifies the labor and fiscal impacts from elderly entrepreneurship.

Third, the sample size of this study is sufficient but not big; there are totally only 51 observations. According to Kline (1998), the adequate sample size is recommended to be at least 10 times (or ideally 20 times) of the number of parameters and 5 times or less is insufficient for significance testing of model effects. In this path analysis model, totally four variables are modeled, with one exogenous variable and three endogenous variables. In this case, the sample size, 51, is more than 10 times of parameter quantities and thus is sufficient, based on Kline (1998). However, the sample size is not as big as 20 times of parameter quantities, which is the threshold for an ideal sample size. A bigger sample size could enhance the model estimation. Unfortunately, with the Social Security data available only at the state level, the total sample size can only be limited to 51. Adding additional variables in the path analysis would introduce more degrees of freedom and thus makes the sample size, 51, even relatively smaller for the regression model estimation. In this case, panel data, instead of cross-sectional data, could largely enlarge the sample size and would be helpful for future studies, assuming data were available in the future.

Last, this path analysis model offers an acceptable model fit for both labor and Social Security effects of elderly entrepreneurship. Still, other models, such as simulation models, would worth further exploration and investigation in future studies.

5. Conclusion

Elderly entrepreneurship is tested in the empirical evidence to have a strong association with a state's employment sizes and the Social Security fund contribution. The total labor effect and total the Social Security fund effect of elderly entrepreneurship shown in this study are not close to be small, instead, they are as strong as 0.75 and 0.74 respectively. This situation indicates that provoking more elderly entrepreneurship and developing a bigger quantity of elderly entrepreneurs (or knowledge-based elderly self-employers and business owners) could relate to a large increase in employment size and a large increase in the Social Security fund contribution. Therefore, developing elderly entrepreneurship could greatly help mitigate the prognostic labor force shortage and the Social Security fund exhaustion that is predicted to result from the aging population in the next decades. The regressions used in this path analysis model also identify spatial impacts. Geographic proximity is also a factor in the labor and Social Security effects of elderly entrepreneurship.

Summary

- Elderly entrepreneurship is tested in the empirical evidence to have a strong association with a state's employment sizes and Social Security fund contribution.
- Based on this path analysis model with spatial analysis, the total labor effect and the total Social Security fund effect of elderly entrepreneurship are as strong as 0.75 and 0.74 (with reference point normally as 1) respectively.
- Therefore, provoking more elderly entrepreneurship and developing a bigger quantity of elderly entrepreneurs could relate to a large increase in employment size and a large increase in Social Security fund contribution; developing elderly entrepreneurship could greatly help mitigate the prognostic labor force shortage and Social Security fund exhaustion that is predicted to result from the aging population in the next decades.
- Geographic proximity is also an important factor in the labor and Social Security effects of elderly entrepreneurship.

End notes

[65] Labor force is the combination of total employment and the unemployed. To control for the regional economic factors that affect unemployment rates, only total employment is used to represent the labor force. Since unemployment only contributes a very small portion of the labor force, total employment can basically represent the labor force.

[66] **Spatial Lag Model:** $y = \rho Wy + X\beta + \varepsilon$,   where

y : dependent variable

X : independent (explanatory) variables

β : regression coefficients

ε : random error term

ρ : spatial autoregressive coefficient

Wy : spatially lagged dependent variable.   (10.a)

Spatial Error Model: $y = X\beta + \varepsilon$, where $\varepsilon = \lambda W\varepsilon + \xi$,   where

y : dependent variable

X : independent (explanatory) variables

β : regression coefficients

ε : random error term

λ : autoregressive coefficient

$W\varepsilon$: spatial lag for the errors

ξ : normal distribution with mean 0 and variance σ^2.   (10.b)

[67] Instead of PUMS 5% samples and previously used Health and Retirement Study (HRS) data. This dissertation consistently uses 1% PUMS samples data because of the flexible geographic identifiers. HRS data, although used heavily in previous aging related studies, is not used because of its limited age information beyond age 57.

[68] Again, the size of total employment represents the labor force participation for this analysis.

PART 8

CONCLUSION...

CHAPTER 11

CONCLUSION AND FUTURE RESEARCH

This book provides several contributions to the fields of public policy, economics, geography and social gerontology. It explains the implications of an aging population. It introduces the problems resulted from an aging population and raises the question whether the elderly can be one type of resource to mitigate the crises associated with an aging population. It interprets why elderly entrepreneurship becomes critical in this background and why elderly entrepreneurship becomes possible in the "knowledge economy" and becomes necessary for the U.S. aging population. It addresses and evidences the economic, labor, and fiscal roles of elderly entrepreneurship in the "knowledge economy", topics that have to date only been scantly addressed, if have ever been addressed, in the literature. It recognizes the elevating economic role of seniors' human capital and interprets this changing role in the setting of the "knowledge economy". It challenges the conventional notion that entrepreneurship is a privilege of only the young and examines the effect that people's age has on their propensity to be entrepreneurs. It looks at and controls for other individual level variables and explores the impact of social and policy factors on the entrepreneurial propensity of an individual. The analysis also tests the impact of elderly entrepreneurship on regional economic growth. This is done by extending the Solow growth model so that it includes elderly entrepreneurship as an input and captures spatial spillovers. It also provides a set of other empirical models that can be used to better understand senior's propensity to be entrepreneurs and the impact that their participation in the labor force as entrepreneurs could have on the economy and society.

This book integrates theories across three fields: economic growth theories, social gerontology theories, and utility maximization theory, and elements from each set that relate to entrepreneurship. Endogenous growth theory and other related economic theories characterize the "knowledge economy" and claim that entrepreneurship is a driving factor behind regional economic growth. Social gerontology theories talk about the controversial role of seniors in the economic society. The utility maximization theory outlines and interprets how seniors choose entrepreneurship to maximize their utility.

The three categories of theories provided the basis for the research questions and hypotheses explored in this book. These hypotheses include the following: (1) seniors are more likely to be entrepreneurs than the young, (2) social factors play an important role in seniors' propensity to be an entrepreneur, (3) elderly entrepreneurship has positive impact on regional economic growth, and (4) elderly entrepreneurship can help to mitigate the potential labor shortage and Social Security fund bankruptcy. Those hypotheses were tested empirically using descriptive statistics, logit model testing, economic growth modeling, spatial econometrics, and path analysis. The following sections summarize the historical background of this book research, major findings, policy implications, future research directions, and concluding remarks.

1. The Socioeconomic Environment for Elderly Entrepreneurship

The U.S. population is aging and consequently, so is its labor force. This has the potential to result in a labor force shortage and Social Security funds exhaustion. While seniors are said to be a possible source of these problems, they could alternatively help to ameliorate the labor force and Social Security crisis. Seniors could provide a valuable source of human capital through their participation in the labor force as entrepreneurs and have a positive impact on the economy. This situation relates to the economic background. This book offers theoretical and empirical evidence to support this notion.

The "knowledge economy" is a fertile environment for elderly entrepreneurship. The "knowledge economy" is centered around knowledge,

innovation, and entrepreneurship. The occupations that are said to characterize the new economy are generally less physically demanding than
those in the "Fordist" economy. It is in the setting of the "knowledge
economy" that elderly entrepreneurship has become more possible than
before. Seniors have a variety of skills that are well suited for knowledge-
based occupations: they have years of cumulated job experience, know-
how, and valuable business ties. This book recognizes the role of elderly
entrepreneurship in the "knowledge economy" and finds that elderly
entrepreneurship contributes to regional growth in the "knowledge
economy".

Encouraging more elderly entrepreneurship could also help to improve
social attitudes toward seniors and enhance seniors' life satisfaction. As
the population ages, the well being of seniors is a rising social concern.
Recognition of the value that seniors provide to the economy and society
could help to mitigate social discrimination against seniors, provide
greater confidence to seniors who would like to re-enter or continue working through their retirement years, and overall, enhance the well being of
seniors.

2. Major Findings

Although the aging population posts a historical challenge to our labor,
fiscal, and economic development, "knowledge economy" facilitates the
approaches to mitigate the aging resulted crises. This is done through
offering special entrepreneurial opportunities to the elderly. In this background, elderly entrepreneurship becomes a particularly critical potential
asset to the aging but knowledge-based economy.

The descriptive analysis reveals that seniors have higher self-employment
rates than their younger cohorts and that these rates for seniors are generally highest in knowledge-based sectors. The higher self-employment
rates among seniors than among the younger working-age people were
consistent for all of the major occupations. The elderly self-employed also
tend to concentrate in knowledge-based occupations (measured by the
"creative class"), with the exception of two sectors, *computer and math*

and *arts and entertainment*. This conclusion supports the argument that the "knowledge-based" economy is a fertile ground for seniors' entrepreneurship.

Another important finding from the descriptive analysis is that elderly self-employers tend to have a lower retirement rate than elderly wage-and-salary employees. Therefore, promoting self-employment among the elderly could help retain seniors in the labor force for a longer period.

Several individual level factors were also found to increase a senior's propensity to be an entrepreneur. The propensity is higher for those who are men, of Caucasian or Asian decent, highly educated, married, and less responsible for grandchildren. This suggests that public policy should support mechanisms that can help to encourage females and minorities (such as Blacks and Natives) to be involved in entrepreneurial activities.

Social factors were also found to have a significant impact on a senior's propensity to be an entrepreneur. The analysis specifically examined the influence of tax policies, R&D performance and culture openness or racial/ethnic diversity. Seniors who live in areas with lower taxes and higher levels of cultural openness were found to be more likely to be entrepreneurs. Both of these factors contribute to the entrepreneurial milieu. Tax policies offer a necessary institutional stimulant, while cultural openness and diversity spur more intercultural exchange and enlightenment. Lower corporate and personal income tax rates increase a senior's propensity for entrepreneurship, although this factor has a smaller impact than the social tolerance level (or cultural openness and diversity).

Elderly entrepreneurship was also found to be a significant and positive factor driving regional economic growth. This economic impact of elderly entrepreneurship seems to be stronger than other factors that are widely accepted in previous literature (i.e., physical capital and knowledge capital) and also stronger than entrepreneurship of the young. In this context, enhancing elderly entrepreneurship could help to boost regional economic growth. Encouraging elderly entrepreneurship through various social and individual factors addressed in Chapter 7 could be an effective economic development tool. When budgets are tight, the priority could be given to implementing policies to foster elderly entrepreneurship. The focus of the Small Business Administration and many local enterprise incubation efforts should incorporate elderly entrepreneurship. Investing in the elderly is not just a welfare strategy; it could also be an effective strategy to help the economy to grow.

Elderly entrepreneurship was also found to affect the size of labor force and the Social Security fund. The path analysis provided in Chapter 10 found a strong association between elderly entrepreneurship and labor force size and between elderly entrepreneurship and the Social Security fund contribution. To mitigate the labor force and Social Security crises, implementing policies to encourage elderly entrepreneurship could be an effective strategy. The results of the path analysis, conducted in Chapter 10, support this notion. Developing elderly entrepreneurship can not only sustain our economy better, but also provides a stronger Social Security guarantee for our seniors in next many decades.

3. Policy Implications

The above findings suggest the necessity to foster more elderly entrepreneurship. To build a stronger elderly entrepreneurship milieu, there are three possible approaches. First, it is critical to retain entrepreneurs with their continued entrepreneurship after average retirement age (the age of 62). As argued in this book, seniors have valuable human capital that is crucial to the knowledge-based economy, such as accumulated working experience, mature interpersonal skills, and well-established business network. Seniors' entrepreneurship has been tested to positively associate with regional economic growth and help mitigate aging-resulted labor shortage and the Social Security fund exhaustion. In this case, entrepreneurs who have been involved with entrepreneurial activities would continue to contribute to the economy and generate crucial economic externalities. For many elderly entrepreneurs, their continued entrepreneurship helps satisfy their continued need to be active and to be of control or for more income; on the other hand, their continued entrepreneurial activities are often not as overwhelming as when they started up. That partially explains why self-employed seniors tend to retire much more gradually than seniors in wage-and-salary employment.

The second possible approach to strengthen the elderly entrepreneurial milieu is to attract to entrepreneurial activities those seniors who are retired or with a wage-and-salary job but would like to become an entrepreneur. Many seniors are managers or executives who have had years of entrepreneurship-related working experience. At the retirement age, they might want to continue staying in the labor force, but various factors discourage them to continue staying in their wage-and-salary employment and thus make self-employment a more attractive option. Those discouraging factors include seniority principle for salary distribution, certain pension penalty for working after certain age, difficult bosses, lack of time flexibility in wage-and-salary employment, and age discrimination, as was delineated in Chapter 2. Many other seniors who have had the thoughts of running their own businesses for years or even had their own businesses before would like to try entrepreneurship when they approach retirement age. Many seniors also tend to have more assets than their younger counterparts, which makes entrepreneurship after or around retirement age more possible. All the above helps to explain why seniors have a much higher self-employment rate than the younger ones.

The third possible approach to obtain a stronger elderly entrepreneurship is to encourage younger entrepreneurship and help those businesses established by younger entrepreneurs to succeed and sustain. Entrepreneurs with successful businesses would naturally tend to stay in their entrepreneurial activities, even after retirement age. This would help to build a larger pool of elderly entrepreneurs who retire more gradually than wage-and-salary employment. This would eventually enlarge the labor force participation rate and mitigate the Social Security fund exhaustion.

The above approaches suggest the following policy implications. First, public attention to entrepreneurship should not just focus on the young. The elderly should be included as the new focus and priority for entrepreneurship initiatives, particularly in this aging era. For example, mass media could report new elderly entrepreneurs or entrepreneurs who are seniors as new stars; enterprise incubators can help entrepreneurs who are approaching retirement age retain with their entrepreneurship, can target the markets to include retired seniors who have the skills and interest to start businesses, and can also help younger entrepreneurs to succeed. Enterprise incubating efforts could also try to motivate other seniors to identify their special market value and start their own businesses for more financial freedom and elevated social value and respect. Successful elderly entrepreneurs, including both seniors who have just established their own businesses and who have been entrepreneurs since younger ages, can also be invited to seminars for programs of community development, entrepreneurship, and aging studies. It is very important to foster an entrepreneurial milieu for seniors so that seniors as well as other social members are aware of, respect, and encourage elderly entrepreneurship. The public efforts to promote such a milieu could extend to various aspects of our social life.

Second, government economic investment should give priority to developing elderly entrepreneurship because elderly entrepreneurship has a stronger impact on regional economic growth than physical capital, knowledge capital, and younger entrepreneurship. The U.S. government has various tax policies to reduce small business owners' tax burden. Certain level of tax incentives could be preferred to the elderly entrepreneurs to encourage entrepreneurs to retain in the labor force and encourage other seniors to be involved in more entrepreneurial activities. In addition, government agencies, such as U.S. Administration on Aging and Small Business Administration, could design some social programs that relieve seniors from various social barriers (such as social discrimination and difficult working environment) to become entrepreneurs so that entrepreneurs after retirement age are more likely to remain entrepreneurs and other seniors who are interested in being an entrepreneur could be more possible to jump in. Government agencies could also design low cost or even free entrepreneurship training and forum programs for the elderly. For those who are senior and skilled in entrepreneurship, the programs can set them as examples; for those who have ideas but do not have enough knowledge, skills, or access to starting a business, necessary trainings on writing business plans, learning financial management, familiarizing with business starting procedures, and referring to the correct network would be very helpful.

Third, females and minority seniors (such as Blacks and Natives) deserve more attention in policies that are intended to encourage elderly entrepreneurship. This situation is particularly critical for the elderly. Among the elderly population, female population takes a bigger proportion than males, while males are typically more possible to become entrepreneurs. Females and minorities have been a general rising focus on entrepreneurship development, but these efforts do not typically address elderly females or elderly minorities. For the traditionally underpowered groups, female and minority seniors in particular, more social concern and encouragement would be helpful. One way to empower them is through organizing unions and connecting them to appropriate network. Policy programs that help them to identify and market their own uniqueness would be extremely enlightening. This effort could benefit both younger and elderly underrepresented entrepreneurial groups, i.e., female and minority entrepreneurs.

Fourth, to develop elderly entrepreneurship, policies could center around increasing cultural openness and racial diversity in a region, lowering corporate income tax rates and personal income tax rates for seniors, fostering a better education and marriage environment, and relieving seniors from involuntary responsibility for grandchildren. Reducing social segregation and zoning is a direct way to increase culture openness and diversity. It is also important to promote intercultural communication. Cultural training and organizing cultural events would be helpful to promote a more tolerant society in general. Many senior centers have put efforts to provide training, education, and even dating services. These efforts would provoke more communication and thus more knowledge spillover, and therefore could be helpful to developing elderly entrepreneurship. Offering low-cost day care services for children or connecting day care needs and demands through an organized network could help liberate both seniors and females from their involuntary responsibility for taking care of children.

Fifth, developing elderly entrepreneurship should be treated as a national strategy to effectively mitigate the labor and fiscal crises resulted from an aging population. It is the time to seriously consider elderly entrepreneurship as a national strategy for our long-run economy. Efforts could start with treating elderly entrepreneurship as a variable in data collection and forecast projection for BLS, BEA, Social Security Administration, and U.S. Census Bureau.

Last, more public attention should be drawn to elderly entrepreneurship and it should be elevated as an important research topic for further studies and practice. Essentially, more research on the topic of elderly entrepreneurship would be the immediate academic efforts to promote elderly entrepreneurship. Research grants, fellowship, conferences, and journal focuses should be directed to this direction to foster more interest and studies. This will fundamentally help to build the elderly entrepreneurial milieu and result in various public attention and policy initiatives.

4. Areas of Future Research

The research conducted in this book provides a base of knowledge on elderly entrepreneurship. It also suggests some needed and potential areas of future exploration on the topic. First, further analysis should explore alternative definitions of entrepreneurship. The definition of entrepreneurship used in this book is legitimate but constrained by data availability. In defining elderly entrepreneurship, this book made an effort to consider both data availability and the proper characterization of entrepreneurship. It extended the measurement of elderly entrepreneurship from elderly self-employment to elderly incorporated and unincorporated self-employment in only knowledge-based sectors. However, this definition has some limitations.

While a relatively widely accepted measurement of entrepreneurship is business ownership and quantity of new startups, data on business ownership among seniors who are aged 62 or above is not available. The use of unincorporated and incorporated self-employment in the knowledge-based sectors as a measure does not accurately reflect the notion of business ownership. The data from Public Use Microdata Samples (PUMS) is self-reported and therefore, the numbers may be somewhat inaccurate.

Additionally, while incorporated self-employment refers in many cases to business owners outside of sole proprietorship, some seniors claim themselves as self-employment only for a tax sheltering purpose.

Further analysis should look more closely at business creation, if data permitted. The definition of entrepreneurship that many people use considers business ownership, particularly *new* businesses. Looking at self-employment numbers for a single census year does not accurately reflect the newness of the business ownership. Rather, it reflects business ownership at a snapshot in time. The temporal growth in self-employment was once considered to be a better measurement; however, this measure does not necessarily provide a good estimate of *new* business creation, either. The death and migration of businesses contribute to the marginal change as well. The compound effects of business exit, migration, and birth would not sing out the creation of *new* business and thus would not offer an advantage to measure entrepreneurship, compared to the definition used in this book. On the other hand, although this static business ownership measure through self-employment data is not the ideal definition of entrepreneurship, the status of being self-employed in the knowledge-based sector does reflect a person's entrepreneurial propensity, compared to being a wage-and-salary employee. The stock of self-employment in the knowledge-based sectors, in contrast to the stock of wage-and-salary employment, characterizes the degree of entrepreneurship within a region.

Future research on elderly entrepreneurship should examine new and different model specifications. There is a remaining question of whether or not the independent variables used in the logit models are all necessary and offer the best combination, whether some have been missed and whether the mathematical formats (e.g., the linear or non-linear formats or interactions) of the variables are the best. This warrants further investigation. Although regression diagnostics can help to detect obvious problems, diagnostic methods cannot suggest all potential good models and do not necessarily detect all possible specification issues. Future efforts exploring different models to compare the model fit and the construct validities could be helpful.

Alternative growth models should also be explored. The model used in this book was based on the Cobb Douglas production function and made some stringent assumptions. Cobb Douglas function is only a simple format of the growth model. To enhance the estimation, a more sophisticated model exploration might help. For example, growth models with various translog formats would be worth exploring to reach a better estimation of the economic role of elderly entrepreneurship.

The path analysis presented in this book was intended to be exploratory. Further research could focus on improving this model and adding more complexity to the formulation. Although the direct effects in the individual regressions test the causal relationship, the total effect reflected in the path analysis is not essentially a measure of the causal relationship. The path analysis model, though offers a good fit for the labor effect of elderly entrepreneurship, does not offer a very good model fit for the Social Security effect yet. To test and also forecast how senior entrepreneurship could affect the future labor force and fiscal situation, simulation models might be useful for future exploration.

It is also important to focus on collecting better, more comprehensive and timely data. Better datasets could improve the measurements of key variables and enhance the results of the estimation. A dataset that has senior business owners' complete demographic and socioeconomic status and even the characteristics of the businesses they own would be an ideal dataset for further exploration of elderly entrepreneurship. Conducting a new survey is an option. A more cost effective way is to extend current datasets that offers relevant information. *Characteristics of Business Owners Survey* that offers detailed demographic and socioeconomic characteristics of business owners of all age groups needs to offer more updated data. This survey only offers information up to 1997 and no newer data is found. *Health and Retirement Survey*, a longitudinal survey describing detailed information of seniors up to age 59, needs to expand its age information. Various U.S. census products, such as *PUMS* and *CPS*, can help to add variables on business ownership status. In addition, more flexible geographic identifiers and more years of data would always be very useful.

Last, distinguishing knowledge-based incorporated elderly self-employment from knowledge-based unincorporated elderly self-employment would generate some interesting observations. Incorporated self-employment is different from unincorporated self-employment in terms of their employment legal formality and other related properties. Distinguishing the propensity for those two types of knowledge-based self-employment and their roles in the economy might generate more specific policy implications. This could be a potential future research topic for elderly entrepreneurship.

5. Concluding Remarks

This book has shown through empirical and theoretical analysis that seniors are valuable asset to the economy, not a burden on the society. In the era of aging, when people complain seniors to be the hurdles of economic growth and blame seniors to be the direct cause of a prognostic labor shortage and Social Security fund bankruptcy, there is actually ways to utilize seniors' human capital and solve the aging-resulted problems. The elderly not only deserve respect from the younger generation after contributing their own hearts and souls to our economy and society for many years, they are also a valuable source of cumulated human capital and this can help the economy to grow. Seniors' human capital assets become increasingly important and contributive in the "knowledge economy". They are valuable not just through mentoring and enlightening the young, but also directly contributing to our economy. Although seniors may suffer more physical difficulties than the younger ones and their working process might be slower at certain ages, it does not necessarily mean they are less productive. Seniors can offer value through their cumulated wisdom, experience, and business ties, and outstanding language and interpersonal skills. This book research has empirically shown that entrepreneurship occurs more often to the elderly, as long as they are active in the labor force. Seniors' entrepreneurship not only has significant impact on the regional economic growth, this impact is even stronger than that from the young. Recognizing and calling for attention to the role of elderly entrepreneurship would further spur more seniors to join in economy and eliminate the social discrimination against older age, which offers social benefits in addition to its positive economic and fiscal impacts.

Moreover, seniors' participation in the labor force as entrepreneurs could have a benefit to themselves. Health permitted, many seniors appear to be interested in being more involved in the society: to continue career values, stay respected, and to earn more income. Being an entrepreneur not only helps them to achieve those goals, but also gives them more mental fulfillment, financial freedom (compared to leaving the labor force), time arrangement flexibility for their own needs (compared to wage-and-salary employment), and therefore enhances their life satisfaction.

More public attention and public efforts, including research and practice on enhancing elderly entrepreneurship, is necessary and important. Seniors, after many years' cumulated working experience and skills, often like to share their experience, skills, and insights, which would be mutually beneficial to seniors and the young, eventually beneficial to the whole society. Elderly entrepreneurship has not been paid much attention to, though the U.S. society, as well as many other societies, has already been experiencing an aging economy. However, it is never too late! The sooner that the notion of elderly entrepreneurship can be recognized by the general public, the earlier the positive impacts of developing elderly entrepreneurship would show up and the more positive externalities would be generated to our society.

Policy implications

- Public attention to entrepreneurship should not just focus on the young. Those new efforts could come from the mass media, enterprise incubators, universities, schools, communities, etc.
- Government economic investment could give priority to developing elderly entrepreneurship because elderly entrepreneurship has a strong impact on regional economic growth, and even stronger impact than knowledge capital and younger entrepreneurship.
- Certain level of tax incentives could be preferred to the elderly entrepreneurs to encourage more elderly entrepreneurial activities.

- Government agencies, such as U.S. Administration on Aging and Small Business Administration, could design some social programs that relieve seniors from various social barriers to become entrepreneurs. They could also design low cost or even free entrepreneurship trainings and forums to the elderly.
- Females and minority seniors (such as African Americans and American Natives) deserve more attention in policies that are intended to encourage elderly entrepreneurship. One way to empower them is through organizing unions and connecting them to appropriate networks.
- Reducing social segregation and zoning and promoting intercultural communication can enhance culture openness and diversity, and thus develop elderly entrepreneurship.
- Offering low-cost day care services for children or connecting day care needs and demands through an organized network could help liberate both seniors and females from their involuntary responsibility for taking care of children and thus develop entrepreneurship from those seniors and women.
- Elderly entrepreneurship should be elevated as an important research topic for further studies and practice. Efforts could start with treating elderly entrepreneurship as a variable in data collection and forecast projection for Bureau of Labor Statistics, Bureau of Economic Analysis, Social Security Administration, and U.S. Census Bureau.
- The sooner that the notion of elderly entrepreneurship can be recognized by the general public, the earlier the positive impacts of developing elderly entrepreneurship would show up and the more positive externalities would be generated to our society.

AFTERWORD

David W. S. Wong
Professor & Chair
Earth Systems & GeoInformation Sciences
George Mason University

"Demography is destiny" is a catchy phrase these days and may be a cliché, but overlooking the significance of population and demographics has been the fundamental flaw of many public policy decisions. Even in natural science, the roles of human beings and population growth have been taken out of the equations when evaluating global and environmental changes. This monograph by Ting Zhang adds to the literature that population demographics play a significant role in many societal issues, especially in the future of the society and even in the global economy. In addition, her focus on addressing the potential societal burden due to the aging demographic is insightful and has significant long-term policy implications.

In early 2008, Virginia Congressman Tom Davis decided not to re-run for his congressional seat, citing the reason that the Congress had ignored addressing some critical social issues, including the imminent breakdown of the Social Security system. His decision highlighted the fact that the impacts on changing demographics in our society was often of lesser concern to politicians and policy makers. While the trouble with the Social Security system is primarily driven by demographics, and there is not much we can do to change the existing demographics, Ting Zhang's monograph, which was based on her Ph.D. thesis in the School of Public Policy at George Mason University, does provide a glimpse of hope that the magnitude of the problem may be lessened. Ting's analysis addressed both the size and the quality of baby-boomer cohorts, and highlighted their importance and economic roles they might play as part of the "creative class", a notion coined by Richard Florida. With their economic flexibilities and vibrancies, which are some of the characteristics of the creative class, the baby-booming cohorts or the soon-to-be-retired population segments may extend their economic productive lifespan well into their normal retirement age. These relatively well educated and entrepreneurial individuals fit into the knowledge-based economy very well even after they "retire." Their levels of engagement in the economy may be driven by their economic needs, but also by their personal desire to be active both physically and intellectually. Their economic engagement will likely reduce the burden on or delay the need of drawing from the fragile Social Security system.

Many studies have documented the economic and political power of the baby-boomers in the U.S. and other economies. Many studies also have assessed the impacts of the baby-boomers on the economy and the social security system when they retire, but few studies have investigated how potential negative impacts from their retirement may be minimized and their potential positive contributions to the economy. This monograph provides a detailed description and analysis on the attributes of the baby-boomer cohorts in terms of their economic potential after entering the retirement phase of their lifecycle. The book should be easy to read and understand to the majority of the readers. The more in-depth analytical sections may require some basic background in statistical modeling, but still should be comprehensible for most readers.

REFERENCES

AARP (n.d.), "Employment and Income Security in an Aging World: A U.S. Perspective," Retrieved from World Wide Web on August 28, 2005 at http://www.aarp.org/research/work/employment/a2003-02-11-russell.html.

Achenbaum, W. A. and Bengtson, V. C., "Re-engaging the Disengagement Theory of Aging: Or the History and Assessment of Theory Development in Gerontology," *The Gerontologist*, 34: 756–763 (1994).

Acs, Z. and Audretsch, D. B., *Innovation and Small Firms*. Cambridge, MA: MIT Press (1990).

Acs, Z., Audretsch, D., Braunerhjelm, P. and Carlsson, B., "The Missing Link: The Knowledge Filter Entrepreneurship and Endogenous Growth," *Center for Economic Policy Research*, London, UK, No. 4783 December (2004).

Acs, Z. and Evans, D., "The Determinants of Variations in Self-employment Rates across Countries and Over time," Working Paper (1994).

Acs, Z. and Armington, C., "Job Creation and Persistence in Services and Manufacturing," *The Papers on Entrepreneurship, Growth, and Public Policy*, No. 1604 (2003).

Acs, Z., Armington, C. and Zhang, T., "The Determinants of New Firm Survival in Regional Economies: The Role of Regional Human Capital Stock and Knowledge Spillovers," *Papers in Regional Science*, 86(3): 367–391 (2007).

Anselin, L., Varga, A. and Acs, Z., "Local Geographic Spillovers between University Research and High-technology Innovation," *Journal of Urban Economics*, 42: 422–448 (1997).

Anselin, L., Varga, A. and Acs, Z., "Geographic and Sectoral Characteristics of Academic Knowledge Externalities," *Papers in Regional Science*, 79(4): 435–443 (2000).

Armington, C. and Acs, Z., "The Determinants of Regional Variation in Firm Formation," *Regional Studies*, 36(1): 33–45 (2002).

Arrow, K., "The Economic Implications of Learning by Doing," *Review of Economic Studies*, 29(3): 155–173 (1962).

Atchley, R. C., *The Social Forces in Later Life*. Belmont, CA: Wadsworth (1972).

Atkinson, R. D. and Court, R. H., *The "New Economy" Index: Understanding America's Economic Transformation*. Washington, DC: Progress Policy Institute (1998).

Audretsch, D. B. and Keilbach, M., "Entrepreneurial Capital and Economic Performance," Discussion paper. *Entrepreneurship, Growth and Public Policy*. Jena, Germany: Max Plank Institute (2004).

Audretsch, D. B. and Thurik, A. R., Linking Entrepreneurship to Growth, STI Working Paper Paris: OECD (2001/2).

Ayer, R. (n.d.), Older Workers Make a Difference. The Hartford Financial Services Group.

Barro, R. J. and Lee, J.-W. "Sources of Economic Growth (with comments from Nancy Stokey)" *Carnegie-Rochester Conference Series on Public Policy,* 40: 1–57 (1994).

Barro, R. J. and Sala-i-Martin, X., "Convergence," *Journal of Political Economy,* 100: 223–251 (1992).

Barro, R. J. and Sala-i-Martin, X., *Economic Growth,* London and Montreal, NY: McGraw-Hill (1995).

Barth, M. C., McNaught, W. and Rizzi, P., "Corporations and the Aging Labor Force," in Mirvis P. H. (ed.), *Building the Competitive Labor Force: Investing in Human Capital for Corporate Success,* New York: John Wiley & Sons (1993).

Baumol, W. J., "Formal Entrepreneurship Theory in Economics: Existence and Bounds," *Journal of Business Venturing,* 3 (1993).

Baumol, W. J., "The Free-Market Innovation Machine: Analysing the Growth Miracle of Capitalism," Princeton University Press (2002).

Becker, G. S., Murphy, K. M. and Tamura, R., "Human Capital, Fertility, and Economic Growth," *Journal of Political Economy,* 98: S12–S37 (1990).

Becker, G. S., "The Economic Way of Looking at Life," Nobel Lecture, December 9 (1992).

Becker, G. S., *Human Capital: A Theoretical and Empirical Analysis with Special Reference to Education.* (3rd ed.). Chicago, USA and London, UK: The University of Chicago Press (1993).

Bengtson, V. L., "Cultural and Occupational Differences in Level of Present Role Activity in Retirement," in Havighurst, R. J., Municks, J. M. A., Neugarten, B. C. and Thomas, H. (eds.), *Adjustments to Retirement: A Cross-national Study.* Assen, The Netherlands: Van Gorkum (1969).

Bengtson, V. L., Burgess, E. O. and Parrott, T. M., "Theory, Explanation and a Third Generation of Theoretical Development in Social Gerontology," *Journal of Gerontology,* 52(B): S72–S88 (1997).

Benz, M. and Frey, B. S., "Being Independent Raises Happiness at Work," *Swedish Economic Policy Review,* 11: 95–134 (2004).

Berkovec, J. and Stern, S., "Job Exit Behavior of Older Men," *Econometrica,* 59(1): 189–210 (January 1991).

Blanchflower, D. G. and Oswald, A. J., "Self-employment and the Enterprise Culture," in Jowell, R., Witherspoon, S. and Jowell, R. (eds.), *British Social Attitudes: The 1990 Report.* Aldershot: Gower Press (1990).

Blanchflower, D. G. and Oswald, A. J., "What Makes an Entrepreneur?" *Journal of Labor Economics Perspectives,* 9: 153–167, Summer (1998).

Blanchflower, D. G., "Self-employment in OECD Countries," *Labour Economics,* 7: 471–505 (2000).

Blanchflower, D. G., Oswald, A. J. and Stutzer, A., "Latent Entrepreneurship across Nations," *European Economic Review,* 45: 680–691 (2001).

Blau, D., "A Time-series Analysis of Self-employment in the United States," *Journal of Political Economy,* 95: 445–467 (1987).

Blau, D., "Labor Force Dynamics of Older Men," *Econometrica*, 62(1): 117–156 (January 1994).

Blöndal, S. and Scarpetta, S., "The Retirement Decision in OECD Countries," *OECD Economics Department Working Papers*, No. 202. Paris: Organization for Economic Cooperation and Development (1999). http://www.oecd.org/dataoecd/36/30/1866098.pdf.

Board of Trustees of the Federal Old-Age and Survivors Insurance and Disability Insurance Trust Funds, *Annual Report*. Washington, DC: Social Security Administration (2000).

Bogenhold, D. and Staber, U., "The Decline and Rise of Self-employment," *Employment and Society*, 5: 223–239 (1991).

Brown, S. K., "Staying Ahead of the Curve 2003: The AARP Working in Retirement Study," *AARP Knowledge Management*. Washington, DC (2003).

Bruce, D., Holtz-Eakin, D. and Quinn, J., "Self-employment and Labor Market Transitions at Older Ages," *Center for Retirement Research at Boston College Working Paper* 13. Chestnut Hill, MA: Center for Retirement Research at Boston College (2000).

Burke, A. E. and Fitzroy, F. R., "Education and Regional Job Creation by the Self-employed: The English North-South Divide," *The Papers on Entrepreneurship, Growth, and Public Policy*, No. 0706 (2006).

Burtless, G. and Quinn, J. F., "Retirement Trends and Policies to Encourage Work among Older Americans," in Allan Hunt (ed.), *Ensuring Health and Income Security for an Aging Labor Force*. Kalamazoo, MI: W. E. Upjohn Institute for Employment Research (2000).

Callaban, D., "Heath Care Struggle Between Young and Old," Markson, E. W. and Hollis-Sawyer, L. A. (eds.), *Intersections of Aging: Readings in Social Gerontology*. Los Angeles: Roxbury (2000).

Carrasco, R. and Ejrnas, M., "Self-employment in Denmark and Spain," Institutions, Economic Conditions, and Gender Differences," Universidad Carlos III de Madrid, Mimeo (2003).

Charness, N., "The Age-Ability-Productivity Paradox," Conference processing of a Wharton Impact Conference, *Maximizing Your Labor Force: Employees Over 50 in Today's Global Economy* 10. University of Pennsylvania and AARP Global Aging Program (November 2004).

Christaller, L. W., Die zentralen Orte in Südeutschl and Jena: Fischer (1933).

CIA World Fact Book. Retrieved from World Wide Web (2005). http://www.cia.gov/cia/publications/factbook/geos/us.html.

Ciccone, A. and Hall, R. E., "Productivity and the Density of Economic Activity," *American Economic Review*, 86(1): 54–70 (1996).

Clark, R. L., York, E. A. and Anker, R., "Economic Development and Labor Force Participation of Older Persons," *Population Research and Policy Review*, 18: 411–432 (1999).

Collison, J. (program manager), "Older Workers Survey," SHRM research. Society for Human Resource Management (SHRM), National Older Worker Career Center (NOWCC) and Committee for Economic Development (CED) (June 2003).

Committee for Economic Development, "New Opportunities for Older Workers," Committee for Economic Development (from Fuller, print out copy] (1999).

Cottrell, L., "The Adjustment of the Individual to His Age and Sex Roles," *American Sociological Review*, 7: 617–620 (1942).

Covey, H. (1981). "A Reconceptualization of Continuity Theory: Some Preliminary Thoughts," *The Gerontologists*, 1981(21): 628–633 (1942).

Crown, W. H. and Longino, C. F. Jr., "Labor Force Trends and Aging Policy," in Markson, E. W. and Hollis-Sawyer, L. A. (eds.), *Intersections of Aging: Readings in Social Gerontology*. Los Angeles: Roxbury (2000).

Dalen, H. P. van and Henkens, K., "Early Retirement Reform. Can it and will it work?" *Ageing and Society*, 22(2): 209–231 (2002).

Day, C. and Dowrick, S. "Aging Economics: Human Capital, Productivity and Fertility," *Agenda*, 11(1): 1–20 (2004).

Doeringer, P. B. (ed.), *Bridges to Retirement: Older Workers in a Changing Labor Market*. Ithaca, New York: ILR press, pp. x, 237 (1990).

Domencich, T. and McFadden, D., *Urban Travel Demand*. Amsterdam: North Holland Publishing Company (1975).

Dunne, E., "The Learning Society: International Perspectives on Core Skills in Higher Education." London: Kogan Page (1990).

Duval, R., "Retirement Behaviour in OECD Countries: Impact of Old-age Pension Schemes and Other Social Transfer Programmes," *OECD Economic Studies*, 5(45): i37 Summer (2003).

Estes, C. L. and Associates, *Social Policy and Aging: A Critical Perspective*. Thousand Oaks: Sage (2000).

Evans, D. and Jovanovic, B., "An Empirical Analysis of Self-employment in the Netherlands," *Economics Letters*, 32: 97–100 (1989).

Evans, D. and Jovanovic, B., "An Estimated Model of Entrepreneurial Liquidity Constraints," *Journal of Political Economy*, 97: 808–827 (1989).

Evans and Leighton, "Some Empirical Aspects of Entrepreneurship," *American Economic Review*, 79: 519–535 (1989).

Everitt, B. S. and Dunn, G, *Applied Multivariate Data Analysis*. London: Edward Arnold (1991).

Florida, R., *The Rise of the Creative Class: And How it's Transforming Work, Leisure, Community and Everyday Life*. New York, NY: Basic Books (2004).

Florida, R., *The Flight of Creative Class: The New Global Competition for Talent*. New York, NY: Harper Business (2005).

Foray, D. and Lundyall, B. D., "The Knowledge-based Economy from the Economics of Knowledge to the Learning Economy," in *Employment and Growth in the "Knowledge-based Economy,"* Paris: OECD, pp. 11–32 (1996).

Friedberg, L., "The Impact of Technological Change on Older Workers: Evidence from Data on Computer Use," *Industrial and Labor Relations Review*, 56(3): 511–529 (2003).

Fuchs, V., "Self-employment and Labor Force Participation on Elder Males," *Journal of Human Resources*, 17: 339–357 (1982).

Garofalo, G. A. and Yamarik, S., "Regional Convergence: Evidence from a New State-by-State Capital Stock Series," *The Review of Economics and Statistics*, 84(2): 316–323. The President and Fellows of Harvard College and the Massachusetts Institute of Technology (2002).

Gendell, M., "Retirement Age Declines Again in 1990s," *Monthly Labor Review* (October 2001). http://www.bls.gov/opub/mlr/2001/10/art2full.pdf.

Giannetti, M. and Simonov, A., "On the Determinants of Entrepreneurial Activity: Social Norms, Economic Environment and Individual Characteristics," *Swedish Economic Policy Review,* 11: 269–313 (2004).

Glaeser, E. L., Kallal, H. D., Scheinkman, J. A. and Shleifer, A., "Growth in Cities," *Journal of Political Economy,* 100: 1126–1152 (1992).

Glaeser, E., Scheinkman, J. and Shleifer, A., "Economic Growth in a Cross Section of Cities," *Journal of Monetary Economics,* 36: 117–143 (1995).

Reynolds, P. D., Camp, S. M., Bygrave, W. D., Autio, E. and Hay, M., (GEM Research Committee), Global Entrepreneurship Monitor, *and Global Entrepreneurship Monitor Executive Report.* Babson College, IBM, London Business School, and the Kauffman Center for Entrepreneurial Leadership (2001 and 2004 respectively).

Acs, Z. J., Arenims, P., Hay, M. and Minniti, M., (GEM Research Committee), Global Entrepreneurship Monitor, and *Global Entrepreneurship Monitor Executive Report.* Babson College and London Business School (2004).

Greenspan, A., "The Interaction of Education and Economic Change," *Federal Reserve Bank of Minneapolis,* 13(1): 6–11 (1999).

Greenspan, A., Opening Remarks at a Symposium Sponsored by the Federal Reserve Bank of Kansas City, Jackson Hole, Wyoming (August 27, 2004). Retrieved from the World Wide Web on October 27, 2005 at http://www.seniorjournal.com/NEWS/Money/4-08-27Greenspan.htm.

Gore, C., *Regions in Question: Space, Development Theory and Regional Policy.* London: Menthuen (1984).

Grossman, G. M. and Helpman, E., "Endogenous Product Cycles," *The Economic Journal,* 101: 1214–1229 (1991).

Grossman, G. M. and Helpman, E., "Endogenous Innovation in the Theory of Growth," *Journal of Economic Perspectives,* 8: 23–44 (1994).

Guillemar, A., Taylor, P. and Walker, A., "Managing an Ageing Labor Force in Britain and France," *The Geneva Papers on Risk and Insurance,* 21: 478–501 (1996).

Hagestad, G. and Neugarten, B., "Age and the Life Course," in Binstock R. H. and Shanas, E. (eds.), *Handbook of Aging and the Social Sciences* (2nd ed.). New York: Van Nostrand (1985).

Hamilton, B. H., "Does Entrepreneurship Pay? An Empirical Analysis of the Return to Self-employment," *Journal of Political Economy,* 108: 604–631 (2000).

Hayflick, L., "The Cell Biology of Human Aging," *Scientific American,* 242: 60 (1980).

Haub, C., "The U.S. Birth Rate Falls Further," Population Research Bureau (2003): http://www.prb.org/Template.cfm?Section=PRB&template=/ContentManagement/ContentDisplay.cfm&ContentID=8838.

Henkens, K., "Supervisors' Attitudes about Early Retirement of Subordinates," *Journal of Applied Social Psychology,* 30(4): 833–852 (2000).

Herman, R., Olivio, T. and Gioia, J., *Impending Crisis: Too Many Jobs, Too Few People.* Winchester, VA: Oakhill Press (2003).

Higgins, B. and Savoie, D. J., *Regional Development Theories and Their Application.* New Jersey: New Brunswick (1995).

Hirschman, A. O., *The Strategy of Economic Development*. New Haven, CT: Yale University Press (1958).

Holtz-Eakin, D., Joulfaian, D. and Rosen, H. S., "Entrepreneurial Decisions and Liquidity Constraints," *Rand Journal of Economics*, 25(2): 334–347, Summer (1994a).

Holtz-Eakin, D., Joulfaian, D. and Rosen, H. S., "Sticking it Out: Entrepreneurial Survival and Liquidity Constraints," *Journal of Political Economy*, 102: 53–75 (February, 1994b).

Hooymann, N. R. and Kiyak, H. A., *Social Gerontology: A Multi-disciplinary Perspective*. Boston: Allyn and Bacon. Chapters 1, 8, 9, 12, 14, and 16 (2005).

Human Resources Development Canada, "Older Worker Adjustment Programs Lessons Learned (Final Report): Evaluation and Data Development Strategic Policy," Human Resources Development Canada, Government of Canada: SP-AH093-12-99E (1999). Retrieved from World Wide Web on Aug 30, 2005 at http://www11.hrdcdrhc.gc.ca/pls/edd/OWAP_134000.htm.

Ippolito, R. A., "Toward Explaining Earlier Retirement After 1970," *Industrial & Labor Relations Review*, Cornell University 43(5): 556 (July 1990).

Jarboe, K. P. and Alliance, A., "Knowledge Management as an Economic Development Strategy," *Reviews of Economic Development Literature and Practice*: No. 7. Economic Development Administration, U.S. Department of Commerce (2001).

Jacobs, J., *The Economy of Cities*. New York: Vintage (1969).

Jaffe, A., Tratjenberg, M. and Henderson, R., "Geography, Location of Knowledge Spillovers as Evidence of Patent Citations," *Quarterly Journal of Economics*, 108: 483–499 (1993).

Jin, D. and Stough R. R., "Learning and Learning Capabilities in the Fordist and Post-Fordist Age: An Integrative Framework," *Environment & Planning*, A 30: 1255–1278 (1998).

Johnson, W., "A Theory of Job-Shopping." *Quarterly Journal of Economics*, 22: 261–278 (May 1978).

Johnson, R., "Why the 'Average Age of Retirement' is a Misleading Measure of Labor Supply?" *Monthly Labor Review* (December 2001). http://www.bls.gov/opub/mlr/2001/12/comntry.pdf.

Karoly, L. A. and Zissimopoulos, J., "Self-employment and the 50+ Population," *AARP*, 03 (2004).

King, L. J., *Central Place Theory*. Beverly Hills, CA: Sage (1985).

Kirzner, I. M., "Entrepreneurial Discovery and The Competitive Market Process: An Austrian Approach," *Journal of Economic Literature*, 35: 60–85 (1997).

Kline, R. B., *Principles and Practice of Structural Equation Modeling*, New York, NY: Guilford Press. A Very Readable Introduction to the Subject, with Good Coverage of Assumptions and SEM's Relation to Underlying Regression, Factor, and Other Techniques (1998).

Lazear, E. P., *Personnel Economics for Managers*, New York: Wiley (1989).

Lazear, E. "Enterpreneurship," *NBER Working Paper* 9109. Cambridge, MA: National Bureau of Economic Research (2002).

Lipton, M., *Why Poor People Stay Poor: Urban Bias in World Development*. Cambridge, MA: Harvard University Press (1977).

Long, J. E., "The Income Tax and Self-employment," *National Tax Journal*, 35: 31–42 (March 1982).

Low, S., Henderson, J. and Weiler, S. "Gauging a Region's Entrepreneurial Potential," Federal Reserve Bank of Kansas City — *Economic Review*, 3rd quarter (2005).

Lösch, A., *Die räumliche Ordung der Wirtschaft*. Jena: Fischer. Translated by Woglom, W. H. and Stolper, W. F. (1954). *The Economics of Location*. New Heaven, CT: Yale University Press (1940).

Lucas, R. E. Jr. "On the Mechanics of Economic Development," *Journal of Monetary Economics*, 22: 3–42 (1988).

Lundvall, B. and Johnson, B., "The Learning Economy," *Journal of Industry Studies,* 1(2): 23–42 (1994).

Malizia, E. E., "Economic Development in Smaller Cities and Rural Areas," *Planner's Notebook.* Autumn (1986).

Mankiw, N. G., "Macroeconomics," (5th ed.). New York: Worth Publishers (2005).

Mankiw, N. G., Romer, D. and Weil, D. N., "A Contribution to the Empirics of Economic Growth," *Quarterly Journal of Economics*, 107(2): 407–437 (May 1992).

Marshall, V. W., "Sociology and Psychology in the Theoretical Legacy of the Kansas City Studies," *The Gerontologist,* 34: 768–774 (1994).

Meager, N., "Does Unemployment Lead to Self-employment?" *Small Business Economics*, 4: 87–103 (1992).

Mertens, N., *Loopbaanonderbrekingen en Kinderen: Gevolgen voor de Beloning van Vrouwen*, Ph.D. thesis, Utrecht University (1998).

Meyer, J. R., "Regional Economics: A Survey," *American Econ. Review*, 53: 19–54 (1963) (reprinted in Needleman, L. (ed.), Regional Economics, p. 19ff (1968)).

Miller, R., "Job Matching and Occupational Choice," *Journal of Political Economy*, 92: 1086–1120 (December 1984).

Minkler, M. and Estes, C., *Readings in the Political Economy of Aging*. Farmingdale, NY: Baywood (1984).

Mincer, J., *Schooling, Experience and Earnings*. New York: Columbia University Press for the National Bureau of Economic Research (1974).

Murphy, K. M. and Welch, F., "The Structure of Wages," *Quarterly Journal of Economic,* 107: 285–326 (1992).

Myrdal, G., *Economic Theory and Underdeveloped Regions*. London: Duckworth (1957).

Nelson, A., "Theories of Regional Development," Bingham, R. and Mier, R. (eds.), *Theories of Local Economic Development.* Sage. pp. 27–29 (1993).

Nelson, A. C., "Comparing States with and without Growth Management: Analysis Based on Indicators with Policy Implications," *Land Use Policy*, 16: 121–127 (1999).

Neugarten, B., Havighurst, R. J. and Tobin, S. S., "Personality and Patterns of Aging," in Neugarten B. L. (ed.), *Middle Age and Aging*. Chicago: University of Chicago Press (1968).

Nijkamp, P. and Poot, J., "Endogenous Technological Change, Innovation Diffusion and Transitional Dynamics in a Nonlinear Growth Model," *Australian Economic Papers,* 32(160): 191–213 (1993).

Olson, L. K., *The Political Economy of Aging*. New York: Columbia University Press (1982).

Overbo, B. and Minkler, M., "The Lives of Older Women: Perspectives from Political Economy and the Humanities," in Cole, T. R., Achenbaum, W. A., Jakobi, P. L. and Kastenbaum, R. (eds.), *Voices and Visions of Aging: Toward a Critical Gerontology.* New York: Springer (1993).

Parker, S. C. and Rougaier, J., "The Retirement Behaviour of the Self-employed in Britain," University of Durham, *Working Paper in Economics and Finance,* No. 04/08 (2004).

Perroux, F., "Note sur la notion de pole de croissance," *Economie Appliquée,* 8: 307–320 (1955)., or in Livingstone I., *Development Economics and Policy: Selected Readings.* London: George Allen & Unwin (1979).

Peterson, P. G., *Gray Dawn: How the Coming Age Wave Will Transform America — and the World.* New York: Times Books, Random House (1999).

Picot, G. and Manser, M., "The Role of Self-employment in Job Creation in Canada and the United States," *Canadian Economic Observer,* 12(3): 3.1–3.17 (March 1999).

Polachek, S. W. and Siebert, W. S., *The Economics of Earnings,* Cambridge, MA: Cambridge University Press (1993).

Psacharopoulos, G., *Earnings and Education in OECD Countries* (Paris: Organization for Economic Co-operation; Washington, DC: OECD Publications Center) (1975).

Putnam, R. D., "Bowling Alone: America's Declining Social Capital," *The Journal of Democracy* (6)1: 65–78 (1995).

Quinn, J. F., "Labor-force Participation Patterns of Older Self-employed Workers," *Social Security Bulletin,* 43(4): 17–28 (1980).

Ray, R. E., "A Post Modern Perspective on Feminist Gerontology," *The Gerontologist,* 36: 674–680 (1996).

Reardon, E., "Self-employment in Canada and the United States." Unpublished paper, (June 1997).

Reich, R., *The Work of Nations.* New York: Vintage Books (1992).

Remery, C., Henkens, K., Schippers, J. and Ekamper, P., "Managing an Aging Labor Force and a Tight Labor Market: Views Held by Dutch Employers," *Population Research and Policy Review,* 22: 21–40. Kluwer Academic Publishers, The Netherlands (2003).

Resnick, B., Mills, M. E. and Nahm, E., "Web Use can Improve Quality of Life for Elders," *Maximizing Human Potential,* 11(3): 4, 6. Winter, (2004).

Reynolds, P. D. *et al.,* "Global Entrepreneurship Monitor: Data Collection Design and Implementation 1998–2003," *Small Business Economics* 24: 205–231 (2005).

Rix, S. E., "Aging and Work — a View from the United States," AARP Public Policy Institute, 2 (2004).

Romer, P. M., "Increasing Returns and Long-run Growth," *Journal of Political Economy,* 94: 1002–1037 (1986).

Romer, P. M., "Endogenous Technological Change," *Journal of Political Economy,* 98(5): 71–102 (1990).

Romer, P. M., "Implementing a National Technology Strategy with Self-Organizing Industry Investment Boards," *Brookings Papers on Economic Activity: Microeconomics,* 2: 345 (1993).

Romer, P. M., "New Goods, Old Theory and the Welfare Costs of Trade Restrictions," *Journal of Development Economics,* 43: 5 (1994).

Roper, A. S. W., *Staying Ahead of the Curve: The AARP Work and Career Study*, Washington DC: AARP (2002).

Saxenian, A. L., *Regional Advantage: Culture and Competition in Silicon Valley and Route p. 128*. Cambridge, MA: Harvard University Press (1994).

Schetagne, S., *Building Bridges Across Generations in the Workplace: A Response to Aging of the Labor Force*. Vancouver, Canada: Columbia Foundation (2001).

Schuetze, H. J., "Taxes, Economic Conditions and Recent Trends in Self-employment: A Canada-U.S. Comparison," *Labour Economics*, 7: 507–554 (2000).

Schuetze, H. J. and Bruce, D., "Tax Policy and Entrepreneurship," *Swedish Economic Policy Review*, 11: 233–265 (2004).

Schultz, T. W., *The Economic Value of Education*. New York: Columbia University Press (1963).

Schulz, R. and Salthouse, T. A., *Adult Development and Aging: Myths and Emerging Realities* (3rd ed.). Upper Saddle River, NJ: Prentice Hall (1999).

Schumpeter, J., *Capitalism, Socialism and Democracy* (3rd ed.) New York: Harper and Row (1950).

Shane, S., Prior Knowledge and the Discovery of Entrepreneurial Opportunities, *Organization Science*, 11: 448–469 (2000).

Smith, L., "How We Age is Becoming a Growing Curriculum," Baltimore Sun (December 2006). Retrieved from the World Wide Web http://www.baltimoresun.com/features/custom/modernlife/bal-ml.boomer31dec31,0,3717492.story

Social Security Administration, "Social Security Bulletin, Annual Statistical Supplement," Bureau of Labor Statistics publications (1999), and Web site. See Murray Gendell and Siegel Jacob, S., "Trends in Retirement Age by Sex, 1950–2005," *Monthly Labor Review*, p. 22–29 (July 1992) for more information about the labor force data.

Social Security Advisory Board, *Forum on Implications of Raising the Social Security Retirement Age*. Washington, DC: Social Security Advisory Board (May 1999).

Social Security Administration, *Overview of SSA: SSA's FY 2004 Performance and Accountability Report* (2004). Retrieved on the World Wide Web at http://www.ssa.gov/finance/2004/Overview.pdf.

Sokolovsky, J., "Images of Aging," Markson, E. W. and Hollis-Sawyer, L. A. (eds.). *Intersections of Aging: Readings in Social Gerontology*. Los Angeles: Roxbury (2000).

Solow, R. S., "Technical Change and the Aggregate Production Function," *Review of Economics and Statistics*, 39: 312–320 (1957).

Sterns, H. L. and McDaniel, M. A., "Job Performance and the Older Worker," in Sara E. Rix (ed.), *Older Workers: How Do They Measure Up?* Washington, DC: AARP (1994).

Steuerle, C. E., "Social Security — A Labor Force Issue," Statement before the Subcommittee on Social Security Committee on Ways and Means United States House of Representatives (June 14, 2005).

Stohr, W. B. and Todtling, F., "An Evaluation of Regional Policies Experiences in Market and Mixed Economies," in Hansen, N. M. (ed.). *Human Settlement Systems: International Perspectives on Structure, Change and Public Policy*. Cambridge, MA: Ballinger (1977–1978).

Stolarick, K. M. (n.d.), "Social Tolerance Index," [Data Series] 2000 Metropolitan Area Statistics (Personal Communication) (2005).

Taylor, M. P., "Earnings, Independence or Unemployment: Why Become Self-employed?" *Oxford Bulletin of Economics and Statistics*, 58(2): 253–265 (1996).

Taylor, M. P., "The Changing Picture of Self-employment in Britain," *Institute for Social and Economic Research (ISER) Working Papers* (1997–2009).

Taylor, P. and Walker, A., "Employers and Older Workers: Attitudes and Employment Practices," *Ageing and Society*, 18(6): 641–658 (1998).

Thurow, L. C., *Generating Inequality*, New York: Basic Books (1975).

U.S. Administration on Aging, *A Profile of Older Americans*. Washington, DC (2002).

U.S. Census Bureau, *The 65 Years and Over Population: 2000*. C2KBR/01-10. Washington, DC (October 2001).

U.S. Census Bureau, Population Estimates and American Community Survey (2000). http://factfinder.census.gov/

U.S. Department of Labor, Bureau of Labor Statistics (1994–2005). http://data.bls.gov/PDQ/servlet/SurveyOutputServlet.

Van der Sluis, J. and van Praag, C. M., "Economic Returns to Education for Entrepreneurs: The Development of a Neglected Child in the Family of Economics of Education?" *Swedish Economic Policy Review*, 11(2) (2004).

Van Stel, A. J. and Storey, D. J., "The Link between Firm Birth and Job Creation: Is There a Upas Tree Effect?" *The Papers on Entrepreneurship, Growth, and Public Policy*, No. 3304 (2004).

Wagner, D. L., *Factors Influencing the Use of Older Workers: A Survey of U.S. Employers*, Washington, DC: The National Council on the Aging (1998).

Waldman, D. A. and Avolio, B. J., "A Meta-Analysis of Age Differences in Job Performance," *Journal of Applied Psychology*, 71: 33–38 (1986).

Weeks, J. R., "Population: An Introduction to Concepts and Issues," Wadsworth (2005).

21 Century Workforce Commission, *A Nation of Opportunity: Building America's 21st Century Workforce*. Washington, DC (1996).

Zhang, T., "Age and Elderly Entrepreneurship," *Working Paper*, George Mason University, Fairfax, Virginia (2007a).

Zhang, T., "Social and Policy Factors for Elderly Entrepreneurship," *Working Paper*, Fairfax, Virginia: George Mason University (2007b).

Zhang, T., "The Role of Elderly Entrepreneurship in Metropolitan Economy," *Working Paper*, Fairfax, Virginia: George Mason University (2007c).

Zhang, T., "Labor and Fiscal Impact of Elderly Entrepreneurship," *Working Paper*, Fairfax, Virginia: George Mason University (2007c).

APPENDIX

Appendix 2.1 Age Pyramids

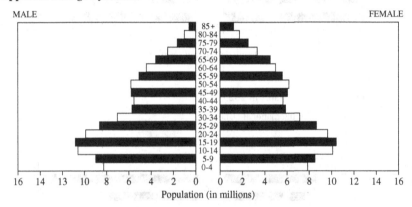

Age Pyramid of the United States in 1975

Source: U.S. Census Bureau, International Data Base.

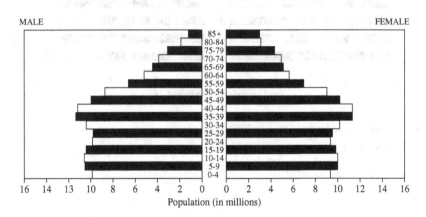

Age Pyramid of the United States in 2000

Source: U.S. Census Bureau, International Data Base.

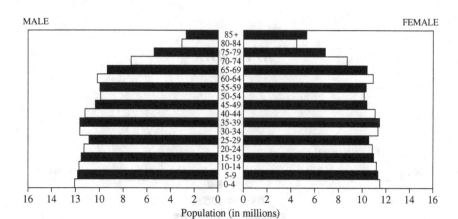

Age Pyramid of the United States in 2025

Source: U.S. Census Bureau, International Data Base.

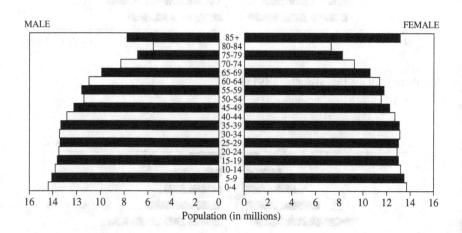

Age Pyramid of the United States in 2050

Source: U.S. Census Bureau, International Data Base.

Appendix 2.2 Labor Force Status Among the Elderly

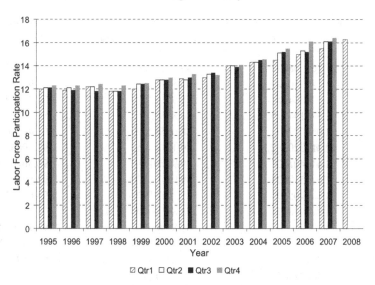

Figure a. Civilian Labor Force Participation Rate (%) for Older Americans (Aged 65 and over), 1995–2008

Source: U.S. Department of Labor, Bureau of Labor Statistics, 1995–2008

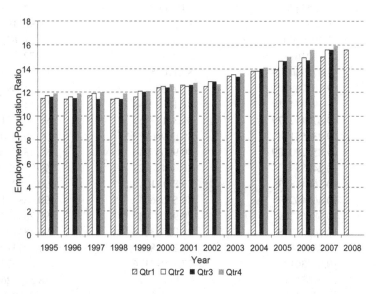

Figure b. Employment-population Ratio for Older Americans (Aged 65 and over), 1995–2008

Source: U.S. Department of Labor, Bureau of Labor Statistics, 1995–2008

Appendix 3.1 Self-employment Rates versus Wage-and-salary Employment Rates in Population by Age

Age	Self-employed	Wage-and-salary Employment	Labor Force
16	1.16310889	43.1143528	47.80397543
17	1.176356429	60.85959571	64.94133889
18	1.37050411	76.97323679	80.71064644
19	1.578194715	84.85828902	88.42130788
20	2.068677457	88.03582099	91.49476003
21	2.313320382	89.13743043	92.59652946
22	2.444401605	89.9170115	93.36200092
23	2.695510628	89.92786478	93.57641836
24	3.064405695	89.82751977	93.68242606
25	3.810838478	88.81596796	93.34932773
26	4.200436942	88.84960583	93.78504882
27	4.600395769	88.25383874	93.52383254
28	4.757822546	88.23478896	93.61934196
29	5.550274854	87.63710787	93.73451436
30	6.053663754	86.95174543	93.52951923
31	6.301690279	86.20912167	93.13477378
32	6.68515097	85.62115294	92.90973401
33	7.229026641	84.91056484	92.65404802
34	7.545547412	84.19009087	92.3297772
35	8.07596726	83.39076523	91.96319135
36	8.2008509	83.03610098	91.81464186
37	9.122161557	81.95376342	91.72444556
38	8.978740763	82.11075869	91.72534396
39	9.60309875	81.16889347	91.41309081
40	9.394834319	81.12899144	91.15304413
41	9.670452779	81.31127452	91.62722174
42	10.23155178	80.60966753	91.39184017
43	9.851290309	80.99057244	91.38953267
44	10.2498592	80.44428227	91.23182206
45	10.56849823	79.81191057	90.97095091
46	10.46940299	79.5760604	90.6686511
47	10.68869289	78.96211737	90.23521315
48	10.80300218	78.99363864	90.38149351
49	10.83492325	78.21448516	89.56431066
50	10.81330122	77.46942136	88.8260346
51	10.90836212	77.0793489	88.57372616
52	11.23914252	76.32982688	88.05797075

(Continued)

Appendix 3.1 (*Continued*)

Age	Self-employed	Wage-and-salary Employment	Labor Force
53	11.01533101	76.01481061	87.63196348
54	11.5781121	73.87271965	86.11071712
55	11.40585763	72.0158389	83.96899556
56	11.78358836	71.33241986	83.70401185
57	11.70414503	70.26631583	82.55819089
58	11.42538506	68.44631048	80.4841438
59	11.1988193	66.56844522	78.31932408
60	11.01902505	64.67528187	76.27454092
61	10.92989386	62.21257293	73.57019181
62	10.41855559	59.2368506	70.22297408
63	10.12013726	56.75786751	67.5666536
64	9.556044676	53.52230517	63.64013548
65	9.343253255	43.44278845	53.54160385
66	8.521090287	40.60157709	49.82898404
67	8.188308984	35.08660253	44.01953491
68	7.287322214	32.32202349	40.38684993
69	6.974381484	30.58953617	38.19775186
70	6.502212003	27.44072795	34.58502582
71	6.365177721	24.2704215	31.24036683
72	6.200510565	22.03901747	28.86785162
73	5.434929166	19.55937531	25.46674276
74	5.006547635	17.97255111	23.60640735
75	4.805691611	16.28347384	21.71464631
76	4.72541769	14.89179231	20.15553532
77	4.097121659	13.56554518	18.21983179
78	3.826695911	12.63324278	17.00649627
79	3.340095721	11.76174828	15.65499157
80	3.720600565	10.07861451	14.57288549
81	2.899265892	9.444175272	12.86511737
82	2.865540687	8.914172817	12.37232583
83	2.338055729	8.303141903	11.54822227
84	2.857585258	7.897099564	11.35028015
85	2.425354665	7.647291751	10.89239345
86	1.81707163	7.129622388	9.729650061
87	2.003503871	7.100195292	9.997923136
88	2.065594639	6.988395041	10.01112859
89	1.529014285	6.641218659	9.047715014
92	1.983907136	7.244426857	9.376071758
93	1.289132903	5.944305578	8.69408692

Appendix 6.1 Classes of Workers for All People Aged 16 and above, 2000

Cohorts	Not Employed	Self-employed	Unemployed	Private Sector Employee	Government Employees	Unpaid Family Workers	Total
Younger	20162559	13357946	945867	118000000	22686759	515749	176000000
Row %	11.46	**7.59**	0.54	67.22	12.9	0.29	100
Column %	42.03	84.55	88.16	93.24	91.46	77.26	81.02
Older	27810597	2440250	127025	8556917	2118136	151832	41214757
Row %	67.48	**5.92**	0.31	20.79	5.14	0.37	100
Column %	57.97	15.45	11.84	6.76	8.54	22.74	18.98
Total	47973156	15798196	1072892	127000000	24804895	667581	217000000
Row %	22.09	7.28	0.49	58.41	11.42	0.31	100
Column %	100	100	100	100	100	100	100

Appendix 6.2 Self-employment, Wage-and-salary Employment, Unemployment, Total Employment, Labor Force, and Population

Age	Self-employed	Wage-and-salary Employment	Unemployment	Total Employment	Labor Force	Population
16	45352	1681117	116039	1747936	1863975	3899205
17	46916	2427231	96128	2493893	2590021	3988247
18	55318	3106890	73951	3183793	3257744	4036325
19	63457	3412033	57221	3498076	3555297	4020860
20	83849	3568326	39942	3668584	3708526	4053266
21	88119	3395423	31255	3495932	3527187	3809200
22	92691	3409627	25017	3515243	3540260	3791971
23	99390	3315858	25207	3425182	3450389	3687242
24	113412	3324468	20325	3446811	3467136	3700946
25	138779	3234404	15846	3383649	3399495	3641692
26	149140	3154679	17428	3312488	3329916	3550583
27	174336	3344456	18633	3525534	3544167	3789587
28	188922	3503597	16456	3700949	3717405	3970766
29	234851	3708224	15618	3950608	3966226	4231340
30	252826	3631464	12260	3893919	3906179	4176413
31	248831	3404087	14768	3662788	3677556	3948639
32	266307	3410770	15700	3685415	3701115	3983560
33	289593	3401496	12191	3699507	3711698	4005975
34	314591	3510076	14375	3835063	3849438	4169227
35	371021	3831086	12136	4212779	4224915	4594137
36	375298	3800006	16769	4184972	4201741	4576330

(Continued)

Appendix 6.2 (*Continued*)

Age	Self-employed	Wage-and-salary Employment	Unemployment	Total Employment	Labor Force	Population
37	415752	3735128	14721	4165716	4180437	4557604
38	419068	3832385	17668	4263462	4281130	4667336
39	451441	3815744	18782	4278541	4297323	4700993
40	449183	3878915	18058	4340124	4358182	4781170
41	439721	3697270	15458	4150884	4166342	4547057
42	470418	3706206	12359	4189581	4201940	4597719
43	443935	3649730	14981	4103364	4118345	4506364
44	452253	3549431	14274	4011134	4025408	4412285
45	460972	3481200	15268	3952662	3967930	4361755
46	431065	3276448	14597	3718575	3733172	4117379
47	429905	3175899	12816	3616493	3629309	4022054
48	425099	3108406	12121	3544398	3556519	3935008
49	413657	2986082	10227	3409170	3419397	3817812
50	401574	2876985	10064	3288672	3298736	3713704
51	395148	2792147	10473	3198050	3208523	3622432
52	413181	2806089	9658	3227589	3237247	3676268
53	401117	2768036	9678	3181390	3191068	3641443
54	324068	2067676	8808	2401406	2410214	2798971
55	319127	2014947	5972	2343415	2349387	2797922
56	329718	1995961	8191	2333941	2342132	2798112
57	331252	1988685	7894	2328677	2336571	2830211

(*Continued*)

Appendix 6.2 (*Continued*)

Age	Self-employed	Wage-and-salary Employment	Unemployment	Total Employment	Labor Force	Population
58	289623	1735051	5596	2034603	2040199	2534908
59	263225	1564672	4487	1836386	1840873	2350471
60	252044	1479352	3718	1740950	1744668	2287353
61	242401	1379738	2733	1628892	1631625	2217780
62	227749	1294914	4023	1531047	1535070	2185994
63	207091	1161451	3594	1379040	1382634	2046326
64	194851	1091338	3181	1294463	1297644	2039034
65	174459	811172	5054	994685	999739	1867219
66	152020	724350	3551	885420	888971	1784044
67	151016	647098	4884	806963	811847	1844288
68	134086	594722	4233	738881	743114	1839990
69	132834	582608	3300	724214	727514	1904599
70	125723	530578	3540	665176	668716	1933542
71	116417	443898	4318	567058	571376	1828967
72	111680	396954	5052	514899	519951	1801142
73	93516	336548	2405	435788	438193	1720648
74	83154	298507	4857	387223	392080	1660905
75	76079	257784	4111	339654	343765	1583102
76	71409	225040	3255	301329	304584	1511168
77	59387	196630	3523	260570	264093	1449481

(*Continued*)

Appendix 6.2 (*Continued*)

Age	Self-employed	Wage-and-salary Employment	Unemployment	Total Employment	Labor Force	Population
78	53092	175275	4020	231930	235950	1387411
79	43778	154159	3286	201901	205187	1310681
80	45931	124421	5491	174412	179903	1234505
81	32373	105453	3697	139954	143651	1116593
82	29472	91682	3702	123547	127249	1028497
83	21890	77738	4962	103158	108120	936248
84	23807	65792	2870	91691	94561	833116
85	19110	60255	4851	80973	85824	787926
86	12082	47406	4071	60623	64694	664916
87	11962	42392	4367	55326	59693	597054
88	10320	34915	3085	46932	50017	499614
89	6449	28011	2698	35463	38161	421775
92	1504	5492	76	7032	7108	75810
93	17009	78430	16968	97743	114711	1319414

Appendix 6.3 Self-employment Rates by Age

Age	In Total Employment	In Labor Force	In Total Population
16	2.594603006	2.433079843	1.16310889
17	1.881235482	1.811413884	1.176356429
18	1.73748733	1.698046255	1.37050411
19	1.814054354	1.784857918	1.578194715
20	2.28559575	2.26097916	2.068677457
21	2.52061539	2.498279791	2.313320382
22	2.636830512	2.618197534	2.444401605
23	2.901743615	2.880544773	2.695510628
24	3.290345772	3.271057149	3.064405695
25	4.101459696	4.082341642	3.810838478
26	4.502355933	4.478791657	4.200436942
27	4.94495302	4.918955568	4.600395769
28	5.104690716	5.082093557	4.757822546
29	5.944679907	5.921271254	5.550274854
30	6.492841787	6.472463243	6.053663754
31	6.793486273	6.7662056	6.301690279
32	7.225970481	7.195318168	6.68515097
33	7.82788085	7.802170327	7.229026641
34	8.203020394	8.172387762	7.545547412
35	8.807036875	8.781738804	8.07596726
36	8.967754145	8.931964155	8.2008509
37	9.980325111	9.945180372	9.122161557
38	9.829288968	9.788724005	8.978740763
39	10.55128372	10.50516798	9.60309875
40	10.34954301	10.30665998	9.394834319
41	10.59343022	10.55412638	9.670452779
42	11.22828273	11.19525743	10.23155178
43	10.81880623	10.77945145	9.851290309
44	11.2749412	11.23496053	10.2498592
45	11.6623177	11.61744285	10.56849823
46	11.59220938	11.54688292	10.46940299
47	11.88734501	11.84536781	10.68869289
48	11.99354587	11.95267057	10.80300218
49	12.13365717	12.09736687	10.83492325
50	12.21082552	12.17357194	10.81330122
51	12.35590438	12.31557324	10.90836212
52	12.801537	12.7633449	11.23914252

(Continued)

Appendix 6.3 (*Continued*)

Age	In Total Employment	In Labor Force	In Total Population
53	12.60823099	12.56999224	11.01533101
54	13.49492755	13.44561105	11.5781121
55	13.6180318	13.58341559	11.40585763
56	14.12709233	14.07768648	11.78358836
57	14.22490109	14.1768429	11.70414503
58	14.23486547	14.19582109	11.42538506
59	14.33386009	14.2989223	11.1988193
60	14.47738304	14.4465308	11.01902505
61	14.88134266	14.85641615	10.92989386
62	14.87537613	14.83639183	10.41855559
63	15.01704084	14.97800575	10.12013726
64	15.05265118	15.01575162	9.556044676
65	17.53912043	17.45045457	9.343253255
66	17.16925301	17.10067033	8.521090287
67	18.714117	18.60153453	8.188308984
68	18.1471712	18.04379947	7.287322214
69	18.34181609	18.2586177	6.974381484
70	18.90071199	18.80065678	6.502212003
71	20.5299987	20.37484949	6.365177721
72	21.6896906	21.47894705	6.200510565
73	21.45905807	21.34128112	5.434929166
74	21.47444754	21.20842685	5.006547635
75	22.39897072	22.13110701	4.805691611
76	23.69801778	23.44476401	4.72541769
77	22.79118855	22.48715415	4.097121659
78	22.89138964	22.50137741	3.826695911
79	21.682904	21.33565967	3.340095721
80	26.33477054	25.53098058	3.720600565
81	23.13117167	22.53586818	2.899265892
82	23.85488923	23.16088928	2.865540687
83	21.21987631	20.24602294	2.338055729
84	25.96438036	25.1763412	2.857585258
85	23.60045941	22.26649888	2.425354665
86	19.92972964	18.67561134	1.81707163
87	21.62093771	20.03920058	2.003503871
88	21.98926106	20.63298479	2.065594639
89	18.18515072	16.89945232	1.529014285
92	21.38794084	21.15925718	1.983907136
93	17.40175767	14.82769743	1.289132903

Appendix 6.4 Self-employment Rates versus Wage-and-salary Employment Rates in Labor Force by Age

Age	Self-employed	Wage-and-salary Employment	Unemployed
16	2.433079843	90.18988989	6.225351735
17	1.811413884	93.71472278	3.711475698
18	1.698046255	95.36937218	2.270006483
19	1.784857918	95.97040697	1.609457663
20	2.26097916	96.21952226	1.077031683
21	2.498279791	96.26433189	0.886116897
22	2.618197534	96.31007327	0.706643015
23	2.880544773	96.10099035	0.730555308
24	3.271057149	95.88513401	0.586218712
25	4.082341642	95.14366104	0.466128057
26	4.478791657	94.73749488	0.523376566
27	4.918955568	94.3650793	0.525737077
28	5.082093557	94.24846096	0.442674392
29	5.921271254	93.49502525	0.393774838
30	6.472463243	92.96716817	0.313861705
31	6.7662056	92.56383859	0.401571043
32	7.195318168	92.15520188	0.424196492
33	7.802170327	91.64258515	0.328448058
34	8.172387762	91.18411571	0.373431135
35	8.781738804	90.67841602	0.287248383
36	8.931964155	90.43884428	0.39909647
37	9.945180372	89.34778828	0.352140219
38	9.788724005	89.51807116	0.412694779
39	10.50516798	88.79351168	0.437062795
40	10.30665998	89.00305219	0.414347083
41	10.55412638	88.74139473	0.37102091
42	11.19525743	88.20225896	0.294126047
43	10.77945145	88.62127869	0.363762628
44	11.23496053	88.17568306	0.354597596
45	11.61744285	87.73340255	0.384785014
46	11.54688292	87.76579274	0.391007969
47	11.84536781	87.50698824	0.353125071
48	11.95267057	87.40023602	0.340810776
49	12.09736687	87.32773644	0.299087822
50	12.17357194	87.21476954	0.305086554
51	12.31557324	87.02281392	0.326411872
52	12.7633449	86.68133757	0.298339917

(Continued)

Appendix 6.4 (*Continued*)

Age	Self-employed	Wage-and-salary Employment	Unemployed
53	12.56999224	86.74324709	0.303284042
54	13.44561105	85.78806695	0.365444728
55	13.58341559	85.76479737	0.254193966
56	14.07768648	85.21983389	0.349724098
57	14.1768429	85.11125919	0.337845501
58	14.19582109	85.04322372	0.274286969
59	14.2989223	84.99619474	0.24374305
60	14.4465308	84.7927514	0.213106448
61	14.85641615	84.56220026	0.167501724
62	14.83639183	84.35537142	0.262072739
63	14.97800575	84.0027802	0.259938639
64	15.01575162	84.10149471	0.245136571
65	17.45045457	81.13837712	0.505531944
66	17.10067033	81.48184811	0.399450601
67	18.60153453	79.70689058	0.601591187
68	18.04379947	80.03105849	0.569629963
69	18.2586177	80.08203279	0.453599518
70	18.80065678	79.34280023	0.529372708
71	20.37484949	77.68929742	0.755719526
72	21.47894705	76.34450169	0.971630019
73	21.34128112	76.80360024	0.548844915
74	21.20842685	76.1342073	1.2387778
75	22.13110701	74.98843687	1.195875089
76	23.44476401	73.88438001	1.068670712
77	22.48715415	74.4548322	1.333999765
78	22.50137741	74.2848061	1.703750795
79	21.33565967	75.13097808	1.60146598
80	25.53098058	69.16004736	3.052200352
81	22.53586818	73.40916527	2.573598513
82	23.16088928	72.04928919	2.909256654
83	20.24602294	71.89974103	4.589345172
84	25.1763412	69.57625237	3.035077886
85	22.26649888	70.20763423	5.652265101
86	18.67561134	73.27727455	6.292701023
87	20.03920058	71.01670213	7.315765668
88	20.63298479	69.80626587	6.167902913
89	16.89945232	73.40216451	7.070045334
92	21.15925718	77.26505346	1.069217783
93	14.82769743	68.37182136	14.79195544

Appendix 6.5 Older versus Younger Knowledge-based Self-employment Rate

	Younger Workers			Older Workers		
	Non Self-employed	Self-employed	Total	Non Self-employed	Self-employed	Total
Non-knowledge-based	98359877	7721201	106100000	7978453	1194935	9E + 06
	92.72	7.28	100.00	86.97	13.03	*100*
	69.07	57.8	68.11	72.77	48.97	68.44
Knowledge-based	44039240	5636745	49675985	2985457	1245315	4E + 06
	88.65	11.35	100.00	70.57	29.43	*100*
	30.93	**42.2**	31.89	27.23	**51.03**	31.56
Total	1.42E + 08	13357946	155800000	10963910	2440250	1E + 07
	91.42	8.58	100.00	81.79	18.21	*100*
	100	*100*	*100*	*100*	*100*	*100*

(For younger) Pearson chi2(1) = 7.1e + 05 Pr = 0.000.

(for older) Pearson chi2(1) = 5.2e + 05 Pr = 0.000.

Appendix 6.6 Summary of Variables

Variable	Definition	Data Type	Source	Unit of Analysis
Dependent variable				
Entrepreneurs (or creative class self-employed)	Value of 1: creative class self-employed; value of 0: all other people participating in employment	Dummy	PUMS	Individual
Independent variables				
Key variable under investigation				
Old age	Value of 0: for age 16–61, value of 1: for age 62+	Dummy	PUMS	Individual
Human capital variable				
Education	The higher value, the higher education attainment by degree or level individuals have achieved	Categorical	PUMS	Individual
Employment Disability	Value of 0: no disability; value of 1: with employment disability	Dummy	PUMS	Individual
Demographic characteristics				
Widowed	0: not, 1: widowed	Dummy	PUMS	Individual
Divorced	0: not; 1: divorced	Dummy	PUMS	Individual
Married	0: not; 1: currently married and live with spouse	Dummy	PUMS	Individual
Single	0: not; 1: never married	Dummy	PUMS	Individual
White	0: not; 1: race is white	Dummy	PUMS	Individual
Black	0: not; 1: race is black	Dummy	PUMS	Individual
Asian	0: not; 1: race is Asian and pacific islander	Dummy	PUMS	Individual
Mixed	0: not; 1: mixed race	Dummy	PUMS	Individual
Male	0: female; 1: male	Dummy	PUMS	Individual

(Continued)

Appendix 6.6 (*Continued*)

Variable	Definition	Data Type	Source	Unit of Analysis
Responsibility for grandchildren				
Responsibility for grandchild	The higher value, having had more years of responsibility for grandchildren	Categorical	PUMS	Individual
Immigration status				
Year to U.S.	The value labels the year of entering. The higher value, the later entering the US	Categorical	PUMS	Individual
Wealth				
Property value	Increase with value	Categorical	PUMS	Individual
Household income	Increase with value	Categorical	PUMS	Individual
Sampling weight				
Weight	Sampling weight calculated by PUMS	Numerical	PUMS	Individual

Appendix 6.7 Logit Model Results for Older Age Effect on Entrepreneurship in 2000

Dependent variable
Probability of being an entrepreneur

Logit model estimation: coefficients of independent variables

	Coef.	Std. Err.	$P > |z|$	[95% Conf. Interval]	
Key variable under investigation					
Being a senior	*0.8293655*	0.0011266	*0.0000*	0.8271573	0.8315737
Human capital					
Education	0.1627496	0.0001764	0.0000	0.1624038	0.1630953
Employment Disability	0.0856348	0.0013727	0.0000	0.0829443	0.0883253
Immigration status					
Year to U.S.	0.0000551	7.10E-07	0.0000	0.0000537	0.0000565

(*Continued*)

Appendix 6.7 *(Continued)*

	Dependent variable
	Probability of being an entrepreneur

Logit model estimation: coefficients of independent variables

	Coef.	Std. Err.	P > |z|	[95% Conf.Interval]	
Demographic characteristics					
Widowed	0.1337199	0.004247	0.0000	0.1253959	0.1420439
Divorced	0.1048729	0.0036532	0.0000	0.0977127	0.1120331
Married	0.0664935	0.0034734	0.0000	0.0596857	0.0733012
Not Married	−0.6025368	0.0036137	0.0000	−0.6096195	−0.595454
White	0.5684632	0.0029441	0.0000	0.5626929	0.5742336
Black	−0.331745	0.0036106	0.0000	−0.3388218	−0.3246683
Asian	0.4833203	0.0034542	0.0000	0.4765502	0.4900904
Mixed	0.4255401	0.0042629	0.0000	0.4171851	0.4338952
Male	0.7842681	0.0008722	0.0000	0.7825587	0.7859776
Responsibility for grandchildren					
Responsibility for grandchildren	−0.0525849	0.0013121	0.0000	−0.0551566	−0.0500132
Wealth					
Household income	2.54E-06	4.65E-09	0.0000	2.54E-06	2.55E-06
Property value	0.04619	0.0000683	0.0000	0.0460561	0.0463239
Constant					
Constant	−6.692379	0.0047471	0.0000	−6.701683	−6.683075

Other statistics

Number of observations	168088331
LR chi2(16)	6471557.54
Prob > chi2	0.0000
Pseudo R2	0.1126
Log likelihood	−25495547

Appendix 7.1 Description of the Variables

Variable	Obs	Mean	Std. Dev.	Min	Max
Dependent variable					
Being an entrepreneur	6979586	0.083591	0.276773	0	1
Independent variables					
Social Factors					
Social tolerance index	21477739	0.669401	0.1775	0.15106	0.96254
R&D environment (1/1000)	21477739	25.91896	13.34741	4.853	64.294
Corporate Tax rate	21477739	2.237499	0.919269	0.39984	6.26016
Individual income & employment tax rate	21477739	17.43735	2.512938	10.5122	24.7227
Human capital					
Disability	21477739	0.413292	0.492424	0	1
Education attainment	21477739	8.965125	3.358602	1	16
Wealth					
Household income	21477739	52400.88	61278.74	−10000	1236580
Demographic characteristics					
Married	21477739	0.553448	0.497135	0	1
Widowed	21477739	0.293187	0.455223	0	1
Divorced	21477739	0.086854	0.281621	0	1
Single	21477739	0.051778	0.221579	0	1
White	21477739	0.819646	0.384482	0	1
Black	21477739	0.104575	0.306005	0	1
Native	21477739	0.002629	0.051202	0	1
Asian	21477739	0.039348	0.194422	0	1
Mixed	21477739	0.013704	0.116258	0	1
Male	21477739	0.415433	0.492797	0	1
Responsibility for grandchildren					
Responsibility for Grandchildren	21477739	0.061358	0.518892	0	5
Immigration status					
Year to U.S.	21477739	319.5458	725.2621	0	2000

Appendix 8.1 Nine Census Regional Divisions

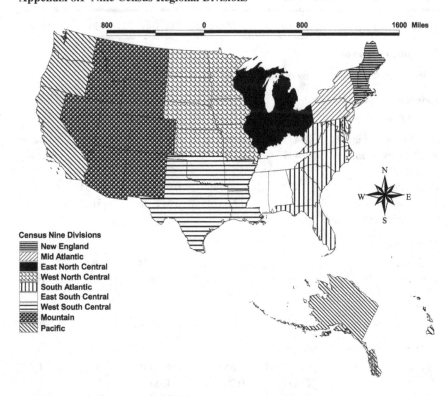

Data source: U.S. Census Bureau 2000 data.

Appendix 9.1 Residual Map of Sampled MSA/PMSA

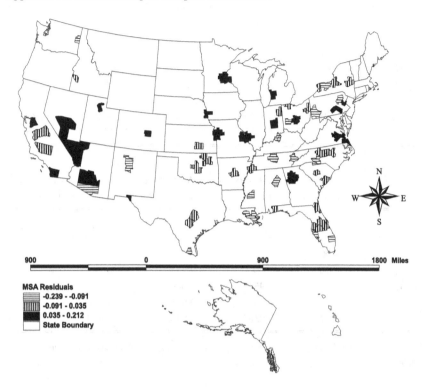

Source: U.S. Census Bureau PUMS.

Appendix 9.2 Summary of the Variables

Variable	Obs	Mean	Std. Dev.	Min	Max
Log (Y/L)	90	10.178960	0.141213	9.679580	10.611000
Log (K/L)	90	12.067890	0.272218	11.400330	12.827560
Log R	90	11.003620	0.925877	9.361859	13.457320
Log E	90	-3.959908	0.315392	-5.003359	-3.303833
Log (Eld. E)	90	-3.666309	0.317785	-5.28401	-3.085954
Log (Yng, E)	90	-3.530132	0.220013	-4.137795	-2.955097

Appendix 9.3 Correlation Matrix for Audretsch and Keilbach (2004) Entrepreneurship Growth Model (R = Postgraduate Education Receivers)

	Log Y	Log K	Log L	Log R	Log E
Log Y	1.0000	—	—	—	—
Log K	0.9546	1.0000	—	—	—
Log L	0.9934	**0.9515**	1.0000	—	—
Log R	0.9576	**0.9610**	0.9578	1.0000	—
Log E	0.9689	**0.9367**	**0.9747**	**0.9600**	1.0000

Y: Economic output; K: Physical capital; L: Labor; R: Knowledge capital (measured by under graduate education attainment); E: Entrepreneurship capital.

Appendix 9.4 Correlation Matrix for Per Capita Entrepreneurship Growth Model (R = Postgraduate Education Receivers)

	Log Y	Log K	Log L	Log R	Log Ee	Log Ey
Log Y	1.0000	—	—	—	—	—
Log K	0.4267	1.0000	—	—	—	—
Log L	0.5543	0.3268	1.0000	—	—	—
Log R	0.2140	-0.3590	0.3357	1.0000	—	—
Log Ee	0.4369	0.2660	0.1733	0.3021	1.0000	—
Log Ey	0.2768	0.1745	0.3735	0.7623	0.3613	1.0000

Y: Economic output; K: Physical capital; L: Labor; R: Knowledge capital (measured by graduate education attainment); Ee: Entrepreneurship capital for the elderly; Ey: Entrepreneurship capital for the young.

Appendix 9.5 Moran's I Spatial Correlogram

Dependent variable: log (median income 2005)

Distance bands	I	E(I)	sd(I)	z	p-value*
[0–5.5]	0.066	−0.011	0.054	1.423	0.077
[5.5–8]	−0.052	−0.011	0.061	−0.679	0.249
[8–11]	0.098	−0.011	0.047	2.325	0.010
[11–13]	−0.011	−0.011	0.060	0.008	0.497

Appendix 10.1 Description of all Variables Used in the Path Analysis

Variable	Obs	Mean	Std. Dev.	Min	Max
Log (Social Security fund contribution)	52	15.5349	1.069531	13.56903	17.8756
Log (Employment)	51	13.83485	1.022344	11.99076	16.04343
Wage-and-salary employment share	51	87.16148	2.646170	79.66628	91.3447
Elderly entrepreneurs	51	19948.47	21870.16	1294	126732

Appendix 10.2 OLS Results — Dependent Variable: SOCIAL SECURITY FUND CONTRIBUTION (IN LOG)

REGRESSION
SUMMARY OF OUTPUT: ORDINARY LEAST SQUARES ESTIMATION

Data set	: **ss test 8**		
Dependent Variable	: **LNSSCTBSD**	Number of Observations	: 51
Mean dependent var	: 9.80392e-008	Number of Variables	: 4
S.D. dependent var	: 0.990148	Degrees of Freedom	: 47
R-squared	: 0.986071	F-statistic	: 1109.05
Adjusted R-squared	: 0.985181	Prob (F-statistic)	: 1.33137e–043
Sum squared residual	: 0.696474	Log likelihood	: 37.1197
Sigma-square	: 0.0148186	Akaike info criterion	: −66.2394
S.E. of regression	: 0.121732	Schwarz criterion	: −58.5121
Sigma-square ML	: 0.0136563		
S.E. of regression ML	: 0.11686		

Variable	Coefficient	Std. Error	t-Statistic	Probability
CONSTANT	1.071848e-007	0.01704584	6.288036e-006	1.0000000
LNEMPLYSD	0.9318842	0.0335118	27.80765	0.0000000
WSEMPLYSD	0.07011949	0.0208303	3.366226	0.0015266
ELDESD	0.03860968	0.03061392	1.26118	0.2134679

REGRESSION DIAGNOSTICS
MULTICOLLINEARITY CONDITION NUMBER   3.625069
TEST ON NORMALITY OF ERRORS

TEST	DF	VALUE	PROB
Jarque-Bera	2	0.5248993	0.7691651

DIAGNOSTICS FOR HETEROSKEDASTICITY
RANDOM COEFFICIENTS

TEST	DF	VALUE	PROB
Breusch-Pagan test	3	2.886281	0.4094928
Koenker-Bassett test	3	3.79142	0.2848857

SPECIFICATION ROBUST TEST

TEST	DF	VALUE	PROB
White	9	10.63702	0.3014118

(Continued)

Appendix 10.2 (*Continued*)

DIAGNOSTICS FOR SPATIAL DEPENDENCE
FOR WEIGHT MATRIX : state2.GAL   (row-standardized weights)

TEST	MI/DF	VALUE	PROB
Moran's I (error)	0.419750	4.9292894	*0.0000008*
Lagrange Multiplier (lag)	1	0.2062607	0.6497141
Robust LM (lag)	1	1.6456109	0.1995574
Lagrange Multiplier (error)	1	18.6461301	*0.0000157*
Robust LM (error)	1	20.0854802	*0.0000074*
Lagrange Multiplier (SARMA)	2	20.2917410	0.0000392

Appendix 10.3 Spatial Error Model — Dependent Variable: SOCIAL SECURITY FUND CONTRIBUTION (IN LOG)

REGRESSION
SUMMARY OF OUTPUT: SPATIAL ERROR MODEL — MAXIMUM
LIKELIHOOD ESTIMATION

Data set	:	**ss test 8**			
Spatial Weight	:	**state2.GAL**			
Dependent Variable	:	**LNSSCTBSD**	Number of Observations	:	51
Mean dependent var	:	0.000000	Number of Variables	:	4
S.D. dependent var	:	0.990148	Degree of Freedom	:	47
Lag coeff. (Lambda)	:	0.711461			
R-squared	:	0.991881	R-squared (BUSE)	:	—
Sq. Correlation	:	—	Log likelihood	:	46.927040
Sigma-square	:	0.007960	Akaike info criterion	:	−85.8541
S.E. of regression	:	0.0892187	Schwarz criterion	:	−78.126778

Variable	Coefficient	Std. Error	z-Value	Probability
CONSTANT	0.03346457	0.03722525	0.8989751	0.3686659
LNEMPLYSD	**0.9824113**	0.02342698	41.93504	**0.0000000**
WSEMPLYSD	**0.05506256**	0.01873747	2.938634	**0.0032968**
ELDESD	0.01558146	0.0202569	0.7691927	0.4417788
LAMBDA	0.7114615	0.1019393	6.979263	**0.0000000**

(*Continued*)

Appendix 10.3 (*Continued*)

REGRESSION DIAGNOSTICS
DIAGNOSTICS FOR HETEROSKEDASTICITY
RANDOM COEFFICIENTS

TEST	DF	VALUE	PROB
Breusch-Pagan test	3	1.326521	0.7228453

DIAGNOSTICS FOR SPATIAL DEPENDENCE
SPATIAL ERROR DEPENDENCE FOR WEIGHT MATRIX : state2.GAL

TEST	DF	VALUE	PROB
Likelihood Ratio Test	1	19.61471	**0.0000095**

Appendix 10.4 OLS Results — Dependent Variable: EMPLOYMENT SIZE (IN LOG)

REGRESSION 2
SUMMARY OF OUTPUT: ORDINARY LEAST SQUARES ESTIMATION

Data set	: **ss test 8**		
Dependent Variable	: **LNEMPLYSD**	Number of Observations	: 51
Mean dependent var	: −2.61229e-017	Number of Variables	: 3
S.D. dependent var	: 0.990148	Degrees of Freedom	: 48
R-squared	: 0.736099	F-statistic	: 66.9431
Adjusted R-squared	: 0.725103	Prob (F-statistic)	: 1.30195e−014
Sum squared residual	: 13.1951	Log likelihood	: −37.8903
Sigma-square	: 0.274897	Akaike info criterion	: 81.7806
S.E. of regression	: 0.524306	Schwarz criterion	: 87.5761
Sigma-square ML	: 0.258727		
S.E. of regression ML	: 0.508652		

Variable	Coefficient	Std. Error	t-Statistic	Probability
CONSTANT	7.835138e-008	0.07341757	1.067202e-006	1.0000000
WSEMPLYSD	**0.3468118**	0.07445423	4.658053	**0.0000256**
ELDESD	**0.7539539**	0.07445423	10.12641	**0.0000000**

REGRESSION DIAGNOSTICS
MULTICOLLINEARITY CONDITION NUMBER   1.095091
TEST ON NORMALITY OF ERRORS

TEST	DF	VALUE	PROB
Jarque-Bera	2	17.52881	*0.0001562*

(*Continued*)

Appendix 10.4 (*Continued*)

DIAGNOSTICS FOR HETEROSKEDASTICITY
RANDOM COEFFICIENTS

TEST	DF	VALUE	PROB
Breusch-Pagan test	2	16.35471	*0.0002809*
Koenker-Bassett test	2	10.19105	*0.0061241*

SPECIFICATION ROBUST TEST

TEST	DF	VALUE	PROB
White	5	28.66795	*0.0000269*

DIAGNOSTICS FOR SPATIAL DEPENDENCE
FOR WEIGHT MATRIX : **state2.GAL**   (row-standardized weights)

TEST	MI/DF	VALUE	PROB
Moran's I (error)	−0.036353	−0.0700213	0.9441766
Lagrange Multiplier (lag)	1	0.3297148	0.5658271
Robust LM (lag)	1	1.3991996	0.2368577
Lagrange Multiplier (error)	1	0.1398548	0.7084254
Robust LM (error)	1	1.2093396	0.2714630
Lagrange Multiplier (SARMA)	2	1.5390544	0.4632320

Appendix 10.5 OLS Results — Dependent Variable: WAGE-AND-SALARY EMPLOYMENT SHARE

REGRESSION 3
SUMMARY OF OUTPUT: ORDINARY LEAST SQUARES ESTIMATION

Data set	:	**ss test 8**		
Dependent Variable	:	**WSEMPLYSD**	Number of Observations	: 51
Mean dependent var	:	−9.80392e-008	Number of Variables	: 2
S.D. dependent var	:	0.990148	Degrees of Freedom	: 49
R-squared	:	0.008206	F-statistic	: 0.405431
Adjusted R-squared	:	*−0.012034*	Prob (F-statistic)	: 0.527262
Sum squared residual	:	49.5897	Log likelihood	: −71.6508
Sigma-square	:	1.01203	Akaike info criterion	: 147.302
S.E. of regression	:	1.006	Schwarz criterion	: 151.165
Sigma-square ML	:	0.972347		
S.E. of regression ML	:	0.986077		

(*Continued*)

Appendix 10.5 (*Continued*)

Variable	Coefficient	Std. Error	t-Statistic	Probability
CONSTANT	−9.271051e-008	0.1408681	−6.581371e-007	1.0000000
ELDESD	0.09058805	0.1422698	0.6367343	0.5272617

REGRESSION DIAGNOSTICS
MULTICOLLINEARITY CONDITION NUMBER 1

(Extreme Multicollinearity)

TEST ON NORMALITY OF ERRORS

TEST	**DF**	**VALUE**	**PROB**
Jarque-Bera	2	8.074578	0.0176452

DIAGNOSTICS FOR HETEROSKEDASTICITY
RANDOM COEFFICIENTS

TEST	**DF**	**VALUE**	**PROB**
Breusch-Pagan test	1	0.06844044	0.7936212
Koenker-Bassett test	1	0.05493566	0.8146872

SPECIFICATION ROBUST TEST

TEST	**DF**	**VALUE**	**PROB**
White	2	5.670406	0.0587066

DIAGNOSTICS FOR SPATIAL DEPENDENCE
FOR WEIGHT MATRIX : **state2.GAL**   (row-standardized weights)

TEST	**MI/DF**	**VALUE**	**PROB**
Moran's I (error)	0.514850	5.7229256	0.0000000
Lagrange Multiplier (lag)	1	29.2423817	*0.0000001*
Robust LM (lag)	1	6.0689888	*0.0137576*
Lagrange Multiplier (error)	1	28.0522600	0.0000001
Robust LM (error)	1	4.8788671	0.0271875
Lagrange Multiplier (SARMA)	2	34.1212488	0.0000000

Appendix 10.6 Spatial Lag Model — Dependent Variable: WAGE-AND-SALARY EMPLOYMENT SHARE

REGRESSION3
SUMMARY OF OUTPUT: SPATIAL LAG MODEL — MAXIMUM LIKELIHOOD ESTIMATION

Data set	:	**ss test 8**			
Spatial Weight	:	**state2.GAL**			
Dependent Variable	:	**WSEMPLYSD**	Number of Observations	:	51
Mean dependent var	:	−9.80392e-008	Number of Variables	:	3
S.D. dependent var	:	0.990148	Degrees of Freedom	:	48
Lag coeff. (Rho)	:	0.697242			
R-squared	:	0.473004	Log likelihood	:	−59.2797
Sq. Correlation	:	—	Akaike info criterion	:	124.559
Sigma-square	:	0.516663	Schwarz criterion	:	130.355
S.E. of regression	:	0.718793			

Variable	Coefficient	Std. Error	z-Value	Probability
W WSEMPLYSD	0.6972425	0.1053229	6.620043	**0.0000000**
CONSTANT	0.001568446	0.1006529	0.01558271	0.9875672
ELDESD	0.01681775	0.1016528	0.165443	0.868595

REGRESSION DIAGNOSTICS
DIAGNOSTICS FOR HETEROSKEDASTICITY
RANDOM COEFFICIENTS

TEST	DF	VALUE	PROB
Breusch-Pagan test	1	0.0007422072	0.9782655

DIAGNOSTICS FOR SPATIAL DEPENDENCE
SPATIAL LAG DEPENDENCE FOR WEIGHT MATRIX : **state2.GAL**

TEST	DF	VALUE	PROB
Likelihood Ratio Test	1	24.74209	**0.0000007**

INDEX